CAREERPRENEURS

CAREERPRENEURS

LESSONS FROM LEADING WOMEN
ENTREPRENEURS ON BUILDING A
CAREER WITHOUT BOUNDARIES

DOROTHY PERRIN MOORE

DAVIES-BLACK PUBLISHING
Palo Alto, California

PUBLISHED BY DAVIES-BLACK PUBLISHING,
an imprint of Consulting Psychologists Press, Inc.,
3803 East Bayshore Road, Palo Alto, CA 94303
800-624-1765

Special discounts on bulk quantities of Davies-Black Publishing books are available to corporations, professional associations, and other organizations. For details, contact the Director of Book Sales at Davies-Black Publishing, 3803 East Bayshore Road, Palo Alto, California 94303; 650-691-9123; Fax 650-623-9271.

04 03 02 01 00   10 9 8 7 6 5 4 3 2 1
Printed in the United States of America

Library of Congress Cataloging-in-Publication Data
Moore, Dorothy P. (Dorothy Perrin)
    Careerpreneurs : lessons from leading women entrepreneurs on
building a career without boundaries / Dorothy Perrin Moore.
        p. cm.
    Includes bibliographical references and index.
    ISBN 0-89106-144-4
    1. Self-employed women—United States. 2. Women-owned business
enterprises—United States. 3. Businesswomen—United States.
4. Entrepreneurship—United States. I. Title.
HD6072.6.U5 M66 2000
658.4'21'0820973—dc21   00-022628

FIRST EDITION
First printing 2000

CONTENTS

PREFACE

This book is for the woman who wants to examine the challenges and barriers to her career advancement and consider the boundaryless career, including opening or expanding a business venture of her own. It includes valuable real-life lessons from accomplished women entrepreneurs. Most spent years in organizational life working for someone else. Many are members of the Committee 200 or have been recognized as outstanding entrepreneurs by *Working Woman,* Ernst & Young, the National Association of Women Business Owners (NAWBO), or the Small Business Administration. Some have been designated Entrepreneur of the Year for their city or state or selected as delegates to the White House Small Business Conference. Others have received the *Crain's* Award, the National Women's Hall of Fame's President's Twenty-first Century Leadership Award, Al Gore's Hammer Award, the Ben Franklin Emerging Business Award, their city's Honor Roll of the Year Award, or other forms of special recognition. Many of these entrepreneurs have been on the list of "Top Twenty-five to Watch" in publications such as *Newsweek, Time,* and *Entrepreneurial Edge.* Particularly notable is the number of these women who have been recognized by their employees for excellence in benefits and working relationships.

In focus interviews, these women shared their experiences, triumphs, doubts, fears, and metaphorical cuts and bruises. From their stories, the reader gains an insight into what it takes to build a career or a business. Success seldom came easily.

The possibilities have never been more exciting. In 1997, U.S. labor force participation rates increased to an all-time high for white women (59.9 percent) and black women (64.0 percent) over the age of twenty. Fifteen years ago, women held only one-third (33.6 percent) of the managerial and executive positions in America's companies and accounted for slightly less than half of the professional positions (48.5 percent). By 1995, women held nearly half of all managerial/executive positions (48.1 percent) and accounted for more than half (52.8 percent) of the people employed in professional occupations. Women now earn more than two-thirds (69 percent) of the associate's degrees in business and marketing and nearly half (48 percent) of the bachelor's degrees.[1] The playing field is not level yet, but the opportunities for women have never been better.

The world of work is changing rapidly. A career is no longer a straight line but often a weaving path. For example, the pattern of working for someone else prior to starting a business, a trend now well established, appears to be the shortest road to owning your own business. Sound strange? It shouldn't. Until recently, people tended to think of work in distinct categories—either working in someone else's business or in one's own. The distinction between being an employee and being an entrepreneur was clear. The rapid changes in the economy in the past two decades, however, have blurred the lines. People quickly came to understand that the idea of being employed had irrevocably changed; one could no longer depend on the traditional arrangements of lifetime jobs and corporate or professional advancement. What counts now are portable skills and knowledge, meaningful work, on-the-job learning, and contacts. In such a world, people move readily from one position to another, into entrepreneurship and back again. Today's female entrepreneur is not just someone who manages a business. She is someone who has managed her career. Owning and operating the business is part of it. This book inquires into the career dynamics of women who head some of the nation's most successful firms.

Individually and as a group, the entrepreneurs featured in this book are impressive. Their businesses range from manufacturing firms to high-technology research enterprises to innovative service providers. They exhibit creativity, risk taking, vision, and courage. They are intelligent and independent. They stand out from the crowd. As individuals, they are goal oriented and willing to take on challenges. They continually reexamine their aspirations and business endeavors. They are remarkably socially conscious.

Diverse in their origins, these entrepreneurs have a number of characteristics in common. Early on they came to appreciate the indispensable value of a good education. Some had to struggle to get one. Nearly all worked in corporate environments where they acquired the training and specialized knowledge that would serve them well. They became good managers, planning well, readily identifying key elements that related to their operations, and adapting quickly. They do not manage autocratically through traditional organizational hierarchies but operate through networks and teams. They work extremely hard.

Like many other entrepreneurs, female and male, the women prominent in this study founded their businesses in search of new challenges, to make money, to be in charge. Some saw opportunities where the managers in their corporate environments did not, and left to pursue them. Others sought to escape stifling corporate environments. Several were influenced by the special effects that gender confers: work environments hostile to women, lingering discrimination, inequitable compensation, and differential treatment.

Each of these business owners has her own individual story, but the origins of nearly all of their firms have an important common feature: At a critical time in the entrepreneur's career, someone with whom she had connected offered encouragement, pointed out an opportunity, provided financial backing, or in some other important way lent a hand. The commonality of incidents cannot be dismissed as good luck, except in terms of the adage that chance favors the well prepared. A two-part explanation is both simpler and sounder. Up to that point in their careers, these women had continually worked toward constructing networks, and with extensive networks with many people they had multiplied the possibilities that they might obtain assistance at a propitious moment. Then they decided to take the plunge. Networking and independent judgment make up an important part of their stories.

The path these women entrepreneurs have set is becoming well traveled. Women-owned businesses have doubled in the last twelve years to more than 9.1 million, 38 percent of all firms in the United

States. These businesses have increased employment fourfold since 1987 to 27.5 million. Women owners generate $3.6 trillion in sales yearly. One in eight of these businesses (13 percent) is owned by a woman of color.[2]

What do we know about women's paths prior to their massive entry into entrepreneurship? We know that cultural patterns have helped shape the structure of all women's careers. During the first third of the twentieth century, in the main, women were relegated to the private sphere of domesticity. When the 1930s depression economy forced women to enter the workplace in increasing numbers, popular culture reflected the change. Helpless womanhood was replaced by Hollywood images of self-assured, wisecracking, working girls such as Katharine Hepburn. During World War II, real-life women poured into the war factories, volunteered for war work, and even joined the armed services in large numbers. Many would remain in the workforce, refusing to surrender their independence. But the prevailing opinion was that women were being called on only for the duration, and official wartime propaganda repeatedly emphasized that when the war ended women were expected to gracefully surrender their war jobs to the returning male veterans and head back to the kitchen. Efforts to turn back the clock continued into the 1950s, when, in the words of one observer, "female power was either domestic or sexual, father knew best, and the ability to please men was essential to the survival of women, from Marilyn Monroe to Harriet Nelson."[3]

In the 1960s occupational and management barriers began to break down, and in the 1970s there were enough women entrepreneurs for people to notice. Before then, on the infrequent occasions when women going into business for themselves were the subjects of research studies, the findings suggested their motivations, psychology, and management styles followed a pattern different from men. The typical female entrepreneur, said the early researchers, usually lacked experience with finance, marketing, and routine business operations, and consequently faced major problems in obtaining loans. Her background, domestic orientation, and limited access to capital led her into sole-proprietor service businesses that tended to be low income, low equity, small, and slow growing. Self-employed female managers and professionals in specialty occupations fared somewhat better, but still earned less than their male counterparts.[4]

Interest in women entrepreneurs has risen steadily ever since the 1980s when they were first identified as the fastest-growing segment of the small business population. The simultaneous and clearly related exodus of successful and creative women from corporate life was also drawing attention.

The new female entrepreneurs were different. Where traditional women entrepreneurs had focused on providing domestic types of services and skills, their modern counterparts entered a wide variety of occupational fields, including the male-dominated business areas of finance, insurance, manufacturing, and construction. Where "Traditional" female entrepreneurs typically had needed assistance in acquiring capital, determining the availability and the use of credit, and managerial training, the "Moderns" more often valued advanced counseling in communication skills, training programs, and new business opportunities. Moderns heading corporations prized assistance in the sophisticated business areas of short- and long-term planning, planning for cash flow, networking, and identifying and expanding into new markets. Demographically, this second generation of hardworking female entrepreneurs tended to conform to a pattern of white, older, married women with some postsecondary education and a background in management or administration.[5]

What was really different about many in this wave of second-generation entrepreneurs was the fact that they had considerable business experience. Researchers found that women transferred their experience to businesses of their own, in essence, using corporations as training grounds and sources of business contacts. Perhaps more important, the management experiences gained in previous organizations correlate with success in the new ventures. The new women entrepreneurs brought to their businesses professional expertise, technical and planning skills, network contacts, and an average of ten to twelve years of wisdom, insight, and judgment gleaned from the business world. They were accustomed to exercising authority and control.[6] Many had left a former organizational environment for opportunities not available in the massively bureaucratic and structured systems. They intended to be their own bosses, to exercise their educational and technical skills, and, not incidentally, to make money. By 1982, the Moderns represented the fastest-growing segment of female-operated businesses. And their companies had success rates comparable to those of businesses owned by men.[7]

Many of the women entrepreneurs you will meet in this book are path breakers and Moderns. Their careers model the way for women in the next generation. Their stories have much to offer to those presently in organizations contemplating a new path and to those who are in a business they're hoping to expand.

This is also a book for the career pather in an organization, offering tips on how to more successfully build a career inside your company.

In the first chapter, "Careers," the reader will meet many of the entrepreneurs who will be followed throughout the book and get a glimpse into the various patterns their lives have followed. While these women have many characteristics in common, their business careers have been diverse. They include intentional entrepreneurship, delayed or blocked progression, organization and boundary spanning, niche and thrill seeking, careerbanding, graduating from corporate environments, business lives as intrapreneurs and copreneurs, and even pandemonium careers. If some of these terms are unfamiliar to you, see Chapter 1 for an explanation.

Chapter 2, "Organizational Transitions," further examines career progress as the entrepreneurs moved out of the organizational incubators to new opportunities. In Chapter 3, "Networks," we explore a phenomenon nearly unique to women business owners: the construction of a three-dimensional enterprise with the owner at the center of an organizational sphere connected to subordinate managers and employees on the organizational surface. Chapter 4, "Leadership, Management, and Entrepreneurship," examines how women manage in a new and interactive style. Along the way, the chapter visits some of the more common myths about women in management. Chapter 5, "Negotiation," deals with a topic that is at the heart of developing one's career in the modern environment of flattened organizations and instant, far-flung communications. Chapter 6, "Growth, Transitions, and Success," examines growth and development of careers and businesses, along with the changing patterns in the lives of entrepreneurs. Chapter 7, "Development and Entrepreneurship," focuses on the requirements for opening a successful business and provides advice from those who have done it. It talks about the nuts and bolts of starting a business, creating a business plan, and finding financial backing. It provides a guide to the vast array of available information, including Internet resources.

Exercises offer the reader help in developing a sense of career options, and what might be done to improve them. For organizational women, the analysis focuses on three career options: staying where you are now, moving to another organization, and entrepreneurship. Women already in business can consider the alternatives of operating their businesses as they are now, assessing what is necessary to move to another stage, or the possibility of returning to organizational life.

At the back of the book, the reader will find listings and brief biographical sketches of more than a hundred entrepreneurs who agreed to be featured in this book. There is also a listing of the conference centers, businesses, and academic institutions that made facilities available for the research undertaken for this project. Without the cooperation of all, this book would not have been possible.

ACKNOWLEDGMENTS

I have many people to thank. Entrepreneurs gave freely of their time to participate in my study in focus groups and individual interviews, and took additional time to review portions of the manuscript for accuracy. While several preferred to remain anonymous, I am happy to acknowledge others by name. By arrangement between Sage Publications and Davies-Black Publishing, research from *Women Entrepreneurs* is incorporated here. Much of this research has been updated for *Careerpreneurs*.

Focus sessions were hosted by the University of California, San Diego, the University of New Orleans, and the Berkley Center for Entrepreneurial Studies at the Leonard N. Stern School of Business, New York University. My thanks to the warm and friendly people at these institutions. Research support was provided by The Citadel Development Foundation.

Special thanks go to Melinda Adams Merino for championing the book and for her continued support and guidance through the first draft of the manuscript. The highly qualified team at Davies-Black has shown much perseverance, diligence, dedication, and skill in the final production of the manuscript. My thanks go to Lee Langhammer Law, Divisional Director, with whom I have been in close contact since August. I especially appreciate the professional work of Jill Anderson-Wilson, Managing Editor, and the Davies-Black production team. I have found Laura Simonds, Director of Sales, to be most knowledgeable and helpful. It is difficult to know which of these people to thank the most because the project was fully a team effort. I am deeply indebted. I acknowledge all the people who reviewed advance copies of the book. This was a special challenge added on to already busy schedules and special appreciation goes to John P. Gardner, coauthor of *Chicken Soup for the Entrepreneurial Soul;* Myra M. Hart, professor of management practice, Harvard Business School; and Lisa A. Mainiero, professor of management, Fairfield University.

Thanks go to my son, Jamie L. Moore, an assistant vice president at Chase Manhattan Bank, for his substantial contribution to the chapter on negotiations. This chapter would not have been possible without his dedicated work and "due diligence." This book is dedicated to my husband, Jamie W. Moore, my confidant, supporter in the face of adversity, and editor. Without his encouragement, thoughts, advice, tolerance, criticism, perseverance, and unlimited support, the book would not have been possible.

ABOUT THE AUTHOR

Dorothy Perrin Moore, Distinguished Professor of Entrepreneurship, The Citadel, Charleston, South Carolina

My interest in the study of businesswomen spans many years of my professional career. But it really started when I was a child. Born in the bluegrass region of Kentucky on a hundred-acre farm, the middle child, I learned the value of a day's hard work at an early age as I accompanied my father in routine chores from tending the livestock to ploughing, cutting-hiring the land, setting and harvesting tobacco, and hanging the stalks from the tall tiers in our barn. Clearing and preparing the land and tending crops, carpentry, and hunting in the forest with a rifle were unisex operations. In the ninth grade, after my father's death, I packed up my belongings and went away to boarding school on a work-study scholarship at Pinkerton High School in Midway, Kentucky, a school for girls. There and later at Midway College I learned a new kind of independence and found new role models. I grew to love and appreciate the school for all the wonderful new windows of opportunity it opened for me, and the idea that challenges were not obstacles but motivators. An award from Midway College is one of my proudest honors.

When I first began looking at masculine and feminine organizational roles in the 1980s, the male-dominated organizational environment was the norm. Much has changed since then. My research and writing have taken me down many avenues, into corporate boardrooms across America, and into many university settings. As the entrepreneurs who made this book possible demonstrate, there are many opportunities for professional and entrepreneurial women who want to take charge.

1. CAREERS

In terms of business years, we're not very old. In 1994, I started SKIRT! with an idea and about $400. In case that sounds romantic and daring, let me assure you that it is merely insane. Someday I may look back and laugh about "SKIRT!—The Early Years," but not unless I'm sitting in a rocking chair in the Caribbean and clutching a retirement plan and a health insurance card. Like many small business owners, I think "health insurance" is one of the most romantic, sexy phrases in the English language.

NIKKI HARDIN

The successful entrepreneurs you will meet in the following pages add dimension to our understanding of women's career strategies. Through their stories you may capture a new view of how expansive career development paths have become in the age of the "protean career" where the individual must be in charge.[1] At the completion of this chapter you will have the opportunity to profile your career development to see what path you are on now and how your strategy compares to those of these successful women.

Women business owners come to entrepreneurship by one of three modes. For some, an entrepreneurial career develops early in life. Others become entrepreneurs after a substantial period in a corporation or other organization. Still others follow a career without boundaries, winding between entrepreneurial and corporate job options. The entrepreneurs within these groups follow a rich variety of paths to business ownership. Some eyed a business of their own from the beginning; they are the *Intentional Entrepreneurs.* Others began with a talent, knowledge, skill, or creative base that transmuted from professional development into *Lifetime Business Ownership.* There are the *Family Business Owners,* women who inherited or succeeded to ownership. These are different from the *Copreneurs,* the little-studied group of dual career business owners who overlap home and family in the firm they jointly operate full-time. There are the *Delayed Entrepreneurs,* women who first took time out for a family, and the *Organizational Entrepreneurs,* women who emerged from the corporate or public sector. In the latter group, some had *Blocked Careers,* others followed *Parallel Paths,* and still others were *Corporate Spanners, Boundary Spanners, Spiral Careerists, Professionals* or *Experts,* and *Careerbanders.* The paths of some of these entrepreneurs led through sequences of *Punctuated Careers, Challenged Careers,* and even *Pandemonium* or *Protean Careers.* Some, the Intrapreneurs, stayed in organizations but nonetheless created entrepreneurial environments in the areas they manage. You will also meet *the Corporate Graduates,* the *Market Creators,* the *Market Expanders,* and the *Mavericks,* those outliers who spanned corporate and entrepreneurial boundaries.

CHANGING DEFINITIONS OF CAREERS

Until recently, career planning was relatively straightforward. Careers developed within the environments of traditional organizations. Bureaucracy, hierarchy, and the security of lifelong careers characterized company life. This is no longer true.

Historically careers have been classified into four categories. *Organizational* (or bureaucratic) careers meant advancement through a sequence of positions in a formally defined hierarchy, with people moving from job to job with accompanying changes in titles, tasks, and work groups. This advancement in positions, responsibilities, and income took place within one or several firms. Companies were characterized by large numbers of dedicated employees who looked to their organizations for recognition, rewards, and job security in long-term employment. What it took for the ambitious to get ahead—the skills, experiences, and professional development—was largely defined by the corporations. Who got promoted was determined by the formal and informal selection procedures of the employing firms.

Within organizations, *intrapreneurial* careers were marked by the advancement that occurred as one added something of value to the company, created a new product or market niche, or in other ways redefined businesses with improvements to the bottom line.[2]

Professional careers were traditionally defined by the development of a talent or skill. Because professional employment tends to be continuous and stable and the talent or skill is portable, the movement of professionals is often to more challenging, important, or rewarding positions, and often to new organizations as one achieves recognition.

For both organizational and professional careers, the most common path to success starts with general education or specific training that opens a place somewhere on the visible job ladder.[3]

In the traditional career universe described above, the distinction between working for others and owning your own business— the *entrepreneurial* career—was clear. Until recently, the gap between the two was viewed as a chasm, primarily because it was thought that the behavior of people in organizations was governed by one set of values, acquired as one developed the skills to cope with a bureaucratic hierarchy, and the behavior of the self-employed by another set of values, with the internal motivation to be independent and in control at the core.[4] In this world, the word "career" meant a sequential set of positions held together by the subjective sense of where one was going, to be reinvented as the person or the environment changed.[5]

With today's rapid technological change and evolving organizational structures, the downsizing, rightsizing, streamlining, working smarter (and other now-passé buzzwords that mean companies trying to do more with fewer long-term employees), no one can count on continuing corporate loyalty. Spawned with this new transitional organizational structure and temporal career environment is the changing job contract that shifts the burden of career planning to the individual.

Savvy employees today plan a career independent of rather than dependent upon traditional organizational career arrangements that may not exist in the future. The hallmarks of the self-managed career are portable skills and knowledge, meaningful work, on-the-job learning, the development of multiple networks, and, above all, taking responsibility.[6] The old meaning of being employed was one's occupation or business. The new meaning is that current employment may be one in a series of temporary stops in an evolving career.[7]

The change from an organization-based to an individual-based career reflects the modern environment of rapidly changing technology and a global economy, a landscape where job security is measured in the skills you have at your command rather than a position you hold within a single company. Continuous learning and recognizing and using one's talents to the fullest are required.[8] Most people will follow less predictable, discontinuous, and even zigzagging career paths, often extending beyond retirement. Today's savvy careerwoman must be a social entrepreneur, constantly managing her pre- and post-retirement strategies and everything in between.[9] The managing includes bridging the old chasm that divided entrepreneurship from working for others. Owning your own business may well be a part of your rich new career. Perhaps business ownership will be for a lifetime, perhaps it will be one of many positions you will hold as you move through your working life.

What all this means is that routes that you may not have thought about exploring, except in your imagination and dreams, can become a reality, as they did for the entrepreneurs you will meet in this book.

What is most striking about these entrepreneurs is that most acquired a package of skills while working for others. In incubator organizations they benefited from advanced training programs and made key contacts. Many enrolled in company-supported MBA programs. When they started their businesses, they were already familiar with product diversity, quality, service, operations, cost control, focusing on the customer, and all the other important elements in their fields—or they were in business with someone who was. As with men, the majority of these women have businesses that provide a service that was generated from an entrepreneurial idea. They represent the employment principle of the new organizational era—the career without boundaries.[10]

ENTREPRENEURS

Intentional Entrepreneurs

These women entrepreneurs know from the beginning what they want to do and consciously work toward the goal of founding a business, organizing their education, training, and early employment along the way.[11]

Rebecca Smith is the founder and president of A. D. Morgan Corporation, a commercial general construction company with offices in Tampa and Melbourne, Florida. Rebecca is a Class A certified general contractor. Her firm's projected total revenues currently exceed $35 million annually. She and her company have received numerous awards.

Introduced to building and construction by helping her father on home projects and watching him prepare engineering drawings in the evenings, Rebecca's fascination with the technical world of architecture and construction led her to take a woodshop course in lieu of home economics in junior high school. One of the projects was to design a house. Rebecca's design won first place in a competition among area schools. After earning her B.A. degree in architecture and her M.S. degree in building construction from the University of Florida, she pursued the practical experience that later would make it possible for her to open her own firm at age twenty-nine. Her business was not an overnight success, and during the first months of operation she chased every conceivable construction contract. "When I was working for another company," Rebecca recalls, "I was building huge multimillion-dollar public-use facilities with costs exceeding $30 million. When I started my own business, for lack of capital, I was building anything short of a doghouse that rolled in." Her hardest task was getting her first big contract.

It was with a real estate company in Tampa that owned a number of office buildings and retail properties around the state of Florida. Even though the construction industry was depressed, there was still frequent turnover in office space and therefore a constant need for renovation. I had been trying to win this company as a client for some time but was met with the response, "We already have a contractor that we're happy with." One Friday afternoon I caught the facilities manager just as he had hung up the phone. His contractor had refused to start a new project that afternoon. It was a rush job that had to be finished in two weeks. Completion of the construction was key to the tenant signing the lease agreement. He looked across the desk and said, "Here's one for you, Rebecca. Are you interested?" I stood up, shook his hand, and said, "Consider it done." With no other employees, I called a subcontracting company with whom I had worked in my past corporate life and called in a favor. They agreed to give up their Friday night and weekend. I headed home to change from being a president to being the project manager and head laborer. In jeans and work boots, I arrived back at the job site and began working along with the crew. The project was successfully completed on time. As a result, A. D. Morgan became the contractor for the real estate firm. We performed all of the work for this client around the state for the next two years. A. D. Morgan is like the little engine that could. I just kept pushing in the face of potential defeat and it brought success.

Like many other intentional entrepreneurs, Rebecca came from a family in which women grew up self-reliant and often were encouraged in their career choices. Focused and determined to start her own business, she exhibited the self-reliance, independence, and motivation characteristic of intentional entrepreneurs. Like many others, she also had spent time in the corporate world to learn the skills she needed.[12]

Lifetime Business Owners

Lifetime Business Owners differ from Intentional Entrepreneurs in that most begin by pursuing a profession or following a skill and wind up starting a business early in life. Sometimes the business is based on a talent. At other times firms are founded on specialized knowledge, ability, or the early identification of a market niche.

Talent-Based Professional

A talent-based professional, Suzy Spafford has spent most of her working life as chief executive officer of Suzy's Zoo. Though she didn't know it at the time, her successful entrepreneurial career began to take shape while she was studying art at San Diego State University and, she thought, heading for a professional career as an art teacher. To pay for her studies, in summer Suzy would set up her card table in La Jolla selling "serious" watercolors and thinking about illustrating children's books. "I was drawing whimsical animals and animal characters that came out of me," she says. "They sold for three dollars apiece, and it was easy to draw them on the spot. Kids and parents would watch me, and I was able to sell the drawings over and over again."

A couple visiting from Berkeley stopped by one day and suggested that Suzy's artwork could be reproduced in some form. Soon the three of them were in business selling boxed notes illustrated by Suzy's drawings. Today, Suzy's Zoo has diversified far beyond the traditional boxed notes, cards for all occasions, and stationery. Product lines include *Alphabetical Soup* and *Witzy and Zoom Zoom*—the two children's books the young art student dreamed of writing. Suzy has more than 900 designs on the market and has worldwide export and licensing arrangements. Her stationery products are translated into eleven languages. Her art is licensed to more than sixteen major U.S. companies, including Gerber Baby Products. In 1996, she was the winner in the greeting card division of the National Cartoonist Society.

Knowledge-Based Professional

A knowledge-based professional, Gail K. Naughton, Ph.D., president and chief operating officer of Advanced Tissue Sciences, Inc., is a company cofounder and coinventor of the firm's core technology. She has been a director since the company's inception in 1986. She received her M.S. and Ph.D. degrees from the New York University Medical Center in dermatology and stayed on as an assistant professor of research for two years before moving to the City University of New York in 1985.

Gail had planned to be a medical researcher and had never thought of working in a private firm. But while a faculty member she came up with an idea for growing tissues in three dimensions for testing purposes. The procedure could be packaged. With friends, she obtained patents and formed a company. It soon received an offer to go public, and when it did, in 1988, it was one of the few public biotech companies in existence. Today, Advanced Tissue Sciences is a world leader in tissue engineering. Products include TransCyte™, a temporary skin substitute and the first human-based tissue engineered product for the treatment of burns to be approved by the U.S. Food and Drug Administration, and Dermagraft®, a human dermal replacement for the treatment of diabetic foot ulcers (available in Canada and the United Kingdom). Both are sold worldwide by a joint venture partner, Smith & Nephew, PLC, a leading worldwide healthcare company with over $1.6 billion in sales annually. With over sixty patents, Gail's company is an industry pioneer, having defined the concept of human-based tissue engineering.

Market Creator

Where Suzy Spafford's quick grasp of a market for her drawing talent and Gail Naughton's perception of the business potential of her research propelled them into entrepreneurship, Ruth Ann Menutis is a skill-based Market Creator. The term describes entrepreneurs who sought and then filled a niche for new, interesting, or challenging projects or services.[13]

Ruth is president and owner of Natural Energy Unlimited, Inc., The Grove, a natural snack retail and wholesale specialty fruit firm earning more than $20 million annually in nineteen major airports in the United States.

> Born in Lafayette, Louisiana, the daughter of a French-speaking rice farmer, I received my formal education in a rural high school. My graduating class totaled seventeen. My first job was at age fifteen. I watched my father work twelve-hour days. I watched my mom help him while raising four children. They gave us love and support, and they gave me confidence that I could achieve and be anything I wanted. I believe my parents, more than anyone else, prepared me to weather the rocky roads I traveled during my business career.

Ruth started her first business at age twenty, a fashion boutique financed with $2,000 in savings and clothing-manufacturer consigned merchandise. Soon after, she expanded into a three-store chain. Then financial misfortune struck her husband, leaving Ruth to become the sole family provider. She sold her store in Houston and opened one in the New Orleans French Quarter, moving her two small daughters with her while her husband continued to recuperate. For the next fifteen years, Ruth owned, merchandised, managed, and operated retail clothing stores in Houston, New Orleans, and New York. The businesses were all a precursor to her present ownership of The Grove. Ruth now has built three successful companies. She has twice served as the Louisiana chair to the National White House Conference on Small Business. She was president of the French Market Corporation for eight years and is a recipient of the Chamber of Commerce Person of the Year and the State of Louisiana Small Business Program awards.

Copreneurs

Copreneurs are a special group who face unique challenges. As with large numbers of women entrepreneurs, the increase in husband-and-wife entrepreneurs sharing business ownership equally is recent. Nearly 70 percent of women-owned businesses were started after 1980 (69.3 percent), and 29 percent after 1990. Between 1980 and 1989, the number of entrepreneurial couples rose by 66 percent, and by the early 1990s, there were 1.8 million couple-owned businesses.

The number of successful entrepreneurial couples is impressive. Of the companies in *Working Woman's* 1995 list of America's fifty top women's businesses, nine of the women CEOs shared ownership with their husbands and six employed their husbands full time.[14] As Kathy Marshack, author of *Entrepreneurial Couples: Making It Work at Work and at Home,* points out, the most productive partnerships are those where the owners exhibit complementary talents and take on distinct responsibilities. "Not only do these partners negotiate with each other for love, sex, status, and support, but they also depend on the relationship for their own self-definition." In a copreneurial couple, each partner is committed to a meaningful career and works full time in the joint venture. Both organize their lives to keep the business manageable.[15]

Cathy M. Brienza is a principal of Waller-Sutton Media Group, Inc., a private equity fund that focuses on the media and communications business, a new venture looking for investments in private companies. She spent over twenty years as a business owner in cable television and cellular telephone businesses, and prior to that a couple of years on Wall Street. Her family provided the copreneurial role model.

I sort of always knew I'd be an entrepreneur. My father was a small business owner in the trucking and warehousing business in New York. My mother worked with him a couple of days a week as the company's bookkeeper. I always saw family working together in a little business. I guess maybe I had a natural interest. My father always discussed business with me. I was always interested and so there was always an assumption that at some point I would find a business. My father encouraged me to go into business because I could control my own destiny. Maybe he saw things in my personality that said to him this might be the right thing for me. I had a very supportive father, particularly in that regard, and my mother was very supportive as well.

After receiving her master's degree in finance-investments from New York University, Cathy became the first woman in the corporate finance department in a company on Wall Street. It was a difficult environment; firms were merging and downsizing. In a single day, her company fired all but 300 of its 1,500 people. While her job was still intact, Cathy and a friend began thinking about something else they could do. Both left to start a financial partnership. Later, they would turn the partnership into a copreneurship. They successfully raised equity capital and merged eighteen different partnerships in the media business, and in 1994–1995 sold them for a substantial sum. Then they made their next entrepreneurial decision.

We looked around again for what we might want to do. We felt that we were young, we had a young child, and wanted to be able to give of our experience, our knowledge, and our relationship to a new business in a different way, not necessarily as the persons who made all the decisions all the time, but to guide other people as part of a larger group. We decided that the way to use our experience, knowledge, and contacts in the business was to go out and raise a private equity fund, which we did. We raised a little over $100 million to invest in other companies where we can help other people be entrepreneurs.

Family-Owned Business

According to the Family Enterprise Center at Kennesaw State College in Georgia, three-quarters of American corporations are family owned or family controlled, and they employ half of the U.S.

workforce and generate half of the gross national product. In increasing numbers, women are coming to power in businesses started earlier by male family members. *Working Woman*'s 1995 list of America's fifty top women business owners included twenty-two women who inherited companies: one who took control of her husband's business after a divorce, eighteen daughters who took over from their fathers, and four widows who headed firms after their husbands died. The numbers of family businesses headed by women can be expected to grow. The 1997 Arthur Anderson/*Mass Mutual American Family Business Survey* found that more than a quarter of family businesses plan to choose a woman as their next chief executive.[16]

Joan B. Anderson is president and CEO, James H. Anderson, Inc., Melrose Park, Illinois, the country's largest woman-owned heating, ventilating, and air-conditioning design/build company. Though she had entered the workforce as a young woman, by coincidence working for an air-conditioning company, and then went on to be a manager with TWA, following her marriage she spent the next twenty-five years at home rearing two children and participating widely as a community volunteer. Through her volunteer activities she developed the strong management skills that culminated in her bringing diverse groups together in a series of initiatives that were implemented in the Oakbrook Terrace, Illinois, Community Park District, which attracted national recognition. In 1976, the Joan B. Anderson Cultural Arts and Community Center was named in her honor for her outstanding service to and achievements in the community.

In 1974, Joan had been elected to the board of directors of and became a shareholder in the family-owned company James H. Anderson, Inc. During the divorce and under her husband's management, the business spiraled downward. In order to see the business prosper in the future, Joan urged her husband to make dramatic changes in the company. He refused. Eventually, Joan was not permitted to enter the premises and was only allowed to operate in the background as an "idea person." By 1993, the corporation was scheduled to be sold for liquidation value. In her divorce settlement, Joan asked for and got the right to purchase the remaining shares of the corporation. She became the sole owner and stockholder. Joan reflects now on the transitions this brought about in her personal life:

I had to move from the role of the woman to the role of the entrepreneur. My marriage had always been the most important to me, but all my life I never fit the role of the "stay-at-home wife." Of course, I cooked, maintained our home life, and all of that, but my other interests were always on the side—all the volunteer activities and my behind-the-scenes work for the corporation. I was always looking for new challenges and new goals to meet.

When I walked into the company the first day to take over, my former husband was waiting for me. He said "The money you thought was here to meet the payroll is not here. There is no money." There has never been a moment in my life that hit me like that. Chicago is a union city. I knew that I not only had a responsibility to each individual employee, but to the families as well. I simply had to find a way to meet payroll—the survival of the company and its employees depended on it.

Since that moment, the James H. Anderson Company ("We had a good name. I kept it.") has regained its competitive standing within the industry. Under Joan's tireless leadership, the number of jobs bid has increased by 150 percent, and the sales volume from $11 million to $30 million. These achievements were the direct result of the teamwork approach Joan inspired between the union and her employees. In 1998, she launched a second company, Advanced Cleanroom Technologies LLC, to conduct dust-free manufacturing facilities for technology firms. For her turnaround success, Joan was recognized in 1999 by *Working Woman* as one of America's seven most successful businesswomen nationwide.[17]

Delayed Entrepreneurs

In return for freedom from the constant pressure to work long hours and weekends, some women delay a business career for family time, and then move into the workforce.[18] Iris Newman, of Veritas Medical Services, Inc., and winner of the 1998 Ben Franklin Emerging Business Award for the most innovative service (for computerized credentials verification for physicians), married when she was very young and concerned herself with family. She became interested in entrepreneurial ventures as her children grew.

Iris began her entrepreneurial career in 1983 when she received her securities license, formed a broker-dealer firm, and became the in-house broker-dealer for a real estate syndicator in Atlanta, Georgia. Moving to Rochester, New York, in 1986, Iris networked with the business community and, in 1987, founded InConcepts, Inc., a consulting firm that specialized in developing and implementing strategic business, marketing, and public relations plans for a diverse group of emerging and established firms. Through InConcepts, Iris developed the Entrepreneurial Venture Capital Conference for High Technology of Rochester. Over an eight-year period, the conference grew to include companies in upstate New York and parts of Canada, bringing businesses together with investors and assisting in raising over $40 million in capital for companies.

In 1995, Iris formed Veritas ("Truth") Medical Services, a firm with the mission of delivering more efficient, cost-effective, and reliable physician credentials verification to the healthcare industry while maintaining high standards of quality, confidentiality, and security. Her career is consistent with research that suggests that women see their personal and business lives as intimately related, where, at different times, concerns for personal and family relationships and concerns about career influence choices.[19] Reflecting on her own career transitions, Iris says, "I've decided there's a season for everything."

Organizational Entrepreneurs

Many entrepreneurs began businesses after a long period in a private or public sector environment where the linear and pluralistic structures no longer worked to deal with the high level of technological and global change. Many among those organizational women left and started business ventures of their own. Some had been *Corporate Climbers,*[20] others had *Blocked Careers,* and still others followed *Parallel Paths* or *Spiral Careers.* Among these entrepreneurs are those who are *Career Challengers* and those who coped using various forms of *Career-banding* and *Broadbanding.* A few careers were *Pandemonium* or *Punctuated.* And some have used the newer *Protean* form. Among those who stayed behind in the organization are the *Intrapranuers,* the organizational entrepreneurs.

Blocked Careerist

Many women intend to climb the career ladder in their firms. But somewhere along the way careers get blocked or career paths are altered. Some women discover that no matter how long the ladder, it is never tall enough to reach the top. It is not uncommon for professional and managerial women who reach this plateau to exit organizations.[21]

Carol A. Vincie, president and founder of two companies—New Era Consulting and Productivity Tools International, in New York—worked at a Fortune 100 technology company for twenty-five years. She never had any idea of owning her own business until she spent four fruitless years trying to convince the company to shift its focus. After conducting an intensive survey of client technology demands, she pinpointed a new trend in the computer industry, which she felt the company needed to adapt to and accept. However,

> Instead of applauding my breakthrough information, company leaders made it very plain to me that they were disappointed with findings that challenged the party line. Rather than getting recognized for my innovation, I was accused of being a subversive—the exact word used. That really offended me because I had taken my position and responsibility very seriously. All the large clients I had been working with clearly identified the fact that we needed to transition, primarily because the business was changing. The traditional large mainframe environment was no longer responsive to the needs of our market. Regardless of how smart, powerful, or dominant the company was, or how much money it had, the PCs provided an opportunity for this transition. I left within ten days without a business plan or any idea what I was going to do. I became a computer consultant. What else? Within six months I realized I really didn't care about technology—an interesting observation—and that my real skill was problem solving. When I look back at how I managed departments, I realize I was an entrepreneur. I had managed my department as if it were my own business. There was much to be learned from this incubator experience.

Parallel Pather

This more ambitious term differentiates simultaneous job holding from the more common "moonlighting."[22] For disenchanted organizational women planning for an exit, it can be a low-risk way to test the entrepreneurial waters. Denise L. Devine is founder and president of Devine Foods, Inc., in Philadelphia. Her achievements have been recognized by business publications such as *Entrepreneurial Edge* (Rising Entrepreneur of 1993), *Business Philadelphia* (25 Companies to Watch and Women to Watch), and *Working Woman* (Women to Watch). Denise holds an MBA degree from the Wharton School of the University of Pennsylvania, an M.S. degree in taxation from Villanova Law School, and a B.S. degree in accounting from Villanova University. Her company is a technology-based manufacturing business with a portfolio of competitive patents that use grains and vegetables in an interesting format. She started as a CPA by training with Arthur Andersen in the late 1970s and found out very quickly that career life and having a family were mutually exclusive.

> I knew that I was going to have a family and that it would take precedence over building that kind of career. From Arthur Andersen and Company I went into the corporate world. I worked for Campbell Soup for six years in finance, doing all the investment strategy and finance on Wall Street. But I felt disconnected from adding value to the business. I enjoyed making money. Actually, I made a lot of money, but I knew how hard it was to jump, particularly for a woman, into a line position. It just was never going to happen. I wanted to do something that was more directly in touch with the end results of the product. I had an idea that stemmed from the time when I had had young children and became interested in children's nutrition. Being in the food business, I was a very frustrated consumer because there were few nutritional products for children. I got to thinking about something better. My husband, who was starting a business in the financial services area, said, "Why don't you come and help me and start this thing on the side?" So from my senior management position at Murray, Devine and Company, I started my business part-time until I could get involved in it full-time. We took three years to do the research and development. We have developed a number of products and enlarged our product line.

Working one job while pursuing career alternatives offers the tremendous payoff of allowing one to study and explore—to fully prepare for entrepreneurship—while drawing a regular paycheck.

The best strategy, advises one authority, involves compartmentalizing your life, picking a business that is not labor- or travel-intensive, and knowing your company's policy toward moonlighting.

Gwyn Myers launched Cymry Communication Company, a Whittier, California-based education and training consulting firm, while working as a senior manager at Price Waterhouse. Before that, she had experimented with a variety of business ideas, "none of them rip-roaring successes. . . . If I had been out on my own, I might have poured a lot of money into one of them to force it to work," she says. But because she had a job she felt she wasn't stuck with a bad decision. "Knowing that you can always continue to draw your paycheck if things don't work out gives you a stressless view of the situation a normal start-up owner doesn't have, so you make smarter business decisions."[23]

Spiral Careerist

When organizational structures began changing in the eighties and nineties, the operative word was flexibility. Managers were encouraged to bring together sets of skills and strengths from diverse areas on a temporary or permanent basis—that is, to react to opportunities and problems in an entrepreneurial way. [24] People who developed this talent found they could apply it to their own careers. Women who did this repeatedly followed spiral career paths.

Claire H. Irving is the founder and principal of Investigative Consultants International, LLC. She is a licensed private investigator with more than twenty-five years of senior management and business experience in the investigations field, and her women-owned firm does corporate investigative work for major corporations, investment banks, and attorneys. She is a long way from her beginnings as an organization woman. "I was the first woman hired for an executive career path at Banker's Trust outside the Trust Department," she remembers.

> I went into an area that nobody knew anything about. We started the Mergers and Acquisitions Department, now known as the Corporate Finance Department. I have gone to five different companies over a period of twenty-two years, not unusual in the merger and acquisition business. I worked as the Director of International Mergers and Acquisitions at Arthur Andersen and Company, Senior Manager

of Corporate Financial Services at Ernst and Whinney, and Director of Mergers and Acquisitions at Lepercq, de Neuflize and Company. In each company I was in a small group starting up a new business center for the respective firms. My last position was with a major bank, which decided to switch its investment banking personnel from corporate bankers to investment bankers. Two and a half years into the change, all the managing directors were brought into a conference room where a thirty-two-year-old guy said, "Hi, my name is X, I am your new boss, and I would have fired you all but they wouldn't let me." I turned to a colleague and said, "I don't think we're on the A team anymore."

Like many talented individuals have done in similar situations, Claire immediately began managing her future outside the company's internal labor market.[25]

I took out my business Rolodex and called people who had recently switched jobs. I said, "You don't know me from a hole in the wall, but I'm interested in learning how you switched careers. Let me buy you coffee (or lunch), and let's discuss how you did it." I made this my mission. I had enough business at the bank and I knew they wouldn't get rid of me for twelve months, so I spent 75 percent of the time for me and 25 percent of the time for them. Word got out that I was looking, and a headhunter called, saying, "We have this new job. We need somebody who can talk with bankers, companies, and attorneys, who knows what a deal looks like and how it's put together, and can supervise a team of eighteen researchers." That was my introduction into the investigation business. I found that being an investigator isn't difficult; it's due diligence at a different level connecting legal, business, and problem solving. My side of the investigations suffered during the downturn in Wall Street in '91. We went from fifty-four cases a week with eighteen researchers to nineteen cases a week. My suggestions for dealing with the change were not accepted. So here I was. Six years later I moved from Wall Street to a new business I liked. I had found a new occupation but had nowhere to practice. I tried to buy another investigative agency but the owner could not afford to sell at a reasonable price. I thought, "This is crazy. I can do this thing. I have this incredible Rolodex." I just couldn't sit there and let all this newfound fun disappear. So I started my own business.

Careerbander

Entrepreneurial spirits who move in and out of organizational environments in a seemingly erratic way may be practicing a new strategy—careerbanding. Movement is often fluid between organizational and entrepreneurial environments. The term is related to the organizational broadbanding that has brought flatter company structures, the clumping of salary and employment ranges, reduced job classifications, fewer middle management positions, temporary job hires, fierce competition for the few available promotional opportunities, and jobs with no long-range, single organizational anchors.[26]

Loretta Soloway, fashion consultant with The Carlisle Collection, New York, began her career working between two companies for about eight years. Because of father-son rivalries in one company, she started a freelance business and within six months had five major accounts.

> Then it got so frenetic that I found myself racing across a runway with my suitcase to catch a private plane because I had just finished a sales meeting for one shoe company and I was supposed to be at another company at the same time. I had a diversified list of clients who wanted my handbags, shoes, and slippers. When they heard I was available, it was very easy for me to get these different positions.

After about a year of trying to be in more than one place at the same time, Loretta went back into corporate life with a major firm. After two unsatisfactory years she went to a headhunter, who said, "I know you did runway shoes for Anne Klein. Manhattan Industries owns a division looking for someone to be head of the Anne Klein Scarf Division. Do you think you could do it?" "I have a color sense, so I accepted this job and took a business from zero to $2 million within a year," Loretta recalls. Eight years later, she had started a family, was renovating a house, and was dealing with new job demands at the firm. When it got to be too much, she left. As soon as she did, "Barr & Beards, who handled the Bill Blass line, called me to ask if I might be interested in freelancing," Loretta was successful, but, "when you're freelancing in the fashion industry, if you're not there all the time, they start thinking you're getting paid too much and you're not producing enough, or they want you full time and they don't want you to work for anyone else." So she looked around for something else. She answered a blind ad in the *New York Times* and forgot about it until one day a district manager with Carlisle called and asked if she would be interested in speaking with them. "That's my story from beginning to now. I can't say how it will end."

Punctuated Careerist

Career paths have forks and branches, forcing choices. Entrepreneurial members in this group do not always follow the obvious course.[27]

Aliza Sherman is president and founder of Cybergrrl, Inc., a Manhattan-based new media company that produces web sites, Internet resources, and other tools for women and girls to enable them to learn about technology and computers. She has also created an online comic strip, *Adventures of Cybergrrl*. Although she has been in business for only four and a half years, she is considered a veteran in the industry.

Only in retrospect are the connections between the various jobs in Aliza's career and her current business apparent. After attending college for four years, Aliza had the opportunity to choose between working in a bank or managing three agents in a growing music booking agency in North Carolina. Young and inexperienced, she did not realize it was blatant discrimination when she was told, after working for three months, that the agency was not ready for a woman agent. But through this position she had become acquainted with an agent from ICM in New York. The contact led to her being hired by top bands. "I ended up working for four years in the music industry overseeing some of the most popular heavy metal bands at the time," she says.

> Then I found out the men who were at the same level made twice as much as I did. I asked why, and my bosses said because the men were married, they had families. I picked up a copy of *MS Magazine* in 1994, my first issue, read it cover to cover, and realized that the way I was being treated was wrong. I had met a photographer who took pictures of rock bands and also documented domestic violence. I started helping her part time, then quit the music business to run her nonprofit organization on domestic violence awareness. I worked with the mayor's office and the governor's office, and spent

over a year in domestic violence work. Then I was held up at gun-point. The attackers were caught just before I left New York City for a little sabbatical in Santa Fe, New Mexico, where I discovered the web. I took a class, came back to New York, and pitched my business idea to a friend of mine. He asked, "What is keeping you from starting your own business?" I never thought I would start a business. It was fear. My biggest fear was not being able to pay my rent. I said, "I have no money." He said, "Well then, I'll pay all of your bills until you get on your feet." Basically he helped me pay my rent and expenses as I founded my own Internet consulting business. So that's three totally different careers in about an eight-year span.

Career Challenger

The pattern of movement from firm to firm, and from organization to entrepreneurship, is becoming more common. In part, this is because companies make decisions that affect people, causing them to involuntarily interrupt their careers.[28] For reasons having to do with dual careers, timing, and personal or family relationships, when this happens, women generally have less flexibility.[29]

Like Suzy Spafford, Katherine Kennedy was born with a tremendous talent and worked hard to refine it into a career. "My mother was a singer with Tommy Dorsey," Katherine relates, "and I thought all of my life that was what I was going to do, too." She studied voice for thirteen years and earned a teaching degree and a master's degree in vocal performance. Katherine taught voice at Mesa College and San Diego State University after graduation, a dual-career decision to avoid long absences from her spouse. She was also singing in the San Diego Opera. Professional singers suggested she go to New York and get a manager. For the next four years, Katherine went back and forth between her home and husband in San Diego and singing in operas and concerts in Manhattan. Then three men mugged her.

While one held a knife to my throat, the only thing I could think about were all the voice lessons I had taken to create the stage performance, the long hours, the lessons that I had worked so hard to teach to pay for the pauper life I was living in New York. An opportunity to sing in Philadelphia was coming up in eight months. And here this kid was going to cut my throat.

Katherine lost her cash, rings, and airline tickets, but talked her way out of physical harm. It was a defining moment. The pauper life she had led in New York to make her way as a singer, the absence from her husband, the two distant lives all flashed before her eyes. As a singer, she says, "you're just auditioning all the time. Until you get something, you're unemployed, and defeated unless you're picked as the star performer. Second best isn't good enough. There is no in-between, especially for a young singer. So I made a commitment to cancel all the contracts I had, including one with Pavarotti." Katherine then went "to a fellow who owned a personnel service I had worked in for four months while I was trying to get back into school in California."

> I said "Look, I've known you for a long time. It's been ten years since I've seen you. I can't do anything except sing in three languages in front of anybody. I'll talk in front of anybody, but I can't type and I don't have any skills. What do you suggest that I do because I don't want to go back to teaching—it's just too isolating for my personality. He said, "I'll hire you in marketing." He hired me to market and I did that for two years with major marketing corporations.

Working on these projects, Katherine learned that the creativity she had developed in the theater and stage carried over to her new job. As she learned the rudiments of marketing, she chafed at the fact that many of her ideas were not being accepted. Eventually she heard "no" from her boss so many times that she decided to try something on her own.

> I went to some guys who owned a moving and storage company that would benefit by a relocation company like mine being in business and I said, "Will you help me start this business?" They said, "Why don't you come to work for us?" I thought, as long as they're in control, they're going to say "no" when it gets too risky or gets a little bit more creative or there's a soft side to it. I had $350 and I was referred to a really great attorney. I went to him and said, "I want to start my own business. Teach me. I have $350—how much are you?" "I charge $150 an hour," he answered. I said, "Talk fast. Teach me how to incorporate. Teach me what I have to do to sell stock. I want to do it legally and I have some guys I think I can sell it to." He gave me a lot more than the two and a half hours. He

helped me understand what to do. I went back to the moving guys and sold them stock in my company—preferred nonvoting stock. With that money, I rented space in the moving company. I worked with these guys as partners for the first six months. I took no salary because I wanted this thing to really fly. I now have a successful corporation in an area that did not exist before.

Pandemonium Careerist

Researchers have suggested that many people are experiencing what they call "career pandemonium"—that is, making major moves across occupational areas and disciplines.[30] If, as one research study defines it, "a career is the evolving sequence of a person's work experiences over time,"[31] then taking charge and managing it takes on a special challenge—which is likely to go beyond organizational boundaries for the woman with an entrepreneurial spirit.

Barbara Bry took her ivory tower experiences and applied them in the private sector, but only after several career changes, which involved work-family choices. A University of Pennsylvania undergraduate and Harvard MBA, Barbara first served as a business writer for the *Los Angeles Times* and then as director of programs for CONNECT, the Program in Technology and Entrepreneurship at the University of California, San Diego, internationally recognized for its work in linking emerging technology companies with technical, managerial, and financial resources. That work and her accumulated expertise in technology, business, and marketing led Barbara to found ATCOM/INFO, now a leading provider of home-away-from-home Internet and e-mail services in public locations such as hotels, airports, and convention centers. In addition, she took on the position of Vice President, Sales & Marketing, for www.proflowers.com in La Jolla, California.

In her first job, Tara Stephenson, now president of The Woodward Group, Ltd., Media, Pennsylvania, an advisory services company for mergers and acquisitions, raising capital valuations, and pretransaction services, worked in a large Chicago financial firm. She moved to other large firms and then changed to head up a small regional investment and merchant banking company. There she discovered something important: "Hey, I can do this myself!" She compares the decision to go into business for herself with one other major decision—"marrying my husband, where I thought, I can't live without this person." Reflecting on her organizational experiences in the investment banking world, Tara says,

> For me the difficulty of starting your own business and being on your own is absolutely worth not worrying about the angst of corporate America, the decisions that are outside your purview. All the difficulties, the burden, the loneliness, the decision making, and the risk, I can honestly say, are worth it.

Bink Cook, M.P.A., is founder and president of The Brighter Side, in Solana Beach, California, a boutique for women with cancer, which provides ancillary products during and after medical treatment. She was recognized as a Woman of Distinction in 1997 by the Salvation Army and as Local Hero by the Komen Foundation Drive for a Cure in 1997. She received the Women Who Mean Business Retail Award for 1998 and was recognized as Advocate of the Year by the local chapter of the National Association of Women Business Owners. Bink worked in the corporate environment as the executive director of first a small hospice and then The Wellness Community. "While at the [Wellness] center, I developed breast cancer and survived it," she says. "This helped make me aware of what patients needed." She started a company to provide services and care that no one else was providing. "All the contacts and expertise through my previous work now became very important to the success of my own business."

Jackie Jennings, president and cofounder of Johnson & Jennings, saw a market and an opportunity. Today, her midsized general contracting firm is among the leading commercial tenant improvement construction firms in southern California and one of the top ten women majority-owned businesses in San Diego. Before opening her business she had twenty years' experience in real estate. She had been sales manager for Chicago Title for seven years, directing all sales and marketing activities, when she ran into a colleague, Tom Johnson, who had left the firm three years earlier and had since obtained his general contracting license. Their research exposed a huge void in the area of tenant improvement construction. Convinced that a tenant improvement firm could succeed by filling a niche for the many building purchasers, the two set up shop in a small older home. The plan was simple: He would build it. She would sell it. The first priority for Jennings and Johnson was to establish an identity. They paid a graphic designer, a friend, most of their $4,000 capital to create a logo and letterhead package that would convey quality and establish immediate name recognition. "It worked. People would look at our business cards and say 'Oh, I've heard of you,'" says Jackie. (Several years later, she married Stuart White, the graphic designer.)

Sales was only a small part of Jackie's role in the beginning. Most days saw her out on the job sites supervising bevies of subcontractors—typically all men—often taking on the job of site cleanup and other chores by herself. One of her secrets to success was that she never pretended to know something that she didn't; instead, she listened to her subcontractors and relied on them to meet her expectations of a quality-built project.

The company today touts a client list that reads like *Who's Who* in southern California's development and property management industries and projects $15 to $17 million in revenues. Several years ago, Jackie's firm was performing the build-out for a well-known law firm's offices in downtown San Diego. A building owner had arranged a meeting between one of the law firm partners and his newly appointed general contractor and space planner to discuss the specifics of the project. As Jackie tells it,

> His jaw dropped about three inches when I walked in to introduce myself, seven months pregnant, together with Kim Lee Jackson of BSHA Design Group, who happened to be eight months pregnant. His first question was whether or not we would be able to finish the job in time, which, incidentally, I did from my hospital bed a few months later. My partner's job, of course, was on time and within budget—unlike babies, which are never according to schedule and always more expensive than planned.

Entrepreneurs have moved from the corporate environment to private ownership in a number of locations and then into franchising their businesses as part of a career progression strategy. Many of these belong to the joint venture group operating in an entrepreneurial mode.

Patricia L. Roscoe, CITE, is chair of PRA Destination Management Company, with offices in San Diego, Orange County, Los Angeles County, Palm Springs, and Santa Barbara. Her company specializes in destination management services, creative special events, and a wide array of interactive multimedia services, including in-house graphic support and web page development. She also offers programs on planning corporate incentives, board meetings, sales meetings, a convention, an association meeting, or any single special event. The Greater San Diego Chamber of Commerce named her the 1998 Entrepreneurial Spirit. In 1999 she was named by *San Diego Magazine* as one of fifty people to watch. She has been a delegate to the White House and has been named Woman of the Year by the Irish Congress of southern California. In 1998, she started another company, Patti Roscoe and Associates, Inc., a national franchising operation.

Intrapreneurs[32]

As Rosabeth Moss Kanter observed a decade ago, any definition of entrepreneurship restricted to an independent business venture or with ownership of a small business is too narrow. Her definition is that entrepreneurship is any activity that produces something—adds value or capacity to an organization.[33]

Mary Lindenstein Walshok is the associate vice chancellor, Extended Studies and Public Programs, of the University of California, San Diego, and a creative entrepreneur. She has been the driving force behind the expansion of the UCSD academic outreach, which includes extension, summer sessions, UCSD-TV, UCSD CONNECT, San Diego Dialogue, and executive education—all self-supporting academic programs of the university. The size of her operation is illustrated by the extension, which alone offers more than 2,000 continuing education courses, annually serving approximately 35,000 students. Mary oversees combined activities that have an annual self-supporting budget of approximately $24 million and a staff of 200. The entrepreneurial spirit started early in her family.

> My parents emigrated from Sweden to the United States as adults and carried with them old country ways. It was a real cultural transition. There we were in Palm Springs, California, at the end of the

1950s. Cary Grant lived two blocks up our street and Bob Hope lived two blocks in the other direction, and here was my formal Swedish father wearing a tie and jacket in the middle of the desert. My father ran a small business, which meant I was expected, from the time I was eleven, to work and contribute. Whether you're a Jewish immigrant in New York or Irish Catholic in Boston, the children of immigrants are expected to make a contribution to the family. I would roll meatballs on Saturday mornings at my dad's restaurant

I'm the typical overreaching, first-generation kid—valedictorian in high school, graduation speaker, full scholarship to a small liberal arts college, got the Ph.D. at age twenty-six. I had used a classic approach for an academic career and yet I always felt that I needed to apply my scholarship in a practical way. My closest college friend, an anthropologist, now the provost at Swarthmore College, and I would engage in conversations about her dreams of being a concert pianist or publishing in scholarly journals and I would talk about Eleanor Roosevelt's columns in *McCall's* magazine. I thought it was very, very important not just to live in an isolated ivory tower academically. I wanted to communicate with a wider public.

Boundary Spanners

People have always moved from one organization to another. Boundary Spanners are people who change not only companies but also fields or disciplines and business areas. Their career movement can be from one organization to another or from organizational life to entrepreneurship, and in some cases back again.

As in the past, many careers are built on a professional or technical specialty. Unlike in the past, instead of leading to the management of a permanent workforce, people now manage themselves while collaborating with others. Sometimes the manager outgrows the organizational boundaries. In this setting, shifting from an organizational environment to entrepreneurship is a natural, short step.[34]

Corporate Spanner

Swiss native Maria-Luisa Maccecchini, Ph.D., founder, president, and chief executive officer of Bearsden Bio, Inc., in Aston, Pennsylvania, grew up in a very conservative environment, one where "women weren't supposed to do anything except get married and have children. I broke all the expected norms."

Maria-Luisa received her Ph.D. degree in biochemistry jointly from the Biocenter of Basel, Switzerland, and Rockefeller University in New York. She continued her studies with two postdoctoral fellowships at the Roche Institute of Immunology in Basel and the California Institute of Technology, received special training in business and patent law, economics, and general and project management from Indiana State University, and followed up with a corporate finance degree from Wharton. Her first position out of graduate school was as an entry-level research scientist in charge of the molecular biology laboratory at IMC Corporation (now Mallinckrodt Group). Responsible for the cloning, expression, purification, and testing of growth factors in animals intended for meat production, she supervised and directed all aspects of two animal programs. She moved on to become general manager at Bachem Bioscience, Inc., and in 1987 founded the company's U.S. subsidiary in Philadelphia. During her four years of responsibility, five new product lines were introduced; the company grew from one to twenty employees and U.S. sales increased from $200,000 to $4 million in 1991.

"At that point," Maria-Luisa says, "I figured that I could probably run my own company."

In 1992 I started Symphony to do brain research and develop drugs for brain disorders, especially the ones for which there was no cure. It went really well for the first three years. We raised a total of $7.5 million and were just about to close on a $10 million deal when, exactly two weeks before we would close, all the dogs died. That meant one of our compounds was toxic. The investors dropped out. Within two weeks we shrank to five people. We gave up the lease to our building and for a while it looked like we were going to die—we were almost dead. So we disappeared for a while. We raised a total of $5 million in grant money because the National Institutes of Health thought the research we were conducting was good. After two years of living on grant money the investors came back in. One said, "I have a company that is as dead as your dogs. Why don't you pick it up?"

Now the CEO of Bearsden Bio, Inc., which resulted from the merger of Symphony Pharmaceuticals, Inc., and Cruachem Holdings, Maria-Luisa's company has locations in Scotland, Japan, and Virginia. The merger with Cruachem, an oligonucleotide company with extensive research in RNA function, complemented Symphony, which was developing drugs for the treatment of depression, epilepsy, pain, and the neurological deficits following stroke and head and spinal cord injury. A year after the merger, the company had over $10 million in sales.

Thrill Seeker

Some Boundary Spanners, bored if a new horizon is not in sight, continually reach out for new challenges. Such an entrepreneur is Carol E. Farren, CFM, IFMA Fellow, the president of Facility Management World Wide Ltd., a management consulting firm specializing in corporate facility management, real estate planning, and operations management. Her career developed through a succession of transitions that commingled corporate advancement and entrepreneurship. A dean's list graduate of Cornell University, her training included special work in interior design at Parsons School of Design and the acquisition of an MBA degree from New York University's Stern School of Business. In 1973, one of her clients asked her to join a major media conglomerate.

> I thought corporate life would be wonderful. The benefits would be much better than they were in the architectural design firm, and maybe a bigger firm would be a lot of fun. I went into the purchasing department, became the chief corporate designer, and did that for a couple of years. Then they said to me, "We are terminating your position. We are not terminating you, we are terminating the position." I went to some of the people I was doing projects for and the next day I was hired freelance. Another executive called me and asked me to do his apartment. Without intending to start my own business, I ended up starting a design practice out of my home. I didn't have a plan; I was planning to look for a job. After nine months and hiring two other people, I thought, "I am serious—I am in business." Then we got an office. I did that for three and a half years while working on my MBA at night. At that point I wondered, "What am I going to do next?"

My business was doing well, but it was lacking something. It was commercial and residential and I realized I really didn't like dealing with husband-and-wife issues. Then the media company I'd worked for asked me to come back. I knew they had a design department so wondered what they wanted me to do. It turned out to be construction management. They had some problems with the current group and wanted me to come back and fix them. We constructed buildings all over the U.S. as the company was expanding. I was there for another nine years and rose up through the ranks to become first the Director of Planning and later the Director of the Facilities Department. I took over maintenance and building operations, department management, and construction management. Then I got fired because another woman decided she wanted my job and she had a lot more political clout than I did. So I said to myself, "I have been here for eleven years. I have a fabulous record, everybody I ever worked for has loved what I've done, and I'm getting fired."

They were kind enough to give me a year's salary to go away quietly and not file a sexual discrimination suit. I decided to start my own company because I didn't want corporate America to do this to me again. I thought, "I don't like my life being out of control because somebody has decided that he or she doesn't want me here anymore. I don't like having my income cut off. But what am I going to do?"

I next set up a business to provide services for small and medium-sized companies that don't have a facilities department but are doing a major renovation or construction project, relocating, etc. Because they don't have the expertise in-house, many things can go wrong, and there is a lot of money at stake. After all, if you relocate a company and the phones don't work, the computers don't work, and the carpet is not on the floor, you are out of business. I had a client before I actually opened for business. I had money in the bank, the business was rolling along, and then I started getting into consulting work. Clients come to me and say, "We think we have a problem, we don't know what is causing it, we don't know how to fix it. We are in the process of renovating our building, and we have spent $20 million. We are over budget, but before we are even finished the building is getting dirty because it is not being maintained correctly, we see spots on the carpet, fingerprints on the wall."

Carol crossed boundaries, but always using her networks in a pattern that kept her highly visible. Oriented to the future and involved in new venture growth, she is presently seeking new challenges for the implementation of a new quality-of-life affordable retirement community concept.

Niche Seeker

A Niche Seeker is a Boundary Spanner whose entrepreneurial career involves an innovative breakthrough with dramatic career consequences.

Audrey Smaltz, who describes herself as "born, bred, buttered, jellied, jammed, toasted, and honeyed in Harlem," is the founder and chief executive officer of The Ground Crew. She is also a fashion authority and has been named three times to the International Best-Dressed List. In 1998, she received a *Crain's* award as one of New York's top six entrepreneurs.

The first African American to be hired by Bache and Company, Audrey trained for nine months, was recommended by John D. Rockefeller, and became a registered representative. She did not particularly like the work but had kept other career options open by modeling and pursuing her interest in fashion. With the combination of fashion, modeling, and a head for figures, she moved to Bloomingdales and then to Lane and Bryant and *Ebony* magazine. As her onstage presence got early recognition, she became the unforgettable commentator for the *Ebony* Fashion Fair shows. After more than 800 shows spanning seven years, fashion devotees in every part of the world had been won over by her sassy style. As she grew older, Audrey realized that it was extremely important to be in a position to make her own decisions. "I knew that I had to be in business for myself," she says. After a couple of false starts,

> I sent out about 100 letters to tell people I wanted to do their fashion shows. They said they didn't need me to do their fashion shows because they did their own. I wanted to do the big shows, but they didn't let me in the front door. So I went in the back door and created an industry called "backstage management." I chose the name "Ground Crew" because a successful fashion show is like an aircraft: The designer is the pilot, but the show can't get off the ground without its support staff.

In the beginning it was difficult to get customers because they said we were charging too much. Why should they pay us when they could get their friends to do the work for free? I said, "Listen, I guarantee that nothing will be missing and you know that backstage at a fashion show there are a lot of nice things for people to put in a bag." The first person to give me a job was a woman. So were the second, the third, and most of my top clients. Finally, one day Helen O'Hagan hired me to do a big show at Saks Fifth Avenue because Donna Karan told her she had used The Ground Crew for her show. I was so happy to get that show. Helen hired me again. Bill Blass and his people were backstage. He said "We've been doing shows for years and we never saw anybody do what you guys do. You're unbelievable." That's all I needed—somebody to see my technique, the way we provide a dependable, methodical calm in the eye of the backstage storm, providing and supervising some of the most expert dressers, pressers, tailors, hair and make-up artists in the business. It was the first big-name male designer assignment after all ladies—Donna Karan, Joan Vass, and Adrienne Vitadini. When Bill hired me, Oscar [de la Renta] decided he had to use The Ground Crew too. We're at a point now where The Ground Crew can take care of themselves.

Corporate Graduate

Corporate Graduates spend a lifetime in organizational service, many of them with the same company. Prior to retirement, something inspires them to become an entrepreneur, or perhaps to recognize the dream they always had. Often taking a golden parachute, they launch a business.

Diane C. Harris is the founder and president of Hypotenuse Enterprises, Inc., in Rochester, New York. She is a Phi Beta Kappa graduate of Catholic University, holds an M.S. degree from Rensselaer Polytechnic Institute, and has been listed twice in *Business Week*'s "Top 50 Women in Corporate America." In 1995, Diane was awarded the President's Twenty-first Century Leadership Award of the National Women's Hall of Fame, the first corporate executive to be so honored. She advanced rapidly with Bausch & Lomb, Inc., where she was Vice President of Corporate Development for more than a decade prior to launching her own business. Then, using the organizational parachute from Bausch & Lomb, Diane established a business that specializes in acquisitions and divestitures. It has even handled a sale for Bausch & Lomb.

Mavericks

A Maverick entrepreneur not only solves complicated problems in a creative way but also breaks out of career walls. Marjorie Alfus, a self-defined Maverick, establishes the role as "one who knows an opportunity when they see it, one who is not bound by convention, tradition, procedures, or job descriptions," someone who "works when and where there's a need, rather than according to schedules and deadlines," who "cares less about why things happen but is interested in making things happen." A Maverick is one who is "easily bored but infinitely curious, marches to the tune of a different drummer, thrives on chaos, and at times creates a little discord here and there to keep ourselves entertained."[35]

Marjorie "did it all" before the expression became fashionable. She was determined to have both a family and a career more than fifty years ago when she received her master of science degree in biochemistry at age eighteen from Ohio State University. Following a stint as a fellow in pediatrics at New York University's Bellevue Hospital, she moved to writing popular science articles, to an editorship at McGraw-Hill, and to producing science shows for television. She took up a career in local television, producing women's daytime fashion and beauty shows with both WNBC and WABC in New York.

In 1951, she quit TV to get married, and joined her husband in running his leather sportswear design and manufacturing business. The product was tremendously successful. Success, however, bored Marjorie. That led to her interest in creating a high-fashion knitwear operation in Italy when apparel importing was in its infancy. Her first factory was in the mountains north of Venice. It consisted of two machines in a loft where, she says, she learned three important rules of business: "how to drink (Grappa) and speak Italian; how to stay warm (it's always colder when you are struggling); and the knit business, the hard way." She developed factories all over Italy, traveling by train at night and working at the plants during the day. Generally credited for introducing knitwear fashions made in Italy to major U.S. specialty retailers, by 1968 she had a $5 million business consisting of four factories and two boutiques in Rome capitalizing on the tourist trade. But as in the leather manufacturing and design business with her husband, once Marjorie again gained success, it was time to chase a new dream.

In the late 1960s, Marjorie attended night school and earned her law degree from New York University, an effort, she says, "to escape" the business life she promised her father she would never pursue. After graduating, she sold her business. Then, quite by chance, she attended a dinner and chatted with an old friend, chairman of the apparel division of the Kmart Corporation, Arnold Bachner. When Bachner made her a job offer, her first response was "no way," but on reflection, she saw an unusual opportunity and climbed aboard the Kmart steamroller as it catapulted from a $2 billion retailer to a $35 billion operation. Starting in 1969, Marjorie served as general counsel and reporting head of Kmart Apparel's Foreign Department for twenty years. She then convinced the company to start its own in-house manufacturing division. As president of that wholly owned subsidiary, Sourcing and Technical Services, she traveled to every corner of the globe setting up plants and related businesses. The division added hundreds of millions to Kmart's operations.

To indicate the full "Maverick" nature of Marjorie's career, it is important to note that even while at Kmart, in her off hours her mind churned with business innovation and investment ideas, which she put into place—all catapulting into a smorgasbord of developments and experiences ranging from ownership of a camp for children to sophisticated housing developments and real estate ventures. Diverse interests are part of being a "Maverick." Since retiring from Kmart, Marjorie has pursued yet another new business direction, "Golfer's Gizmos."

Marjorie has had a most impressive career. But it is not over. As we shall see in a later chapter, she is still blazing new paths. She was one of the first women members of the Young President's Organization (YPO) and is presently on the boards of foundation of Committee 200 and the National Foundation for Women Business Owners. At her initiation and seed funding, the Harvard Business

School is preparing case studies featuring women as protagonist. She has been and is devoted to fostering women entrepreneurship practically, financially, and academically. She has created a new career descriptor through her life example of a "Maverick"—the entrepreneur brimming with creativity and innovativeness that exemplifies the boundaryless career in its fullest sense.

Career Profiles

Individually, the experiences of these entrepreneurs are unique. Collectively, they reflect the demographic, technological, and competitive forces that in recent decades have reshaped corporate structures and altered the way we view careers. They reinforce the lesson that the old view of what constitutes a career is becoming increasingly outdated, and also that something as important as your career is worth a considerable investment of your time.[36]

Though it may not be readily apparent, these entrepreneurs have many things in common. Advancement and success came after hard work, planning, and development. They possessed, expanded on, or learned specific business skills relating to finance, accounting, management, marketing, negotiation, and technology—or they were in business with people who had these skills. Throughout their lives they developed networks, and through them many found the person who, at a critical moment, would offer the advice, financing, or assistance they needed. Most got their practical experience working for others, in incubator organizations. Nearly all had to navigate important organizational transitions.

A comparative assessment of your career profile may help you see patterns not previously considered in personal development. Begin by completing a self-assessment of the three career profiles in the following three exercises, which group entrepreneurial career types into three classifications: women who initially followed a corporate career, women who always used the entrepreneurial approach, and those who feel comfortable moving back and forth between the two. For example, in Exercise 1 you are asked to read each of the twelve statements and provide "yes" or "no" responses.

The number of "yes" answers you record determines your score for corporate style. To determine how strong this style is, compute the percentage of the total responses this style represents. Use a similar procedure for each of the other exercises. When you finish your self-assessment, examine the style in the last column to see which matches yours. Then proceed to Exercise 2 to evaluate your entrepreneurial style. Exercise 3 will help you evaluate how easily you might move from a corporate to an entrepreneurial environment and vice versa. This will give you a method by which you may consider setting a new career path or direction. You will see your career in relation to those of numerous successful women entrepreneurs, many of whom moved from corporate environments to start businesses of their own. The analysis will assist in determining the style most comfortable for you. It may also help you answer some important questions about the long-range direction for your personal career.

EXERCISE 1 — Corporate Self-Assessment

Check all that apply.	YES	NO	Identify Style
1. In my organization I create and initiate work that adds value or capacity, and in the process I have carved out a niche similar to a business of my own, but I do not own the company.			Intrapraneur
2. I have held a sequence of jobs, each requiring new skills where It Is necessary to learn and change, and I measure my accomplishments partly in terms of the satisfaction this brings.			Protean
3. I went to work with every intention of staying put, but I now question the fit. There is little opportunity for me to recognize my potential in this company or industry.			Blocked Careerist
4. I have made deliberate changes in my career, leaving positions to develop a specialty, get more education, or advance myself.			Spiral Careerist
5. In my company, there is a salary system that operates within fixed bands. Moving upward from one to another in jobs and promotions provides me with considerable flexibility.			Careerbander
6. Looking back, my career path resembles a tree with forks and branches everywhere. Though unintentional, my choices have led me into totally different careers in a short period of time.			Punctuated Careerist
7. I have made major moves across occupational areas, specialties, disciplines, and organizations. Sometimes this was my idea, sometimes the choices were forced.			Pandemonium or Career Challenger
8. I feel comfortable when people follow the manual, the SOPs, or written that I am on the fast career track in my corporate or organizational environment.			Corporate Climber

Score for Corporate Style_____

(Total of all "YES" Answers)

To develop an index of the strength of your corporate preference, divide the number of check marks in the "YES" column by 8. Using a similar method in Exercises 2 and 3 will enable you to assess the strength of your propensity to remain in a corporate environment, to launch out on your own, or to move between organizational and entrepreneurial careers.

EXERCISE 2	Entrepreneurial Style Self-Assessment			
Check all that apply.		YES	NO	Identify Style
1. I have an idea, product, or service, and I have always known I wanted to own my own business.				Intentional
2. Recently I have been seriously thinking, planning, and mapping a strategy for a business of my own.				Latent Entrepreneur
3. I am self-reliant, independent, and highly motivated, innovative—in fact, almost driven to accomplish my goals—and one of these is to create a business of my own.				Entrepreneurial
4. Early on I recognized a special talent, knowledge, or skill. When I can I will employ this creative base to start a business and stay with it.				Lifetime Business Owner
5. I have thought about starting a business, but other things, such as family responsibilities, came first.				Delayed Entrepreneur
6. My spouse and I operate a business together with equal ownership and responsibilities.				Copreneur
7. I have been successful in developing patterns from my ideas, knowledge, and expertise, and I have an overriding need to create not just one but many businesses.				Franchiser or Market Expander
8. I will inherit or take over a business that has been in the family.				Family-Owned Business

Score for Entrepreneurial Style_____

(Total of all "YES" Answers)

To develop a comparative Entrepreneurial Style index with your Corporate and Spanner Styles, divide your "YES" answers on this self-assessment by 8.

Organizational/Entrepreneurial Boundary Spanners Passage Self-Assessment

EXERCISE 3

Check all that apply.	YES	NO	Identify Style
1. I have a talent, skill, or knowledge base (artist, musician, writer, computer specialist, engineer, lawyer, etc.) and I make my living using it.			TKS Based Professional
2. In my company, I have figured out some interesting and challenging projects. I was able to convince others to help develop and market them.			Market Creator
3. At least once, I have launched an outside business while still working my job.			Parallel Pather
4. I manage or work with others and adapt easily to new environments. I have used this skill to move around into new jobs and firms with fresh challenges.			Corporate Spanner
5. I look forward to moving upward in my career at this company or one like it, with a comfortable retirement package when the time comes to enable me to try my business idea.			Corporate Graduate
6. Creating products or services with my identity is important to me (i.e., leaving a legacy) and I am seeking the opportunity where I can carry out this dream.			Niche Seeker
7. I have to have something going all the time or I don't feel appropriately challenged. I see patterns of developmental opportunities and relationships where no one else does.			Thrill Seeker
8. I know an opportunity when I see it, I cannot be bound by convention, tradition, procedures, or job descriptions, and I am easily bored, infinitely curious, and thrive on chaos.			Maverick

*Score for Organizational/Entrepreneurial Boundary Style*_____

(Total of all "YES" Answers)

To develop a comparative Spanner Style *index with your* Organizational *and* Entrepreneurial Styles, *divide your "YES" answers on this self-assessment by 8.*

2. ORGANIZATIONAL TRANSITIONS

I live in San Francisco, and I liken the disillusionment in a corporation to a creeping fog. In the nighttime, the fog slowly comes in from the ocean and goes under the Golden Gate Bridge. You are really not aware of it at first, and eventually you hear the foghorns in the distance, and those foghorns indicate a change in the environment, a slow creeping disillusionment.

JILL MARTIN FUGARO[1]

Though women entered the labor force in increasing numbers beginning in the 1980s and made substantial gains, and although pay rates for women slowly crept closer to those for men, the workplace remained unequal.[2] No matter where one looked, women held fewer positions of authority, had fewer executive benefits, and had more limited mobility, particularly in international postings. Although women accounted for 10 percent of all corporate officers, they were a tiny fraction in the highest ranks of corporate leadership (2.4 percent) and were barely represented in the most highly compensated officer positions in Fortune 500 companies (1.9 percent).[3]

ORGANIZATIONAL WOMEN

In addition to the difficulty of rising higher in organizations, women frequently encountered barriers to their continued success that had little to do with their abilities or track records. Investigating why significantly more women than men had dropped off the management track, a *Fortune* study of men and women who received their MBAs in 1976 from seventeen of the most select business schools concluded that one reason was environments insufficiently accommodating to women. The phenomenon came to be called the "glass ceiling," or more recently a "second ceiling," implying barriers to women's progress based on attitudinal and organizational bias.[4] The pervasiveness of the higher ceiling in corporate America is demonstrated by the fact that over 92 percent of executive women say it exists, with consequences to productivity and career development.[5]

The extent of the imbalance was described in the 1991 National Organizational Study (NOS), a multipurpose, multi-investigator survey of the structure, context, and personnel practices of a diverse population of U.S. organizations without limits on type, geography, size, or any other dimension. The extensive, pathbreaking research yielded copious data and the revelation of overwhelming gender segregation in the workplace. Whether private for-profit businesses, public agencies, or nonprofit establishments, most men worked in typically male jobs, most women in typically female jobs. By the criterion of 30 percent to 70 percent male or female, only 19 percent of all American jobs could be called gender balanced. The greatest job segregation was found in firms that had fewer than twenty workers. Upper management positions were dominated by men, with half of managerial jobs typically male and more than a quarter exclusively so.

Gender segregation both reflected and bred inequality. Most female jobs were characterized by low wages, limited access to employee training programs, and little or no chance for advancement. In business fields where the workforce was predominantly female, wages were lower.[6] Researchers disagreed over the reasons why. Some studies suggested the arrival of women caused wages to drift lower, others said that the drop in pay and prestige occurred first, after which qualified white males, traditionally the most desirable hires, ceased to be attracted to the positions, forcing employers to look for the "next-best" alternative. Because they had fewer options, women took these lower-paying jobs. In the 1980s, for example, United Press International (UPI) had a larger number of female bureau managers than other news organizations. This was not because UPI was progressive but because it was near financial collapse and could not pay high salaries. UPI hired women to gain better talent for the money.[7]

The National Organizational Study also disproved the conventional wisdom that men, because they are viewed as breadwinners, are more committed to their companies and jobs than women, which conventional wisdom held to be home and family oriented. The real explanation was much simpler. Men, the NOS noted, were more likely than women to have jobs with commitment-enhancing features.[8]

The lack of organizational access accounts for many of today's female workplace stereotypes, helps explain why most of the literature on power and most business examples and advice are predominantly male oriented, and is the backdrop for the sex role stereotype of passive and compliant women in the business world. The historic imbalance in the workplace is also partly responsible for the dilemma women face when they seek to demonstrate their ability to handle complex business problems and their competence to move up in organizations. It also makes business situations more ambiguous for women than for men, which is one reason consultants advise treading carefully if you are new or the first woman in the position.[9]

The career obstacles to women meant that maintaining one's identity and a sense of what is important in environments shaped and largely controlled by men was usually a struggle, and sometimes absurdly so. Women who valued equality and successfully employed the management techniques of connecting directly with people instead of practicing an authoritarian management style, for example, would unwittingly reinforce sex role stereotypes and—though it sounds ridiculous—leave some men with the idea they did not have the ability to handle complex issues even as they were demonstrating their competence.[10]

THE SECOND CEILING

Women had to learn special skills to survive. In a survey conducted three years after the 1991 National Organizational Study was completed, over 85 percent of the women said that the American workplace was male oriented. A majority of women said they had to be prepared to "compete on the same terms as men" and appear "as much like men as possible." Yet, glass ceilings and second ceilings persist. A 1999 survey of more than 1,000 senior executive women in brokerage, investment, banking, and consulting businesses with more than twenty years of finance-related experience cited as problems a lack of role models, the career-limiting gender issues of corporate culture, no entry into line management, and continuing stereotypes about women's commitment to their careers.[11] A summary of recent research, also published in 1999, suggests that gender segregation not only continues but, while there has been a striking growth of women in the labor force, dramatically increasing men's chances of interacting with women in the same occupation, the changes for women interacting with men have actually declined.[12] In essence, patterns of gender interaction in organizations may tend to place women at a disadvantage, causing them to withdraw from mixed-sex groups, and narrowing their chances to participate in important projects and exert leadership.[13]

For many women, being extremely competent did not help. In a study of 1,251 executive women, the respondents reported that they were consistently expected to outperform their peers, deal with male managers in a style that made men comfortable, and seek out difficult or challenging assignments to continually prove themselves. In short, they had to outperform everyone else on the team on every project, each day, and in each new work environment.[14]

As Gary Powell has pointed out, of the explanations that have been offered to account for the relatively small proportion of women in top management, those relating to an individual's traits, skills, attitudes, and behaviors play a far less important role in explaining the existence of the glass ceiling than do explanations relating to the social system and those examining group norms and organizational cultures and programs.[15] An entrepreneur interviewed for this study said of her former company, "There were no women in management. It really didn't make a difference if you saved the company a million dollars, and I did." Claire Irving, of Investigative Consultants International, describes one of her corporate transitions prior to running her own business.

> I went from Wall Street to a firm influenced by a police mentality. I was the only woman in the managing director ranks. I've never seen anything like it. It was worse than Wall Street would ever be. A "skirt" just had no place in their business life. The fact that I was the only one who could read a balance sheet added to the prejudice. My power was in my training but it also worked against me.

When organizational values clash with gender differences, the organization usually wins. In complex ways, organizations reproduce and reinforce masculine values and subordinate feminine values in processes that both confer to white males the invisible privileges they enjoy and teach women they have to adopt male-like behaviors to get ahead.[16] Such organizational conditions have led to many entrepreneurial start-ups. For some women, it was merely a matter of finding that the attraction of being one's own boss outweighed the advantages of staying put. Elise E. McCullough, president and owner of Staffing Solution in New Orleans, never intended to start a business

> until all of a sudden I found myself without a job, rent due in three weeks. I was tired of people not taking my ideas and moving forward with them or listening to what I had to say. I knew I had things to offer. I was being held back by having to follow their directions, their rules, their policies, and their books. It finally made me decide to become an entrepreneur.

Actually, Elise has always been entrepreneurial. She began working at fourteen, and has been independent ever since.

STEPPING OFF THE CORPORATE TRACK

A 1998 Catalyst–National Foundation of Women Business Owners study revealed that the major reasons women entrepreneurs leave jobs in corporate America are a lack of flexibility (51 percent in private and 44 percent in nonprivate organizations), glass ceiling issues (29 percent in private and 16 percent in nonprivate), unhappiness with the work environment (28 percent private and 17 percent nonprivate) and a lack of challenge (22 percent private and 19 percent nonprivate). Significantly, in the last twenty years, the percentage of women leaving organizations because they had an entrepreneurial idea dropped from 50 percent to 35 percent while the percentage of women leaving because they were unfulfilled, downsized, or victims of a glass ceiling rose from 25 percent to 46 percent. A most telling statistic is that more than 60 percent of the respondents said that nothing their former organization could do would make them return. Unrecognized accomplishments, unfulfilled needs to make contributions that would be recognized, and discrimination, far more pronounced for black women than for other groups, have been strong forces in pushing women out.[17]

Entrenched good-old-boy systems in organizations have been responsible for driving out one in every five women who later start businesses. Women often make $20,000 less than men for comparable jobs. Two-thirds of employed women say they have experienced one or more episodes of discrimination. Remarked one entrepreneur, "I was the pioneering female, the only one for many years. As I got higher up, I really started experiencing more discrimination." What depressed me, said another businesswoman, "was that I felt like a female every single day of my life . . . there were colleagues who would never give me an assignment because I was a female." "I was one of the ten highest-ranking women in a 15,000-person corporation," said still another entrepreneur, "That's when I found the glass ceiling." Dallas entrepreneur Elizabeth Morris, founder of Insight Research, recalled, "They didn't encourage you to be the best you could be. They encouraged you to fit into a niche or slot . . . to fit into their expectations." The entrenched systems of organizational politics drained energy from productive work and created uncertainty about career advancement opportunities. Few women advanced to upper management, and then usually in staff positions, and opportunities in alternate organizations offered little opportunity for improvement.

By 1990, 13 percent of the female professionals leaving Fortune 500 companies were going into business for themselves. They were women like Anne Sadovsky, now CEO of her Dallas-based marketing, consulting, and seminar firm, who looked at her future and concluded that the only way through the glass ceiling was to go out on her own. Jill Martin Fugaro rose high in the management ranks of a major clothing manufacturer before launching a West Coast designer label sportswear company that grossed over a million dollars in the first year of business. She later sold her trademark line. Sudha Pennathur held a variety of corporate management positions over an eighteen-year span, and she filled all of them well. When she left to establish a firm that designs jewelry, accessories, gifts, and other *objets d'art* ranging from reproductions of antiques to unique originals, she was the youngest general merchandise manager in the company's history. Few companies had employees as devoted as Honi Stempler, who worked sixty- to eighty-hour weeks in her corporate job before leaving to found the first of her own companies. Few executives pursued careers as purposefully as Linda Sahagian, who successfully battled her way through a number of organizational discrimination barriers before opening her Chicago specialty snack foods and confections manufacturing company.[18]

The repeated occurrences of capable women exiting firms provide an important wake-up call for corporate career counselors. Creative talent will be drained from organizations that do not pay sufficient attention to the expectations and values of all their employees. Change is possible. The primary change ingredient is the role model at the top. The change in the corporate culture at Hewlett-Packard is attributed to Lewis E. Platt, the company's fifty-eight-year-old chairman. To stem the mass exit of women, he took positive steps to change the company package to accommodate the heretofore incompatible work and home schedules of women by adding flexible work schedules, work days at home, shared jobs, and paid sabbaticals with no questions asked. Having personally learned how difficult it was to juggle the competing duties of father and breadwinner as a rising senior executive after the death of his first wife, he had come to understand the problem.[19] Recently, Hewlett-Packard appointed a woman to be the chief executive officer, making it only the third Fortune 500 company to do so.

The female entrepreneurs who emerged from these corporate environments tended to be internally motivated ("I have always wanted to be my own boss") rather than exhibiting the externally motivated characteristics of men ("I had identified a market need"). They placed a higher value on equality of treatment, both for themselves and for others, than did men. They operated in a more flexible, innovative, action-oriented, integrated, and inspirational management style rather than emphasizing long range, formalized, and strategic planning. For many, a primary business goal was to do the work they wanted to do, as opposed to focusing on money. They were strongly driven to be their own bosses, to be credible, to be independent.[20] Though 59 percent of men business owners are in a business closely related to their previous careers, 56 percent of women owners are not, with 42 percent in a field unrelated to their previous organizational career. However, women who launched a business in an industry sector very similar to the work environment in which they had gained their experience were the most successful.[21]

For many entrepreneurs, research suggests, it is the combination of organizational push and entrepreneurial pull that leads them to found businesses. While the desire to be in charge and to be one's own boss is the most cited reason for starting a business, the actual launching was a gradual process. Women were less likely to quit their current jobs because of plans for their ventures and more likely to layer full-time with part-time work.[22] A common approach is to explore opportunities or even start a business while still employed and remain in the position until it has a firm footing.[23] A more recent approach, often used by corporate graduates, is to have a business firmly launched prior to retirement and to continue to be involved afterwards.

ORGANIZATIONAL INCUBATORS—
THE UPSIDE AND DOWN

Diane C. Harris, a prototype corporate graduate, had a successful career within a corporate environment prior to becoming an entrepreneur. Her experience at Bausch and Lomb as a research chemist led to advancement in the company's technical, marketing, and general management areas. As vice president in the Soflens products group, she orchestrated B & L's successful entry into the contact lens solutions business. As director of corporate planning and as vice president of corporate development, she was deeply involved in the acquisition and divestiture transactions that marked B & L's billion-dollar corporate restructuring program and transformed the company into a global leader in optics and healthcare products. Diane completed 230 transactions (including 47 acquisitions), which put B & L into five new business sectors with worldwide operations and provided half of the company's growth every year for over a decade. And when she had risen as high as she could go on the corporate ladder, as we saw in Chapter 1, Diane founded Hypotenuse Enterprises, a business specializing in the type of acquisitions and divestitures she was doing for Bausch and Lomb.

There are many advantages to working in a corporate environment, including the following:

- Gaining exposure to customers, suppliers, and competitors
- Acquiring specific managerial, technical, and planning skills
- Often learning from less-than-optimal managers and working environments

Diane Harris and an entire generation of entrepreneurs have clearly benefited from organizational incubator experiences. Their careers illustrate the upside of organizational incubation. Research suggests that the more successful of these entrepreneurs launched firms in the sector or industry in which they had gained experience, training, and skills, or in firms that dealt in products and services similar to those of their prior organizations.[24] The lesson of taking advantage of organizational opportunities to obtain the broadest possible range of skills and experiences is underscored by many women now in business for themselves who look back and see what they missed. Interestingly, what these business owners failed to take from their previous organizational environments had a lot to do with their intentions while they were in those positions. Women who had entered corporations intending to go into business for themselves someday tended to concentrate on industry-related skills and marketing and to underestimate the importance of managerial skills. Those who had gone into the companies initially intending to climb the corporate ladder had underestimated the need for marketing and technical skills.[25]

There can be a downside to working for many corporations. Marilyn Sifford, owner of STAR Consulting, in Philadelphia, accumulated experience across six or seven different industries and organizations in her crossbanding career.

> I was a truant officer, then I worked for the state employment security commission. This was followed by a personnel job at a newspaper, and then I got involved in training. After that, I worked for an insurance company and from there went into organizational development in an oil company. The oil company had a major restructuring and eliminated my department. My next job was at a university hospital. The man who hired me died of cancer. The man who succeeded him called me into his office one day and said, "I want my own team." My next job was starting an internal consulting function inside a financial corporation. I'd been there about two years when I was recruited for a job with a major corporation in another state, a position that basically put together everything I had done up to that point. I passed the six-figure mark with that job.

To gain flexibility in her life and control over her work, Marilyn started her own firm.[26] She would be one model for a long line of high-performing women who would exit unsatisfactory corporate environments to start successful businesses of their own.

CHARTING A COURSE

While many people are certain where the path they are following will eventually lead, the evidence from research shows that things will probably work out differently than you suppose. Curiously enough, a strong desire to be an entrepreneur someday is not a particularly good predictor of what women in organizations will eventually do.[27] In doing the research for *Women Entrepreneurs: Moving Beyond the Glass Ceiling,* I was struck by the fact that the largest number came not from the group that had set out from the beginning to found businesses but from the group that had first advanced in corporations and then made step-by-step decisions that eventually led them to start businesses of their own. To manage a career successfully, it is essential to monitor many paths and keep the options open.

Every year, prospective students and parents buy millions of dollars worth of books advising how to choose the right college and, after selecting several, study how to get in. The reason (probably understood better by parents) is that today the most certain path to satisfying and financially rewarding work is to get the right education. There is also considerable evidence, anecdotal and otherwise, to convince people that the better the educational institution, the better the start in life. So the struggle is to get into what the public perceives to be the "right" schools.[28]

The same logic can be applied to selecting a place to begin your work career. *Fortune* magazine has been tracking the 100 best companies to work for since 1998. The annual list is now based on more than 20,000 questionnaires filled out by randomly chosen employees at 238 large and medium-size companies from a pre-selected database. The best companies to work for are distinguished by the relationship management has with employees. Great workplaces not only sound nice, there is a direct economic payoff; the companies also rank in *Fortune*'s Top 100.[29]

The combination of a good working environment in companies that offer learning opportunities and training in the most advanced technology and skills can be hard to beat. Companies currently invest over $30 billion annually in training, according to a recent article by Catalyst.[30] Historically, most of this training focused on skills development or elements related to production and sales. This is no longer true. The widespread downsizing and corporate restructuring not only has resulted in flatter company structures, it has meant that employees must have a broader range of skills. Companies today provide a range of training opportunities to enhance skills. Many of the skills acquired in corporate training programs are portable—technical expertise in particular. Entrepreneurs who have been exposed to training programs find the experience invaluable.

It is a mistake, however, to assume that technical skills alone will allow you to leap diagonally upward through various corporate environments. As top female executives point out, technical competence may be crucial when getting hired, but advancement is based on many other factors.[31]

There are other advantages to spending time in a corporate incubator, some not immediately obvious. The relationship between corporate field experience and new venture creation is strong.[32] Of the group of successful entrepreneurs participating in one study, 92 percent were in a field very similar to that of the organization they had left and 87 percent said there had been a direct transfer of information from the prior organizational setting to the business they now own.

Even where the new business was dissimilar, many of the entrepreneurs said they employed skills similar to those they used in the previous organizational environment. In some cases, the new business came about directly or indirectly from outsourcing by the incubator firm. Diane Harris, for example, did some work for Bausch and Lomb after graduating from the firm. In the case of Elizabeth Morris, who operates a Dallas research firm that has contributed to location decisions affecting the workplaces of more than 1.3 million workers, a succession of positions she held identified the market for the company she eventually formed. "I think the business kind of came and got me," she says.

> It developed out of the previous work I had done. I spent seven years as an assistant city manager. We were responsible to everyone. Everything we said, everything we did was screened through different filters, and perhaps some elected officials. I had moved from that position into real estate brokerage where I saw a totally different business pace but very little research to accompany it. So on one side we had extraordinary levels of research, and on the other side we had none. I moved to a corporation that developed office buildings, warehouses, and apartment complexes. I was in on the ground floor. Inside three years I had an opportunity to build an office building, a shopping center, and a 120-unit condominium complex virtually unsupervised because the company was growing so fast. I got a real quick education as a developer. I became convinced that the industry was going to hell in a handbasket because

the research was not being done to support all the development. Because I did an extraordinary amount of research on my projects, people kept asking me if I would help with theirs. The firm I was with didn't offer the money I needed to make it. So I said, "OK, I've got two kids, a mortgage, and a car payment and I'm going to make a success of this. I want to see if I'm as good as I think I am." I got a white-knuckle grip on the table and submitted my resignation. My research company now has three branches.[33]

INCUBATOR RETROSPECTIVES

What did the new entrepreneurs value most after starting their businesses? For some, it was the experiences they had gained in an organizational incubator in facing major setbacks and achieving success. For others, it was the experience gained from supervising managers and workers. Slightly more than one-third (34 percent) of the entrepreneurs brought from the organizational environment the key contacts that they later used in their own firms. Slightly less than half (49 percent) said they had directly transferred business expertise. Over half of the entrepreneurs had not benefited from either formal or informal organizational training programs. Most commonly, this was because access to training was part of organizational patterns of tracking and grooming men, but not women, for powerful positions.[34]

MENTORS

While mentoring relationships are important for all organizational members, they are essential for women. Mentors can both protect women from discrimination and help them learn what men supposedly learn from the "old boy's network" about how to navigate their way past obstacles to their career success. Mentored individuals (also known as protégés) experience greater career success in objective terms than nonmentored individuals. They are also more satisfied with and committed to their jobs, careers, and organizations; receive more promotions and greater compensation; and have greater career mobility than nonprotégés.[35] Catalyst findings (1998) also indicate that, if one wishes to rise to the level of female executive, mentoring is a key strategy for both breaking through the glass ceiling and overcoming barriers that lie on the other side.[36]

Many women who rise to the top levels in their organizations find new obstacles and shattered illusions. Some turn to other avenues for new opportunities. Increasingly, many are likely to forsake the corporate world to run their own businesses when the mentoring and supportive relationships are missing inside the corporate culture. From the earlier work reported in *Women Entrepreneurs,* we found positive experiences related to mentoring from the small number of women who had benefited.[37]

A recent survey finds that mentoring makes a decided difference in career advancement. Among female entrepreneurs, more than nine out of ten (94 percent) said the experience was crucial or very helpful to their success. Mentoring for women appears to be on the increase in organizations. More than two-thirds (68 percent) of women aged eighteen to twenty-nine say they have benefited from a mentor, compared with slightly more than half (56 percent) of women aged fifty or older.[38]

ORGANIZATIONAL SKILLS AND LEARNING

Nothing is guaranteed. Just working in an organization does not ensure that you are acquiring the skills and developing the expertise to move on. A third of the entrepreneurs in one study said that the skills acquired in previous organizations prepared them in a general way rather than in the specifics of running the businesses they would create. Says Janet McCann, a Chicago interior designer, "I remember thinking after beginning my business, well, I must be nuts, I know nothing about finance, nothing about marketing, I know nothing about any of this stuff. What am I doing here?"[39] Many other entrepreneurs also wished they had better preparation, specifically in human resource management, finance, marketing, sales, and legal expertise before starting their businesses.

Survival Skills

A major value of an incubator organization lies in its importance in teaching survival skills, learning to cope with setbacks, and dealing with special challenges. The credibility that an organization provides is important because it can remove barriers and blocks and lend a special sense of self-knowledge and confidence.

Lillian Coury, who later founded a New York printing company, established three criteria in plotting her course. "First, I wanted to deal with decision makers. Second, I wanted to develop expertise in repeat sales. Finally, I wanted a creative selling environment with input into the sale." Meeting the criteria meant acquiring a job in a male-dominated major company because it was the most influential organization.[40]

Management and Entrepreneurial Passages

Some research suggests that managers in large organizations who do not aspire to become entrepreneurs value management experience more highly because it is key to upward mobility. Other research suggests that women who aspire to be entrepreneurs are more likely to be dissatisfied and frustrated in their organizational employment and less committed to their companies than women who intend to stay in the organizations. Nothing in any of these studies predicts women's career transitions. What has been reported is the general agreement in research findings that success as an entrepreneur is highly correlated with extensive managerial and start-up experience and the ability to react quickly to environmental change.[41] The lesson seems to be that to have a successful and creative career it is essential to survey many paths while still inside the corporation and, particularly, to acquire experience in management and take on demanding assignments and challenging opportunities.

Career barriers and special challenges may surface in even the best organizational environments. The entrepreneurs in this study who ran up against immovable barriers and then left companies have few regrets. As one says, "The only way through the glass ceiling is to go out on your own. . . . The guys still run the major corporations in America today."[42]

DESIGNING A TRANSITIONAL STRATEGY

The best career advancement strategy is to maintain a cutting edge in your field, practice strong business and people skills, and develop portable talents. Most of all, you must be adaptable. Managing your business career instead of letting your work life manage you is a daily challenge. It begins by analyzing where you are now, where you intend to be in five years, in ten years, and by the end of your career. The underlying question is: How ready are you to move on to the next phase? You can begin by selecting the best companies to work for (and, once inside, selecting your boss carefully). The question then is: How do you make the best choices?

The problems of operating in environments largely dominated by men have led many women to continually reassess themselves and their situations. The trick is to do this correctly. Constructing an index of your self-efficiency is a good starting point. It requires simultaneously examining workplace obstacles and your performance in the context of what you expect or would like to see and determining whether one or the other or both need changing. To begin your transition assessment, answer the following questions and carefully analyze your responses.

- What incubator organizations offer the training, experience, and skills I need?
- How do I identify these organizations or entrepreneurial options?
- What package of skills can I put together to get inside?
- Once there, how do I take the best advantage of the environment?
- Will I be able to maintain a positive attitude reflected in:
  - high self-esteem
  - efficacy
  - a mind-set for success
- Am I doing interesting work that gives me visibility?
- Am I moving up, or on?
- Am I managing my own career, or am I just reacting?

- What education, certifications, and/or credentials do I need now and in the future?

Steps in the assessment process can be facilitated by using Exercise 4, Transition Readiness Assessment I. First, identify the values important to you in the work environment, a baseline measure of what you would like to have if you could get it. You do this by rating a list of attributes that are valued highly by employees who consider their firms to be the best places to work in the United States. Exercise 4 includes in the left-hand column a list of attributes that employees have rated as desirable.[43] These attributes are grouped in three categories: *Work Environment, Compensation Package,* and *Opportunities to Get Ahead.* In the right-hand column you will rate each attribute on a scale from 1 (low desirability) to 5 (high desirability). After you complete your rating, you will want to review the list of attributes, removing any that are unimportant to you and adding others that you consider important.

Second, survey the work environments of firms that you personally have identified for values and attributes in accord with yours. This requires some in-depth research on the companies in the field in which you're working or planning to enter. Such listings can be found in a number of places, including *Fortune*'s annual list of 100 Best Companies to Work For, *Working Woman*'s annual list of twenty-five top companies, and *Working Mother*'s annual survey of family-friendly companies that identifies the 100 best national companies based on pay, advancement opportunities, childcare facilities, flexible work schedules, and the like.[44] You may also wish to consult the National Association of Businesswomen's list of award-winning companies that have been identified from the national and international pools of candidates, and the winners of the Catalyst's annual diversity awards.[45] The Catalyst awards list includes organizations that recognize and make strong efforts to promote women based on their abilities, performance, and credentials.

It is important to remember that not all organizations appear on national lists such as those mentioned here, not because they do not have environments friendly to women, but because of the selection criteria. In the case of the *Working Woman* list, for example, the selection pool consists of publicly held companies with more than 3,000

Transition Readiness Assessment I

EXERCISE 4

Workplace Attributes Valued Highly by U.S. Employees	Desirability in My Personal Strategy
	Rate each attribute

Work Environment — low 1 2 3 4 5 high

Will what the company is doing continue to be part of the market? (*Product or Service*)	— — — — —
Does the company have a history of ups and downs? (*Stability*)	— — — — —
Does the industry have a future? (*Industry*)	— — — — —
Is there a cycle of widespread layoffs and rapid hiring? (*Employment Patterns*)	— — — — —
Is the workforce diverse? (*Diversity*)	— — — — —
Does the company have a reputation for treating employees and customers fairly? (*Ethics*)	— — — — —
Is the company state of the art? (*Technology*)	— — — — —
Is the organization hierarchical? (*Work Styles*)	— — — — —
Does the company employ teams? (*Participation*)	— — — — —
Would you like to live there? (*Location*)	— — — — —
How does the company compare with others in the field? (*Credibility*)	— — — — —

Compensation Package

Salary (*Industry Level*)	— — — — —
Employee Package (*Employee stock options, 401K, Flex Time*)	— — — — —
Fringe Benefits (*Medical, Dental, Life Insurance, other*)	— — — — —
Employee-Friendly Benefits (*facilities for child or elder care, laundry services, other*)	— — — — —
	— — — — —

Opportunities to Get Ahead

Are there opportunities for future career development? (*Career Building*)	— — — — —
What access will I have to training programs? (*Training*)	— — — — —
Will the position be challenging? (*Challenge*)	— — — — —
Does the employer pay for college programs? (*Education*)	— — — — —

employees and at least two women on the board of directors.[46] To identify other best companies you might find attractive, examine the award-winning firms in your region or field. Check for companies that receive the local Chamber of Commerce award for employer of the year and local winners of awards such as those given by the National Association of Women Business Owners. Other groups that give recognition and awards to companies for major accomplishments include the Conference Board, the National Council of Women Corporate Advancement, *Crain's New York* and *Crain's Chicago Business,* and industry and trade organizations. Your network of contacts can serve as an additional source of information about good companies. You can get recommendations from customers of your present company, college and university placement services, business associates, colleagues, family, friends, and board associations.

Third, probe more deeply into the firms you identified in the second step to further narrow the field. Sources include company web pages; business outlets such as the *Wall Street Journal, Moody's Industrial Guide, Dun & Bradstreet Report, Fortune, Forbes Database,* the *New York Times,* the *Dow Jones Business Directory,* and the Annual Report Gallery; trade publications; and online career development centers.[47] You can request published information from each organization you're interested in. As you go through this process, examine the information in light of the list of attributes that you have identified as important.

Finally, after collecting the data and developing a competitive profile of companies that might be attractive to you, narrow your choices. Then compare these firms to your present employer. At the end of the book we will add entrepreneurship to the list.

Exercise 5, Transition Readiness Assessment II, provides in the left-hand column a list of valued workplace attributes. In the next three columns, indicate the likelihood (on a scale of 1 to 5) that you will find that valued attribute in your present work environment, in one of the companies you identified after working through Exercise 4, or by going an entrepreneurial route. An assessment of the rating totals for each career choice will enable you to better understand your readiness for a career switch. (A separate worksheet, Exercise 6, is provided to enable you to include other values that are desirable to you but aren't listed on this sheet.) Women who contemplate starting their own business or developing an existing business will need to acquire considerable data on all aspects of entrepreneurship and to complete a business plan. Chapter 7 provides guidance and sources where the necessary information can be readily acquired. [48]

For those in organizations or who are getting ready to enter the workforce, the five-step assessment process we have just explored will yield a comparison of three distinct choices: staying with your firm, making a job change, or going into business for yourself. For entrepreneurs, the choices are: continuing as you are, taking the business to the next stage, or shifting to corporate life. Whether making the decision to remain in the same firm or to transition to another organization, or to entrepreneurship, you need to ask yourself some important questions. Do I have the qualifications to be employed by one of the firms that appear desirable? If not, am I willing to put in the extra effort to acquire the education or skills I need? What specific steps do I need to take? Am I willing to take the entrepreneurial risk? Depending on how carefully you complete this analysis, the exercises can help you take an honest look at the career directions you might pursue and how ready you are to make a transition. A valuable lesson from present research on women entrepreneurs is that they not only develop important skills while inside an organization, working for someone else, but that they also may transfer in and out of entrepreneurship to higher corporate positions with the added skills gained by owning a business of their own. This career assessment at the transition point provides you with the kind of personal information about what you value in a work environment that no other measurement could possibly reveal.

EXERCISE 5 — *Transition Readiness Assessment II*

Comparison of Alternatives Across Choices

Valued Workplace Attributes	Present Company Likelihood of Finding 1 2 3 4 5	Potential Company Likelihood of Finding 1 2 3 4 5	Entrepreneurial Alternative Likelihood of Finding 1 2 3 4 5
Work Environment			
Product or Service	— — — — —	— — — — —	— — — — —
Stability	— — — — —	— — — — —	— — — — —
Industry	— — — — —	— — — — —	— — — — —
Employment Patterns	— — — — —	— — — — —	— — — — —
Diversity	— — — — —	— — — — —	— — — — —
Ethics	— — — — —	— — — — —	— — — — —
Technology	— — — — —	— — — — —	— — — — —
Work Styles	— — — — —	— — — — —	— — — — —
Participation	— — — — —	— — — — —	— — — — —
Location	— — — — —	— — — — —	— — — — —
Credibility	— — — — —	— — — — —	— — — — —
Score			
Compensation Package			
Salary	— — — — —	— — — — —	— — — — —
Employee Package	— — — — —	— — — — —	— — — — —
Fringe Benefits	— — — — —	— — — — —	— — — — —
Employee-Friendly Benefits	— — — — —	— — — — —	— — — — —
Score			
Opportunities to Get Ahead			
Career Building	— — — — —	— — — — —	— — — — —
Training Programs	— — — — —	— — — — —	— — — — —
Challenge	— — — — —	— — — — —	— — — — —
Education	— — — — —	— — — — —	— — — — —
Score			
TOTAL SCORE			

Scoring: On a scale of 1 (low value) to 5 (high value), rate each attribute for each alternative. Add all the ratings in each section and divide by the number of attributes to determine the score for that section. Then total the scores in each column. The highest total score indicates which alternative might be your next desired career choice.

EXERCISE 6 — *Transition Readiness Assessment Worksheet*

Comparison of Alternatives Across Choices

Valued Workplace Attributes	Present Company Likelihood of Finding	Potential Company Likelihood of Finding	Entrepreneurial Alternative Likelihood of Finding
	1 2 3 4 5	1 2 3 4 5	1 2 3 4 5
Work Environment			
_____	— — — —	— — — — —	— — — — —
_____	— — — — —	— — — — —	— — — — —
_____	— — — — —	— — — — —	— — — — —
_____	— — — — —	— — — — —	— — — — —
_____	— — — — —	— — — — —	— — — — —
_____	— — — — —	— — — — —	— — — — —
_____	— — — — —	— — — — —	— — — — —
_____	— — — — —	— — — — —	— — — — —
_____	— — — —	— — — —	— — — — —
Score			
Compensation Package			
_____	— — — — —	— — — — —	— — — — —
_____	— — — — —	— — — — —	— — — — —
_____	— — — — —	— — — — —	— — — — —
Score			
Opportunities to Get Ahead			
_____	— — — — —	— — — — —	— — — — —
_____	— — — — —	— — — — —	— — — — —
_____	— — — — —	— — — — —	— — — — —
Score			
TOTAL SCORE			

Scoring: On a scale of 1 (low value) to 5 (high value), rate each attribute for each alternative. Add all the ratings in each section and divide by the number of attributes to determine the score for that section. Then total the scores in each column. The highest total score indicates which alternative might be your next desired career choice.

3. Networks

The networks of a woman entrepreneur resemble a sphere. She is at the center, the essential core, connecting not only to subordinate managers but also to her employees on the organizational surface. In turn, they link to their neighbors and network to others more distant. The intricate links form a graphic; they are a means of unleashing the creative energy of all.

D. P. Moore

To remain competitive, an entrepreneur must simultaneously deal with day-to-day operating concerns and monitor the continual flow of information. In the corporate environment, one finds experts, mentors, and a range of support facilities. Once in business for yourself, however, gaps in knowledge, training, or information, not recognized in the supportive organizational climate, can surface quickly. Ties to others become critical. That is why the path of business success winds through networks. Entrepreneurs who develop the skills to cross boundaries, make connections, and link resources tend to be the most successful.

Networks of trusted advisors serve women entrepreneurs in a variety of ways. They can be an important confidential sounding board for voicing concerns and sharing solutions. They are usually an integral part of an interactive strategy to build and develop successful businesses. Says Mary Walshok of the University of California, San Diego, networks are the "socialization process that leads us to be different colors in a single hour." Successful networks are based on establishing a deep anchor among a small set of friends or a close professional community. Aliza Sherman, founder of Cybergrrl, Inc., for example, designed the New Girls Network—WEB Girls—as a place where women could go to share resources and information about technology, whether it be learning how to use e-mail, finding out how to buy a first computer, or seeking out venture capital or funding for entrepreneurial efforts.

Networking begins with sharing places and spaces and the quality and quantity of relationships. It thrives on linking people and the activity that the connections generate. As a business owner, your goal is the entrepreneurial equivalent of the profile description of Lois Weisberg, the Commissioner of Cultural Affairs for the City of Chicago. She stands "at the intersection of different worlds, connecting people, creating opportunities, and spreading ideas," wrote Malcolm Gladwell. She connects because "there is nothing more irresistible to a human being than to be unqualifiedly liked by another."[1]

Networking is not an afterthought, something to be done after more important business matters are attended to. As a Chicago entrepreneur pointed out, "Without the personality, networking, connections, and the ability to put the pieces all together, one can't do well." Launching and operating a business requires constant networking. "It's not cold calls" advised another entrepreneur; "it's the contacts and referrals." Female entrepreneurs with mature firms attribute sales growth to network activities that enabled them to gain strategic advantages over larger, more established competitors.[2]

High-level managers as well as business owners understand the importance of networking. Iris Newman, Veritas Medical Services, Inc., founded Philadelphia's Women's Investment Network (WIN) at about the same time she started her own business. It brought together female founders and executive officers in high-technology businesses. The object was to make people aware of the number of women in these high-growth businesses, to provide some of the opportunities that men have had in networks, and to do away with the myth that women who were starting businesses only needed to raise $5,000 to $10,000 to begin a cottage operation. "The president of Citibank in Rochester, New York, acted as WIN's first sponsor and supported the start of WIN," says Iris.

I told him about the idea of creating the Women's Investment Network for high-tech entrepreneurs. He said, "I think it's fabulous. I'll be the first sponsor." I came back to the group and said, "Now we have a sponsor; we'd better do something." One of the women was an attorney with one of the large firms, and she put all our papers together as a not-for-profit. Then we went out to other corporate investors in the Philadelphia area. They each put in $5,000 to $10,000. We hired an executive director to give WIN the attention it needed. Our membership is now up to sixty women. We have a really interesting mix of women who have started networking among themselves and assisting one another. The objective is to have women who will pick up the phone and call five friends and say, "I have a deal. Do you want to come in with me?"

The bottom line is that only an unwise beginning entrepreneur will say, "I can do it all by myself." The notion of the lone wolf —a single individual who can make it unaided in a rapidly evolving technological environment and an increasingly international economy— is not just a romantic relic, it is a dangerous idea.

Women, Men, and Networks

A self-managed career depends greatly on a web of contacts. The world will not beat a path to your door or even know if you have a mousetrap unless someone tells someone else. With contacts, one can capitalize on the resources at the heart of networking, the exchange of ideas and information that enhance knowledge and experience. A successful network can also provide an important support group, offer encouragement at just the right moment, and allow you the opportunity to relieve the tension from feeling alone in your situation. To take control of your career, begin with networking.

Organizational Networks

Male managers and professionals have long operated successfully in organizational networks. As women in organizations increased in number, they followed suit, as the title of a 1997 *Wall Street Journal* article, "New Girl Network Is Boon for Women Lawyers," suggests. Women constructed ties for the same reasons men do: effective

networking is a requirement for organizational success and relationships are vital to a business career. In corporations, researchers
have pointed out, the formal organizational chart shows only the
skeleton of the company. The collective, informal networks, the
really important part of the organization, make up the central ner-
vous system. Networks are the shadow organization behind every
company's organizational chart.[3]

High-Level Networking

Studies show that men and women in organizations do not inhabit
the same networks. There are several reasons for this. The most
important is that the organizations seldom provide identical cultures
and opportunities for men and women. This does not mean that men
and women are necessarily predisposed to form and maintain separate networks. However, the positions that individuals hold within
organizations confer status, determine who speaks to whom, who
defers, and otherwise direct how contacts are carried on. The fact that
fewer women than men occupy the high-level, high-profile positions
creates separate gender effects.[4] As a rule, women have to adapt to
male-dominated, gendered institutions.

The first women to enter formerly all-male environments were
acutely aware of this. Susan Bird, president of Women.future, LLC,
and one of the founders of the Committee 200, calls it the "talking
dog syndrome." "I started practicing law in a firm in which there
were three women," she recalls.

> When I joined the workforce, there was no question about it—once
> you took your place, you were noted because you were so unusual.
> When I worked for IBM, I was the first woman to sell computers. I just
> loved being introduced that way. Then, finally, it dawns on you that
> you're a freak of nature and you realize that the cure is to bring in other
> people like yourself. I think the same thing is happening slowly on cor-
> porate boards, because some women are occupying six or seven board
> seats while others are helping to spread the opportunities. We've just
> formed a relationship with a firm that places women on corporate
> boards. The interest here is in placing women who haven't been heard
> of before.

Women's Networks Under Construction

Extensive networking efforts are being led by Marjorie Alfus and the Committee 200, an elite group of businesswomen whose membership is restricted to women owning companies generating annual revenues of more than $20 million or who manage a division of a U.S.-based company with annual revenues of more than $100 million. One project is a matched-funds gift to Harvard Business School to provide $1 million over the next five years for the purpose of generating between sixty and seventy-five case studies featuring women executives facing management dilemmas.[5] Members of the Committee 200 and others will provide the material and the funds for the first cases. Notes Susan Bird, "The fact that Harvard publishes 96 percent of the case studies around the world and that women are also making up a greater percentage of students in business schools was also a contributing factor in the decision."

Marjorie, a former Kmart executive, a lawyer, and a supporter of the case-study method of instruction, considers the Committee 200 project a great opportunity to help the next generation of women executives along. Her prediction of the future that women executives will face is interesting. "I think a lot of women are smarter than men, more insightful," she says. "Everything is a ball game to a guy. I tell women that they are going to have it much tougher than I did. Their competition is women."[6] As Susan Bird points out, many women have had to deal with the same organizational barriers, but a large number are now in leadership roles, "doing very well, thank you very much." The Committee 200 is now looking at the interest of many members in mentoring. "Some women," Susan says,

> have now run their companies very successfully, some have sold them, some are still operating. Most of our work is through MBA programs like Stern, Columbia, Harvard, and Stanford. We are now deciding our next thrust. Should we be working with women who have small companies that look as if they have great promise, who aren't eligible for membership but would gain from our accumulated knowledge? There are some fairly faint voices asking why do we start with the women who are already focused on this business? Why

don't we talk to high school girls? We have many challenges ahead to continue our networking.

The work of the Committee 200 and other organizations, such as the National Federation of Women Business Owners, to create high-profile women's networks is a direct reaction to the exclusion from networks women experience in business. A Cincinnati entrepreneur summed it up:

> I would be willing to bet that those fellows on the board get together on some things that are not shared with the few women who serve on the same boards. Irrespective of how shrewd or clever a woman is, she will still not have access to the well-kept information that is saved for the good old boys. As women, we are just now learning how to get some of that information from them. But believe me, they network with one another, as women are doing now, and they talk to the point when they say, "Go in and see my banker" and, "I'll call him for you." They call the banker and say, "Help him out." When the person gets there, the banker says, "Well, I'll give you a thirty-day loan and then you can turn it over and you can do this and that." This is information that women have not been privy to. But most of all, we have not been in those boardrooms with men learning how to do things. It's something new for women.
>
> Obviously, while this is not solely learned by sitting in a boardroom, the access to the information is created by that membership. Where you learn it is after you meet that person in the boardroom and you are standing and chatting, or working the crowd.
>
> The trick is breaking into male-dominated networks when you have no ties other than through business associations because much of the information, while related to business, is considered personal. The key to the problem that women entrepreneurs confront may lie in something they are not discussing.[7]

What is happening now is a continuation of a process that started several decades ago. Though men and women build networks equally well, in organizations each gender tended to interact with itself. The net result was that most organizations had two informal and segregated networks, one male and one female. In part, this was because many women had to work their way around the internal structural barriers that constrained them inside organizations by building special types of contacts. Today, women are moving rapidly to build the same kinds of contacts at the higher levels.[8]

Networking and Leadership

Change sometimes involves seemingly little things. In focus groups around the country, women recounted experiences of attending conferences where they had been one of the few women who were not spouses or had been excluded from organized tennis or golf games or other all-male networking gatherings. In 1969, Diane Harris was the only woman member of the Association for Corporate Growth. At an early association meeting, only a handful of women attended, and Diane noticed they were indistinguishable from the spouses. She chaired a committee that changed the badge color to differentiate association members. Diane later became the association's first female president.

Organizational Networking

The research findings on organizational networking suggest two things, one important for women in organizations, the other for aspiring entrepreneurs. In the corporate world, men naturally make the informal organizational contacts that are a well-understood part of the status quo. Women have to learn the networking skills that will enable them to tap into the informal organization. Particularly useful in organizational networking are contacts with those who exercise power. In most organizations, these people are men. But because women usually network with other women, not with the men who hold the power, this means they are often not part of the in-group and may not see themselves as an integral part of the organization. Possibly this is because women, more than men, tend to consider organizational networking "office politics" by another name and are disinclined to participate. When women do play the corporate political game, they often network less effectively than men do because they lack the societal conditioning. This does not have to be the case. Smart networking and smart office politics work the same way, advises Susan M. Barbieri—key skills include "communicating well with superiors, drawing out the best in subordinates, and working easily with colleagues." Organizational networking is necessary because it keeps you in touch with the strategic information you need.[9]

For the aspiring entrepreneur, there are two suggestions. The first is that continuous networking is important and a learned skill. The second is that the old organizational networks and the networking style practiced in a previous corporate environment may not transfer well to business ownership. Entrepreneurs need to build new networks, and the time to start is before the business opens.

PRE-VENTURE NETWORKING

Constructing networks should be a vital part of the business plan. The positive impact networks have on business start-ups is well established. The exchange of information among potential entrepreneurs through networks, often forged in the corporate environment prior to launching a business, is so vital to managerial and entrepreneurial development that it is doubtful that many ventures would be created or successful without these bonds. Among the most important benefits of starting out in corporate life and then moving to entrepreneurship are having established relationships with contacts and potential partners, positioning oneself to spot opportunities and prospective customers, and being able to identify sources of financial backing.

Network resources will not appear by chance. One must strive to establish beforehand the business networks that every entrepreneur finds she needs. In some male-dominated fields, useful networking may not come easily. Recalls Carol E. Farren, president of Facility Management World Wide Ltd.,

> I was in the Building Owners and Managers Association for a number of years. If you want to talk about a good-old-boys' group, that's it. I was very involved. I wrote articles for the newsletter and attended regular meetings. I was on their professional committee. I helped them set up cocktail parties and donated to their charities. I never got one penny's worth of business out of it, and it was a

very expensive organization. I finally dropped it because it was not getting me anywhere. The good old boys don't share.

As in the case of women's networks within organizations, the context of women's pre-venture organizational networks differs from that of men's networks. Effective women's business networks, one team of researchers points out, are "the result of a deliberate strategy of linking women with other women to expand contacts, provide successful role models for each other, generate solutions to problems, and disseminate information."[10] It is not unusual for the new business owner to be unaware of important contacts. Katherine Kennedy, Relocation Coordinates, Inc., in San Diego, was two years into her business.

> Then a woman in Denver called me and said, "I hear you're really good at what you do and there are others of us who want to meet so we can learn how to do what we do better." We all went to Phoenix and met. It was like meeting aliens because the ladies from Cleveland and the woman from Denver didn't do anything like what we do. But we all worked well in our markets, so those people became my mentors.

Network preplanning is important irrespective of the type of business or field one is considering. The Women in Franchising Association, for example, suggests that women considering purchasing a franchise operation should call no fewer than six franchises and ask basic questions.[11] Women considering a home-based business should first decide if they could function effectively away from the frequent interactions of office and business colleagues. If the decision is to proceed to entrepreneurship, the preplanning should include a working schedule with frequent business-related lunch appointments and connections to women's business organizations.

The connections between organizational networking and entrepreneurship can be very close. Marion Gold, who had taken a subsidiary of the large advertising and public relations firm where she was employed from $250,000 in annual billings to $10 million, lost her argument to have the subsidiary spun off into a separately incorporated company. Not wanting to work for a competitor, she went out on her own as an independent consultant.[12] Darlene Thomas, a New Orleans entrepreneur who describes herself as a transplant from Texas, owns and operates Thomas Travel and Cruise, a leisure travel agency that specializes in meeting the needs of the pampered traveler. Before starting her business she was an executive administrator with a legal firm.

> Before I opened my doors I started making networking contacts with all the attorneys I knew. "Hey, I'm going to be opening a travel agency and I want your business." From day one I had a large client base, actually more than I could handle when I first started. Networking is very important to me. By word of mouth—one person telling another person—we grow one on one.

Even when the break with the former employer is deliberate, the old corporate networks can have considerable value. Advises Elizabeth Capen, a principal with a New York advertising firm, as a newly minted consultant you should contact professional acquaintances, attend professional meetings, scan trade publications, contact past organizational clients to remind them about work done for them, and in the process take the opportunity to let clients know that you are available. For the organizationally upwardly mobile, networking ahead may pave the way to entrepreneurship. After studying the corporate trend in her previous organization, Kathy Reed maneuvered her way into a central operating post and also wisely negotiated an employment contract with a generous severance agreement in case something unexpected happened. She then read widely and took classes to prepare for the consulting firm she would begin after departing the organization.[13]

A large number of entrepreneurs networked very hard from the beginning. An example is Elise McCullough, president of Staffing Solution, a temporary and permanent placement service of accounting, financial, data processing, and clerical professionals headquartered in New Orleans, with a territory covering Louisiana, Alabama, and Mississippi.

> I jumped in, got involved, and joined every group I possibly could, actually too many at first. I felt the networks provided the opportunity to develop important relationships and establish a sense of trust and respect in the community. In Louisiana especially, people do business with people they trust and like, so you have to grow that relationship for a long time. I thought seeing the same people

over and over again and letting them get to know me would help establish my credibility. This is especially important in the staffing industry, which is highly competitive. There are seventy-eight other agencies in New Orleans. I knew that I had to stand out among everyone else as a very reliable source.

Successful women entrepreneurs deliberately set out to construct networks with the key components they need. "When I started my business," said the owner of one real estate firm, "it was some women executives and some real estate firms who made sure that some business was thrown my way."[14]

Sometimes there is a happy match between a diversified organization looking for ways to trim some of its costs by contracting out segments of its work and a member of that organization looking to start a business. In such cases, the exiting entrepreneur can take advantage of being in the pipeline already and may be in a position to transfer strong organizational relationships to her new venture. It can take considerable vigilance to spot a portion of the business the incubator organization is not interested in developing. But the payoff can be huge because the ingredients in the transition from organizational member to business can get the new business off to a running start. Terri Parker-Halpin, cofounder of the Cincinnati Chapter of the National ISO 9000 User Support Group, recalls,

> I was in an employment referral for a technical communicator's organization and had been a past president. It was my best networking effort ever. I saw that a firm was looking for someone to document an entire computerized transportation management system. I looked at that opportunity and thought, Why not me?[15]

Becoming an entrepreneur is a major decision. Networks play a role in weighing the potential costs and benefits. For Jean Kelly, a New Orleans architect, her new career opportunity began with an unexpected builder contact that she developed after designing her kitchen table and chairs. After the builder's death she took over his business part-time, and later bought it out. It was a calculated risk. She left an architectural position for an income approximately one-third of what she previously had made on just one big architectural job. She feels the payoff is in building equity in her future through the enhanced marketability of her skills.[16]

For Ruth Ann Menutis, Natural Energy Unlimited, Inc., The Grove, networks have been an important part of her building strategy. After selling fifteen retail stores and while planning her next move, she traveled through Denver and saw something exciting.

I returned to New Orleans and mentioned to my attorney and friend, Paul, that I had seen this unique concept that would do well in the New Orleans Airport. I also asked him if he knew the then-chairman of the board of the New Orleans Airport. Paul immediately called his friend Jerry, the chairman, to explain my idea for this new concept. Jerry said, "If you and Ruth Ann want to put one in the New Orleans Airport, we'll give it a three-month trial." Paul agreed to this and hung up. I told him I could not make an investment of $20,000 for three months. He said, "Let's call him back. Maybe we can get one year." Well, Jerry would not bend. It was a three-month trial, take it or leave it. Sometimes you must gamble, so we took it. We each put up $10,000. During our first two months, we paid for the unit. One year later, we bought the Denver-based company.

But growth didn't come easily, and this is where my second story begins. We now owned a company with the ability to expand but no place to expand to. We had contacted most airports and kept hearing that our company was too small for their airport. We had opened at Lakeside Mall, but the store was only marginally profitable, so we knew the concept was not for shopping malls.

One day Paul and I were purchasing insurance for the business. The salesman was Danny, a New Orleans football player who was selling insurance on the side. We told Danny how we had tried to get into the Dallas–Ft. Worth Airport with no success. Danny said, "Oh, I know the director. I'll introduce you." He arranged an appointment in Dallas for all three of us. The director was an obvious football lover who worshipped Danny. As Danny introduced Paul and me, we got a nod and then it was football talk for one solid hour. I sat there wondering what I was doing there when the big question came, addressed to Danny, ignoring Paul and me. "Well, Danny, what is it you want in my airport?" Danny replied, "Oh, my friends want to put in a 42-square-foot nut stand." He wanted to see a picture, which I pulled out and handed to Danny, who laid it on his desk. After two seconds of looking at it, the director said, "Sure Danny, move it in any time." That was airport number two and the rest is history. Once in DFW, airports all over the U.S. were calling us to set up.

Sources of Network Support

Among the most important kinds of support for starting one's own business are the resources obtained through social networks (material support), emotional support for the idea of starting a business (affective support), and advice on finances, production, and other matters (information support).[17] For some women, emotional support was their only source early on. Patricia Droppelman, president of Pediatric Nursing Care, Inc., in Cincinnati, initially received little encouragement to start her firm. But she networked outward, doing what seemed logical and familiar.

> You had to run a house, you had to pay the bills, and you couldn't pay any more than you had in your pocket unless you wanted to go into debt. Unknowingly, I had established a relationship with a banker, and he helped me when I needed money. My accountant also really believed in my company. I didn't know these areas but I could count on them in the areas where I needed the advice. It always worked out in the way I wanted to do it.[18]

Barbara Bry, Proflowers.com, La Jolla, California, found the affiliations developed in her ten years in the public sector and her experiences as a journalist had built networks that were important in getting her business off the ground. She used those contacts when raising money and in selecting accountants and legal representatives. She also relied heavily on her relationships with the members of Athena, a group of women executives in biotech and high-tech companies where she had been executive director.

Family can be the strongest source of encouragement and support, and also the basis for a business launch. Among the family-launched business success stories is La Tempesta Bakery. This $5-million-a-year firm, which turns out 2 million biscotti a month, was started by Bonnie Tempesta and her mother in 1983 with a $15,000 loan from a family member.[19]

Close longtime friendships can also become effective business support networks. Five female New York professionals who received their MBAs in 1983 get together regularly. All started with well-known companies. Over the years careers and interests changed: two remained single, three moved to the suburbs, and two later started their own businesses.[20]

While informal network contacts can form the basis for access to business necessities, such as formal sources of capital, for women, the real importance of the family and close friendship networks lies in the personal and emotional support one receives. Over 60 percent of the entrepreneurs in one study viewed their work and life as a central point connected to an overlapping series of network relationships that included family, business, and society. In terms of the relative value of different types of personal and operational support for running a business, emotional support received from family (a spouse or significant others) topped the list. All other support dimensions, such as help in running the business, contributing expertise in operational functions, assistance in making business decisions, and providing financial support, ranked substantially lower.[21]

Constructing Venture Networks

While it is important to have internal and external networks well in place when starting a business, it is even more crucial to recognize that the initial networks will need to be updated and refreshed. As Margaret M. Larkin, president and owner of Larkin Pension Services, Inc., in San Diego, says, "You outgrow your networks in professional organizations." Jeanette Scollard Hester, Hester Foods, expressed her philosophy in this crisp language:

> When I got married, I changed my name. As I go from one business to another, I leave networks behind. I keep a master network of accountants, but in terms of industry boards and connections, I have no interest in that. I'm not interested in ever being who I've been, so my network is always changing. There are some stable things. I've had my accountant my entire business career. The kinds of networks I want to be part of are like this focus session.

New network ties become important when moving into a small business because of the change in one's status. "As an executive in a large company," says a Chicago entrepreneur, you are able to present a glamorous and prestigious image. You have the name of the company on your card and everyone wants to talk to you. If it is your name on the card and no one knows who you are, then they don't care because they get five to ten calls a day. You end up having five to ten seconds. . . . It isn't a matter of how smart you are, how much more professional, but whether you can get that strategic window. I discovered early on that affiliations had to be part of my professional life.[22]

Networking can be particularly important to survival in the two industry categories where, according to the National Foundation for Women Business Owners, 60 percent of women open businesses: services, with a failure rate more than 50 percent higher than the national average for all small businesses, and retail trade, where profit margins are low. Interestingly, among these riskiest fields are groups—home healthcare, nondurable manufacturing, environmental products and services, information management and technology, and business financial services—that have been among the fastest growing recently and that are attractive because of the relatively low start-up costs.[23]

The usefulness of networking before you launch your business may be seen in a single statistic. In incubator organizations, women who begin businesses start with an average of 4.9 network contacts inside and 2.8 contacts outside their former organization.[24]

Formal Networks, Business Growth, and Value Added

Contacts are important not only in beginning a business but also for firm development. Business growth appears to be significantly related to the time entrepreneurs spend developing the right contacts within such strategic interest groups as customers, suppliers, and investors. Recent research reveals that belonging to an association or being part of businesswomen's networks can have a significant effect on profitability.[25] Belonging to and building networks can add value and teamwork to a business without the financial strings. Through forming relationships, people in networks can exchange vital information about key resources, potential partners, joint relationships, accessing training programs, and teamwork approaches to acquiring larger market shares. The value-added dimension of network affiliations comes from the quality and level of information exchanged.

The most elementary networking involves building continuing customer relationships. For small service businesses, success or failure can be decided right here. Networking your business advisors is a good idea that is often overlooked. One entrepreneur was advised by her accountant to take as many business deductions as possible to minimize taxes, while her banker advised that it would be necessary to show a profit to get a loan. The suggested resolution was to have the banker and accountant meet together with the entrepreneur to review her financial situation.[26]

> Entrepreneurs craft networks to suit differing interests. One Kentucky entrepreneur designed her networks to support other women. When she started her business, she sought out a female attorney, a female CPA, and a female travel agent to try to use her dollars to support women. She continues this policy to this day.

Sounding Boards

Networks provide important confidential sounding boards of trusted advisors for voicing concerns and sharing solutions. Women entrepreneurs find it helpful to have trusted others to talk with about dreams, ambitions, and implementation strategies and to get support if something doesn't work out, along with encouragement to try something new. A successful sounding board provides a combination of information, a sanity check, and a release. It offers the freedom to have witnesses to business triumphs and can even fulfill the advisory role of the corporate staff meeting in a former organization.[27]

Network functions are especially important in the organizational transition and entry stage of entrepreneurship. One Chicago entrepreneur described how the Women's Information Support Group, a National Association of Women Business Owners subgroup composed of women in business for at least seven years, provided "the opportunity to throw our problems on the table—expansion, bankruptcy, confidential stuff." In Cincinnati, the Women's Business Development Center furnishes needed support. The Forum of Executive Women in Philadelphia provides a similarly valuable sounding board for members. Tara Stephenson, The Woodward Group Ltd., and Marian V. Marchese, VIRTU, Inc., are in agreement about the value of the forum:

It wasn't so important for building business as it was for finding out that no matter what you had gone through, somebody had gone through something worse and could help you build through that. You need this support.

Validation

The establishment of cooperative networks is clearly important to gaining success at various stages of business development and growth, enabling women to establish their credibility and develop a sense of teamwork across organizations. Two recent studies found that women entrepreneurs not only continued the same advertising media used during the first year but also reported greater usage of referrals, community events, telephone directories, and fliers than males, with referrals ranked the highest.[28] The result has led to improved business conditions, gains in customers, and better performance in general.

Entrepreneurs can construct networks to take them where the action is. One can begin with the entrepreneurial development organizations most frequently operational in business roundtables, chambers of commerce, and industrial councils. These loosely structured federations of business leaders, until lately composed almost exclusively of white male managers and entrepreneurs, seek to improve the overall business climate by attracting new industries, protecting existing ones, and managing existing business infrastructures.[29] Affiliations in economic development organizations (EDOs) form important power bases and offer networking opportunities that have largely been untapped by women entrepreneurs. The lack of participation of women business owners in EDOs, which varies by geographic region, may result from continued homophily—that is, the tendency to form same-sex networks.

As noted already, in the past women in organizations had to form special networks to gain instrumental power, and where the hierarchy is predominantly male they continue to do so.[30] If female business owners continue this networking pattern into entrepreneurship, they may be excluded from the important operating networks to which they need to be connected. The solution is to reach out. One suggestion is to become involved in a public service and, by devoting unique resources, reap the rewards of good publicity and avoid tunnel vision. Rebecca Smith, A. D. Morgan, used indirect networking to help her business along.

> I live in an "old world" community where the "old guard" runs the show. By becoming involved in the community, I gain a reputation, which, in turn, helps facilitate business growth. For example, in looking for a banking relationship, I would set up a meeting, present the company, and then request whatever financial support was necessary to run the business. This was only half of the process. The banker would then begin to ask around the community to find out, "Who is Rebecca? Is she credible?" That is where the community involvement and reputation play such an important role. His colleagues would respond, "Yes, I know Rebecca. I met her while we were serving on a board together."

As Ruth Ann Menutis notes, "You can't always do it alone. Sometimes it takes a community. Join them! Become part of it! Simply be positive in your endeavors. Do not allow sexual or racist comments to ever interfere with your drive to succeed."

Network Development

Key to networking strategy, say entrepreneurs, is to stay focused and constantly update the network. The interactive process is continuous. To use Deborah Szekely's analogy for networks, consider networking a part of the business strategy that provides you with "blue sky" time. As an entrepreneur, be sure not to let other activities fill your valuable time and leave you unable to make the right connections or develop the necessary strategies for business and personal growth.

Getting into the networks is just the beginning. There are effective and ineffective networkers. Ineffective networkers, Susan Linn points out, attend networking groups but visit with the same friends each time. "Obviously, this defeats the purpose of networking." The trick is to approach networking like any other aspect of your business. Meet new people in your existing networks by reaching out and move into new networks regularly.[31] The focus, as Patricia L. Roscoe, Destination Management, suggests, is always on one's business.

> For a long time, because I was in a high-profile business I found that all the boards I was asked to join were for men. Women's networks did not exist. The few that did were composed of women who talked about family issues instead of business. This was not what I wanted in a network—it would not help my business.

Tara Stephenson, president, principal, and founder of The Woodward Group, Ltd., in Media, Pennsylvania, speaks of a time crunch.

> I have cut back on much of my networking. I have had to eliminate trade organizations because there simply is no time. The networking I have now is much more pure. For example, I network with individuals who are excellent referrals of business for my firm or who I have selected as co-mentors.

In a society where gender differences carry role stereotypes, female entrepreneurs have adapted skillfully. Darlene Drake, president of Fitness Pro Health and Exercise Equipment in Lexington, Kentucky, deals with fitness equipment in markets that are predominantly male. Networking is the cornerstone of her business. One problem she faced was convincing large organizations to install fitness centers in their corporations. Because most of her corporate contacts were men, she developed a predominantly male sales staff and trained them carefully to deal with potential clients. "When you are talking about weight-lifting equipment and things like that," she says, "customers are just more comfortable. They think men know more about these things. So I send them out to the field."[32]

Researchers commonly agree that networks are most valuable when one enters them without expecting an immediate benefit. As Suzan Kotler, a Cincinnati entrepreneur, explains, "You have to put out more than what you expect to get back and it will usually come back to you more than a hundredfold. If you don't do it that way, you usually end up with zip."[33] Unexpected affiliations can become important in career transition stages. For example, an opportunity to be nominated an "Ernst & Young Entrepreneur of the Year" came to one entrepreneur as a result of a casual speaking engagement. The affiliation in turn led to her selection as a judge for this award at the local and national level. As a judge she became familiar with the Ernst & Young award criteria.[34] Fund-raising events can create the same kind of exposure.

Network Characteristics

Some research suggests that perhaps the ideal number of people for a network (researchers call this network density) is six to eight. Successful entrepreneurs appear to have networks that are more dense in terms of a "percentage of strangers"—that is, people whose presence strongly relates in some way to performance measures. The real secret may be in how many distinct and unique networks each entrepreneur maintains. As one study has noted, "A network with two people has but one possible match, one with four people has six, and one with six people has fifteen. A network base of fifty has potential matches of 1,225 people." The mathematics can apply in real life. Says an Atlanta entrepreneur, "The best thing I have done in years was to join the women's network. The opportunity for interaction with so many really terrific women was great. The contacts I have made and the opportunity to peddle my products has really astounded me."[35]

Strategic alliances are important networks. By strategic alliances is meant connections with larger organizations in the same or similar fields. Discussing the impact of an organizational restructuring on her business, Elizabeth Morris of Dallas offered a compelling illustration of how such contacts had worked for her.

> Some of my clients went to the Northeast, some of them went to the Midwest, and some of them went north, west, and south. So, we tracked them down. And all of a sudden, inside of a year's time, I had a national company. They had liked the quality of our work, so they took us with them as preferred subcontractors to their new companies.[36]

Alliances form in unique ways for each entrepreneur, but the quality of the work appears to be one of the most important ingredients in forging alliances with larger companies. From the hub of one of her networks, Hattie Hill, CEO, Hattie Hill Enterprises, a Dallas-based company, found business opportunities that led her into some seventy different countries. "I've been doing international work for about seven years," she says. "I'm being thrust into the international market through the corporations I work with. That's where the business is going. And you go where the business is going."[37]

Network affiliations forged though professional, social, and civic contacts are becoming increasingly important. This may be one of the underlying reasons so many entrepreneurs are increasing their community activities. According to a study by the National Foundation for Women Business Owners, 78 percent of women business owners are active community volunteers, with half of these women volunteering for more than one charity. This percentage rises among women with children. Regardless of their activity, over half of these business owners encourage employee volunteerism and integrate volunteerism into their lives and businesses.[38]

Networking Opportunities

Opportunities for networking have increased dramatically in the last five years. "One of the best things I have done in the last two years is really get involved in women's networking organizations," says one entrepreneur, "right now with the National Association of Women Business Owners (NAWBO) but prior to that the Women's Business Development Center. I was one of NAWBO's first clients and they are marvelous."[39] With locations in the United States and abroad, NAWBO has been a major facilitator of women's entrepreneurial networks. The association has developed new connections by its identification, in 1997, of leading women entrepreneurs worldwide, which now includes women from more than twenty-five countries.[40] The United States Small Business Administration has developed a "virtual women's center" that works concurrently with fifty-four women's business centers nationwide and more recently has reached out to establish links overseas.[41]

Several international networks have been around for some time. One of the foremost of these, Les Femmes Chefs d' Entreprises Mondiales (FCEM), was started by Madame Foinant, who owned and managed a steel works in France in 1945. In 1998, the network celebrated its forty-sixth world conference with thirty-five member countries and over 29,000 business owners and members. Other international associations of growing strength include American Businesswomen International, founded in 1995 for the advancement of international trade, and the International Federation of Business and Professional Women. In addition to these networks, there are a number of other centers that have sprung up nationally and internationally since 1992. The Centre for Women in Business, Mount Saint Vincent University, received initial funding from the Atlantic Canada Opportunities Agency in 1992. The Centre for Women Entrepreneurs, Simon Fraser University, opened in 1996 at Harbour Centre and is funded by Scotia Bank. Centers in the United States include the New Women Entrepreneur Center in Florida founded in 1992 as a not-for-profit corporation.

Assessing Networks

For the female entrepreneur, personal time is a precious commodity, not to be relinquished easily. (Among other reasons, unlike the male entrepreneur, women still bear more of the responsibilities at home.) So how does one decide which networks are valuable and worth the investment?

From the previous discussion, it is clear that successful network-building strategies involve four types of networks. Each works at a different level. *Personal networks* are developed on the basis of interpersonal bonds and relationships. They are important because women in business have multifaceted relationships. The value of personal networks lies in the emotional and coping support they provide. Bink Cook's personal network was critical to starting her business.

> When I was kind of in-between things, I walked every morning with a couple of friends in my neighborhood and we would talk about our ideas and so forth. One day one of them turned to me and said, "You know Bink, you've heard of 'ready, aim, fire.' I see you as ready, aim, aim, aim." It made me furious because I thought that's not true. But that was what really got me started.

Professional networks have the advantage of offering you renewed energy in your field. Their effectiveness can vary based on the exclusiveness and accessibility of the network. Professional networks that allow valuable information to be shared only among a few exclusive members may confer short-term advantages, but over time the in-group nature can stifle growth because the network lacks the diversity needed to keep it fresh. *Formal organizational networks* consist of more open ways of getting and receiving information. They are limited only by the entrepreneur's field, interests, or such boundaries as an MBA association, alumni groups by year of graduation, and the like. *Opportunistic networks* are created when people come together and individually decide there is a payoff in continuing the association. These networks tend to be intense, interesting, and sporadic. A network originally created because of compelling advantage may or may not evolve over time to equal the value of the integrated networks one develops.

Irrespective of which type of network one creates, it is important to open up the network and realize that the true function is not to remain conservative but to let others share in the rewards. As Claire Irving notes, networks can be valuable when members want to share the resources they gain from their memberships.

> The Financial Women's Association of New York is forty years old and has done an excellent job of educating and reaching out to its core young financial professionals. It has provided scholarships to young women in business schools for thirty years. The New Alliances Committee is trying to establish chapters in a number of major cities—the Boston chapter is three years old, a chapter is forming in Washington, and the San Francisco FWA is aligning with us. We also have allegiances in London, in Japan, and in a Hong Kong branch. We are trying to get them to network, and they're all saying, "Oh, my gosh, where have we been?" The FWN web site will soon link us worldwide.

Developing a Broader Network Strategy

Establishing extensive networks involves commonsense strategies. Maria-Luisa Maccecchini, founder, president, and CEO of Bearsden Bio, Inc., illustrates how she once again is trying networking on a larger scale.

> You have the big boys' organizations and you don't quite belong. You have the more nurturing groups because you like them. But in order to succeed you have to go and work the old-boy networks. I am trying the big boys again, I think for two reasons. Number one,

maybe I am a bigger girl. Number two, the person I merged with in the company with the three subsidiaries on three continents has started to push me to go out there. He feels if I really do want to go public for $200 to $300 million, of course $500 million ideally, I need to go out there. I feel that things have changed a little now because I am being introduced. It is the first time I ever went to a financial meeting and somebody says, "This lady saved two companies." If I were to say the same thing nobody would believe me. But when he says it they all listen. And it is all very interesting because this is the first time that somebody has done this for me. I have never had a mentor in my whole life. I always read with something between envy and disbelief that people have mentors. I seem to have found one.

Business networks are important in information gathering, centrality, building support systems, and maintaining a competitive edge in development and growth. For the woman entrepreneur, networks also link work and personal life, connecting to an overlapping series of relationships that include family, business, and society. While networks may be structured or casual, for women, informal networks take on a special role in providing social, emotional, and financial support. Prior employment clearly leads to the advantages of in-place networks when starting a business. However, as noted in this chapter, it is important to know when to shed old networks and develop new and diverse ones. Research on network centrality and inclusion highlights the importance of networks in making transitions at all stages of career development. Establishing cooperative networks is clearly a by-product of the degree to which the entrepreneur has transferred useful, multiple connections.

Ways to Enhance the Diversity of Your Network

1. Increase the age range of contacts. If you are older, forge links with younger connections and vice versa. This will increase demographic diversity.

2. Begin increasing contacts by self-promoting.
   - Bring your business card and a flier about your company to any meeting you attend. When you introduce yourself,

give this material to the new acquaintance at the same time.

- Be intimately familiar with your own product line or service so you can quickly identify with a new contact.
- Become a broker, bringing together people who have complementary needs.

3. Remember, while gaining from the special advantages of sex-segregated networks, it is important to realize that most of the businesses are still owned by men. Become a member of networks that have been traditionally controlled by men in order to change the connotation of "entrepreneur" to make it a sex-neutral term.

Ways to Change the Direction of an Existing Network

- Take on a leadership role in an existing network.
- Form and maintain active contacts with six to eight trusted advisors.
- Keep your contacts up to date in your computer file.
- Remember the golden rule: Promise only what you can deliver, and deliver quality information that has value to the recipient. Business is acquired by knowing people and building confidence in what you have to offer.

Where are you in the development of network links to enhance your career development? Completing Exercises 7 and 8 will help you assess your present network strategy and provide suggestive insights. Establishing useful networks involves a careful weighing of the value of one's time.

Networking with Multiple Demands and Limited Time

EXERCISE 7

Before entering a network, which requires an investment of your scarce time, consider these questions.

• Is this network worth my time and energy?

• Do I have time to cultivate key relationships in this network?

• Can I take the risk of not developing this networking opportunity?

• How attractive are the members and the businesses they represent?

• What is the network affiliated with that I value?

• What are the collective opportunities that I cannot acquire otherwise?

• Is there a sense of exchange among members?

• If the network contains competitors, what is their impact on my business?

• What exciting programs does the network provide that are unavailable elsewhere?

• What do I bring to the table?

• What do I have to offer in exchange for what I gain?

• What is the personal payback to my business and my profession?

• Is this network too large or too small to be useful?

• Is this the kind of network I need at this stage of my business growth?

EXERCISE 8 — *Networking Self-Assessment Exercise*

Assess the usefulness of your current networks by answering these questions.

• Do you have a propensity to create network connections with people in other branches, divisions, and specialties inside your organization and with individuals in trade, professional, and social organizations?

• What is your degree of network activity—that is, with how many people do you discuss business matters, and how much time do you spend developing and maintaining contacts?

• How dense is your network—that is, to what degree do you reach out beyond personal friends and immediate contacts to discuss business?

• How intense are your networks?

• How many years have you known network members?

• How frequently do you interact with your contacts, and how great is the quality and quantity of the resources you exchange?[42]

Evaluating Your Responses

Calculate how many of your present network contacts know each other. This will give you an understanding of the density as well as the diversity of your network. If the answer is that 50 percent or more of the people in your networks know each other, you need to expand your network options. Leave time for chance meetings. Opportunities escalate through random activities, which permit you to break away from the routines.

4. Leadership, Management, and Entrepreneurship

I am five feet tall and female, and people do not take me seriously right off the bat. You need to be bigger and more masculine to intimidate people. Then they pay attention to you. It's like an elephant. An elephant gets more attention than a mouse. But if the mouse is the president of the company and it needs to be run effectively, then the mouse needs to learn how to manage the elephant. And that is what we do. We manage at least one elephant every single day.

Linda Horn, L. R. Horn Concepts, Inc.

The words *management* and *leadership* are often used as if they are interchangeable. They are not. While the behaviors of a leader and a manager may overlap in narrow ways, there are major distinctions. In business, leaders are predominantly responsible for the vision and direction that allow employees to be inspired and motivated. Management talents are chiefly identified with keeping the organization going: planning and budgeting, organizing and staffing, and control.[1]

As an entrepreneur, you will be the leader responsible for providing the company goal, the plans for attaining it, and the methods of influencing your employees to achieve it.[2] Leaders, it is said, are like "pioneers, venturing into unexplored territory and guiding followers to new and unfamiliar destinations."[3] Most people learn about management while working for someone else. Anyone who has spent time in a large corporation or government bureaucracy has observed that most managers are neither entrepreneurial nor creative leaders. This is because a successful system is already in place in large organizations, and most managers have job descriptions that entail keeping the machinery running and teaching newcomers how the company wants things done.

The words *leadership* and *management* are so often used interchangeably that new meanings have been attached. In the corporate setting particularly, leadership has been redefined. At the midorganizational levels, it has come to mean managing employees in ways that encourage them to sign on to the company goals and ways of doing things—to "share the vision" so they willingly contribute. Only at the highest level does leadership tend to retain its original meaning.

WOMEN AND MANAGEMENT

Few female managers get high enough in the organization to go beyond the mid-managerial definition. While the women who today make up 46 percent of the total U.S. labor force hold a seemingly impressive 48 percent of all managerial and specialty positions, for reasons that have been pointed out in earlier chapters, nearly all of these management jobs are at the middle and lower organizational levels.[4]

When preparing to launch your business it is important to understand the differences between leadership and management. As an entrepreneur you will probably fill both roles, at least in the beginning. Each requires particular skills.

Begin preparing by building on the management skills you are learning in the organizational environment and taking on any leadership opportunities that arise. Supplement this with any special educational and training programs that are available. Formal training is also highly desirable. For women, the figures here, while better than in the past, are not particularly encouraging. Well prepared at the undergraduate level, women earn only 37 percent of the master's degrees in business and marketing and 27 percent of the doctorates.[5]

In your role as the leader of your firm, you may be brilliant. You are sure to be often lonely. Once the business is established, you probably will measure success in ego terms: risks taken, the passion displayed for work, the ability to see things differently than others, and the satisfaction of creating something new. As Mary Lindenstein Walshok, University of California, San Diego, says, "The real competitor one faces is oneself. It's the game that's the challenge." The entrepreneurial spirit is embedded, she says, "in creating, inventing your own systems, your own environment, building your own teams, and defining your own agenda. It is not control in a psychological sense, but it connects to creativity."

In the beginning, most entrepreneurs don't have a choice between exercising a managerial or a leadership role. Both are intricately important to survival and success. Bink Cook, The Brighter Side, advises that initially the balance favors management. "After the start-up phase you learn whether or not you're the right person to continue, if you've got the skills for it." What she means is that once the business gets off the ground, management tasks become increasingly important. All organizations need someone to keep daily operations running smoothly, to hold the long-range objectives firmly in mind, and, at the same time, to remain creative and open to the new directions and approaches that will keep the company competitive and successful.

THE LEADERSHIP/ MANAGEMENT DILEMMA

Management skills are necessary to entrepreneurial success. There are no definitive studies that suggest that one will be more successful if the managerial role is valued over the leadership role. But there is ample evidence that a good number of creative entrepreneurs failed in their ventures because they first failed to manage budgets, people, and materials. Someone must do these tasks. But the requirement to be a good manager creates another problem. It is very easy for the leader turned manager to get bogged down.

Then creativity and vision, the elements that brought the business into being, may begin to disappear. These problems commonly arise when, after a period of operating success, the entrepreneur comes to realize that the business has reached a threshold. Dealing with a threshold decision requires careful thought and planning.

As her company developed, Phyllis Jordan, owner, PJ's Brand Coffee and Tea Company, with corporate offices in New Orleans, discovered that many of the people she had initially brought in were not prepared to grow along with the business. The industry was changing and she had become preoccupied with repeated and prolonged attention to the day-to-day operational details. She needed to move the company forward, but without unduly upsetting the corporate environment that had brought the business this far. Proceeding carefully, Phyllis began by bringing in outside help and examining her company and herself critically. She decided that her real strength was not in running the details of the company or in new store openings but in marketing. She realized that new energy was needed to grow and keep pace with competitors. The most important decision, she concluded, was whether to hire a new chief executive officer to move forward to the next level of competition or to hang onto the personalized image she had started with and keep the company where it was. There was no middle ground. "I realized that the marketing directorship was the one for me, so I had to hire someone to do the CEO stuff," she says.

> But it was not an easy shift. It was a very emotional process, and we talked about it for many days and in many meetings before the change was made. We have a new store that has just opened, and it is out of my direct control. At first, it bothered me when they came and told me how great the store was doing. Of course, I wanted this success, but it was also a validation that it could happen without my direct management, and I had a hard time enjoying it at first. But I had made a conscious decision to control my ego needs in favor of my financial needs.

The decision to hire a CEO, Phyllis says, compares to her childhood experience of looking at the high diving board with awe. "Then one day you get up there, hesitate, there is a split second, then you jump." It was a major leap—and a smart business decision. Phyllis's company is being managed successfully by the new CEO. Today a leader in the specialty coffee industry, PJ's Coffee and Tea Company has gone from relative obscurity to a widely known brand name. PJ's now operates and franchises twenty-six locations across the southeastern United States. The company plans to expand into more airports, working on locations in Denver, Las Vegas, and Atlanta.

Suzy Spafford had to choose between leading or managing Suzy's Zoo. Her orientation is toward doing what she loves: "drawing and laughing and creating those characters." Her life's purpose is "to make people happy, to share the joy you experience if you don't forget what it is like to be a child." Each of the Zoo's more than ninety greeting card characters has a history, a personality, and a story. "I can create something that's unique," she says, therefore

> I want to hire people who have the ability to expand my concept, to add to value, not to redo the designs. It's not as easy as I thought. I want to say to my artists, "Be graphic, have good composition, good words, but let me own the character. I am the little personality." As far as leadership style or management style, I know what I can do best, and that is to create those characters and the personalities that make them come alive. I put people in places to run the business and make it work so that I am free to do what I do best. Essentially that's what I have always done, and I plan to continue doing it. I am CEO just because I own the business, but I have a president, a person who manages, and I have other people with experience.

As the two examples illustrate, it is important for the entrepreneur to be aware where her preference and talent lie. Entrepreneurs with continually growing businesses eventually reach a threshold, the point in their businesses where they must make the important decision to either continue operating as the owner-manager or turn the management over to a professional manager. This subject is discussed in more detail in Chapter 6.

ENTREPRENEURIAL LEADERSHIP AND MANAGEMENT

As a managing entrepreneur, you will be engaged in a number of activities simultaneously. You will deal with people, process information, and make decisions. You will be the organizational figurehead, doing things that are primarily ceremonial in nature, such as posing for a newspaper photograph at the opening of your business. You are the organizational leader who must work with and through your employees to achieve goals. You are the outside organizational contact networking with individuals and groups. You are the information resource for your firm, and you are responsible for ensuring that information is communicated throughout the organization so your employees can do their jobs. You will continually monitor what is going on inside your company to see that things are staying on track. You will constantly scan the external environment to pick up things that are new or useful and pass them on to employees. As the company leader, you will be vision setter, motivator, analyzer, and taskmaster. As the firm manager, you will be the ambassador, driver, auditor, and servant.[6] As the company's spokesperson, you are the official and final voice of the business. As a Georgia entrepreneur explains, "Basically the buck stops here. Anything that anybody falls down on, ultimately it's my liability, my name. I have to deal with the problem effectively, or somebody is disgruntled."[7]

Managers make decisions. You will be called on to resolve problems as they arise, such as dealing with irate customers or suppliers or financial backers and handling disagreements among employees. You will choose where to put your money, your time, and your energy. You will judge whether an employee needs to be counseled, disciplined, or terminated. You will decide which business decisions you will make and which decisions will be delegated, and to whom. There is no escaping decisions because not deciding is a decision not to choose. Female entrepreneurs say decision making is their most important skill.[8] You will come to understand what is controllable and what is not. As Gail K. Naughton, Advanced Tissue Sciences, Inc., notes,

> I set the vision in the company. I have my thumbprint on priorities. But I can't tell people what to do. It took me a long time to realize I'm in control of nothing, I really am in control of nothing except in the morning when I'm feeding the cats. I have to take the circumstances at hand and do the best I can in order to manage them.

Business owners cannot do everything themselves. You will spend considerable time doing something other than working on your product or service. Your most critical decision is where to invest your limited time. You will be dealing with employees whose skill levels are high in areas where yours are low, and vice versa. Katherine Kennedy, Relocation Coordinates, says:

> An entrepreneur's nightmare is trying to own it all and control it all without realizing that she's good at the creative part but not day-to-day management. I get tired of the day-to-day stuff like managing money and facilities and a new computer system or software. It's stuff that I'm really not good at. Sometimes you have to hire a horse, a Clydesdale, who can just plough through. You have to pay the price to have somebody like that on the team because you know you don't have those skills. I recognized that finally. I think it's taken me a while in my business, but I recognized it and I hired myself a Clydesdale who's just been a delight, an absolute delight.

Among the hardest things you will learn is to tolerate employee work that is not as good as the job you could do because you don't have the time to do their work and yours. You will learn to hire competent, high-performing employees. In small businesses, there is little margin for error.

Learning to delegate authority can be difficult but will be necessary. It's very hard to delegate, says a New Orleans entrepreneur, "I want to know everything that is going on. I want that control." A Kentucky businesswoman explained, "We work so hard to get our power that it is hard to turn it over."[9] Gail Naughton remembers that one of her most important lessons involved hiring. A consultant came to her office one day with a set of Russian folk art nesting dolls. Slowly, he removed each doll from the stacked set of successively smaller dolls that cradled the smallest in the set and

placed them in a line on the desk. Then the consultant reached for
the center doll and said, "The reason someone is successful in business is very much tied to who they hire." He picked up the middle doll and said,

> Pretend this is you. Because people want control they tend to hire
> somebody smaller. If they hire someone bigger, they're afraid that their
> selection of the big one will lead to all the others being gobbled up as
> in the case of the dolls when they are stacked inside the nested set.
> But if you hire the smaller person, your company will never grow.

Gail keeps one of those Russian doll sets in her office as a
reminder. "It's very, very scary to hire somebody better than you," she
says, "because you have to realize that you can't control them. But if
you don't hire them, you can't grow your business. If you hire people better than you, you have to say, I am not going to control them."

From her own experience, Katherine Kennedy describes the
problem this way:

> It has very much to do with giving people the freedom, telling them
> they can do it, and helping them if they think they can't. That's
> what I always wanted somebody to say to me. "You're little, but
> you've got the potential for a very big voice." If somebody had told
> me that when I understudied Beverly Sills here, I would have gone
> on and done *Merry Widow* on TV. Instead, I heard, "You're too lit-
> tle but you're good enough for the understudy."

Somehow, Katherine says, "that is our mission as leaders and managers in organizations—to share the power, to let our people know
that they can do it."

Staying Alert

One of the most important things an entrepreneur must do is continually check inside and outside the company for opportunities
that may present themselves or problems that will be encountered
downline. This task involves developing and maintaining contacts—
networking. You will decide which items on the horizon are opportunities, such as a new market or product you can develop, and
whether or not to pursue them. You are responsible for creating

your own intelligence system to warn about pending or distant problems, such as the emergence of a competitive new technology, and the research and development process to deal with emerging issues. The problems will be there and sooner or later you will confront them. If you bury yourself so deeply in the day-to-day operations of your business that you are oblivious to what is going on, you may pay a price.[10] As Katherine notes,

> You always have to be developing another level in the business. Things die. They have a cycle. You might have a vision and get a contract for three years, but you have to keep coming up with something new—looking ahead and seeing what the next market is. God help you if you get a sore throat and don't perform the role—you constantly have to see what the next generation of whatever it is should be and could be and where your market is.

There are no set rules that fit all situations. Saralyn Levine, an Atlanta entrepreneur, opened up as a narrowly based gourmet dinner delivery service. Customer requests for more menu items led her to expand into a full-scale catering business. By contrast, Karen Kline, who received the 1992 Chicago Woman Business Owner of the Year Award, has consciously resisted all temptations to expand the lines in her store beyond city memorabilia because the narrow focus was what made her successful.[11]

You will spend considerable time negotiating with someone about something. The area of negotiations is so important and so little understood that the entire next chapter is devoted to it. Here, you need only to keep in mind that while gender does have some effect in management situations, women are as effective as men in negotiating sessions. [12]

Management Theories

Like understanding the local geography, an entrepreneur can benefit from knowing about management theories—where they came from, why they developed, and when they apply.

The first theories of management came into being when large business organizations arose as a consequence of the nineteenth-century industrial revolution. David Nadler and Michael Tushman have suggested they were as logical an outgrowth of the industrial age as the physical architecture of the new buildings. The combination of new building materials (structural steel), new company needs (centralizing workers in production units, controlling numerous business units over vast geographic areas), and collateral technology (factory and office machines, telegraph, and telephone) provided the capability to build massive factories and modern skyscrapers and to create the large firms necessary to manage far-flung operations.[15] Organizing work in the image of the machine—structured, orderly, and impersonal—evolved naturally.

The management theories that emerged during this period are collectively referred to as the *traditional style* of management. Among the most important of these theories was *scientific management,* which focused on the individual worker and the best ways to perform tasks—managing the work. A factory would be a typical setting for its application. Scientific management involved developing standards for each job; selecting, training, and supporting the workers; and supervising them, most commonly by foremen familiar with what the people under them were doing. Money, it was thought, was the best way to motivate the workforce. *Organizational management* dealt with the many levels and functions of firms with diverse and far-flung operations. It required dividing management levels by function (staff, line), authority, and responsibility, with rules for operating at each level. Power was centralized and concentrated at the upper levels of the organization. Authority flowed downward through a single chain of command. In this pyramid-shaped hierarchy, unity of purpose would be achieved under a system of comprehensive rules and procedures that described how all organizational duties were to be performed.

It quickly became apparent that the idea of machine-like management operating in a fixed organizational structure did not fit reality. Organizations changed internally as they responded to an unpredictable world. Soon, organizations were being described in biological terms of complex evolving systems. Contrasting ways of managing employees in this setting were set out by Douglas McGregor in his *Theory X* and *Theory Y* propositions. Each rests on assumptions about employees. Theory X describes managers who assume that most people are not ambitious, don't want responsibility, dislike work, and try to avoid it. Managers who view employees this way give detailed and complete instructions and strive to maintain control. Theory Y describes managers who assume that employees are internally motivated and capable of self-direction and self-control in working toward organizational goals. (A later addition, *Theory Z,* advocates trusting employees and making them feel an intimate part of the organization and suggests this will lead to improved operations.)

Quantitative theories of management appeared when computers allowed people to process huge amounts of information. Using mathematical models of the decision-making process, quantitative management compared alternative courses of action as precisely as possible. *Systems analysis* viewed complex organizations as a collection of related subsystems. For example, consider a restaurant. The diverse items going into the system (capital, land, equipment, materials, customers, and information) are called inputs. What comes out of the system (meals, service) are called outputs. The system itself is called the transformational process. Open subsystems (waiters serving customers) interact with the external environment. Relatively closed subsystems (the kitchen staff) infrequently interact with the external environment. Decisions made independently at the subsystem level (the cook decides to buy the cheapest ingredients available rather than the best, the front end manager schedules too few waiters to serve customers) can affect the organization negatively. The systems perspective thus assumes that the whole is greater than the sum of its parts. Because any change in a subsystem can affect other parts of the organization, the organization must be managed as a coordinated entity.

Contingency theory offered a way to pull everything together. The theory assumes that the effectiveness of a particular management style varies according to the situation. Any of the above management perspectives can be used alone or in combination depending on the situation. In a construction firm, for example, once the project has been settled on and the goals agreed to, the entrepreneur might manage architects using Theory Y because they are creative professionals and possibly disinclined to do their best work in an overly structured environment. She might employ scientific management principles to decide the best way to perform component tasks (whether to pour concrete walls at the site or use preset slabs). Elements of the traditional management style with strict rules and bureaucratic regulations (such as a fixed start time and work schedule and requiring hardhats to be worn) might guide workers on a job site. As the team's project supervisor for the construction of Baltimore's Oriole Park at Camden Yards, Janet Marie Smith moved between facilitative and hierarchical management styles as circumstances dictated.[14]

The above perspectives do not exhaust the way organizations are viewed. The *stakeholder view* of the firm assumes that both primary stakeholders (owners, suppliers, customers, employees) and secondary stakeholders (consumer groups, media) have views that affect or may be affected by the firm, and therefore should be taken into account by the management. The stakeholder view also assumes that as organizations grow and change, their stakeholder base widens. Advocates of public responsibility and social responsibility have suggested that the responsibilities of a business go beyond the simple maximization of profits.[15]

Effective Management

What works best? There is no one simple answer, but considerable research points to a direction in which answers may lie. Tom Peters and Robert Waterman examined some of America's best-run companies and found common characteristics. Best-run firms responded to conditions quickly, had a relatively simple structure with few hierarchical levels, and stayed close to their customers. They focused on increasing productivity by raising the desire of employees to make improvements, giving them authority and recognizing accomplishments. They had clear organizational goals and a strong organizational culture. Firm managers set clearly defined limits but allowed great freedom and authority within those limits.[16]

Effective entrepreneurial managers exhibit similar attributes. They plan well, understand something about the different management perspectives, are capable of identifying and understanding key variables that relate to their organization, are prepared to select elements from the various management perspectives appropriate for each situation, and are adaptable. They do not manage through the traditional organizational hierarchies but employ a new team-oriented management style. [17] Ruth Ann Menutis uses this management style at The Grove.

> Our company is divided into teams and each team leader has five airports that he or she is responsible for. It is a very delicate balance. Each manager must have a certain level of autonomy. There are many little things that you have to be careful about to make the strategy work smoothly. It takes an insider to make it work.

Nadler and Tushman conclude that just as the elements of the industrial revolution led to the creation of hierarchical organizations and bureaucratic management, the new information technologies that make timely information immediately available to a better educated workforce have called forth a new organizational architecture. Organizational efficiency, they suggest, requires creativity, and that means managing teams of people to use their collective abilities. As an entrepreneur interviewed for this study says, "I am a firm believer that all brains have to be at the table."[18]

Elements of the new management style have been popularized as reengineering the organization. One most colorful description contrasts the old firm structure of the CEO with loyal employees waiting in the herd with a new firm structure of organizational members as "self-directed geese, flying in formation." Reengineering doesn't imply that the management processes of planning, organizing, leading, and controlling are no longer needed. It means instead that managers have to understand that unpredictability is a naturally occurring phenomenon and therefore they must be willing to replace command-and-control leadership with the decisions of well-trained employees. Among the practitioners of the new philosophy is the U.S. Army, which discovered that local units acting on their own with timely, accurate information and adequate resources make better decisions and are far more effective than units that must wait for direction from a remote higher-ranking officer. As David Holzmann observed in 1991, the various employee empowerment programs that began sweeping the country in the 1980s had, at the bottom, a few common ingredients for success: management had to gain the trust of employees by behaving with honesty, openness, and integrity; employees had to be able to make decisions without fear for their jobs; everyone from management to the newest worker should feel responsible for the company's welfare; and—the most difficult— for employees to have power, management had to give it up.[19]

Though precise styles may vary, effective managers do the same key things. For example, they plan ahead. Linda Isenhour, general manager of BellSouth's phone network operations in southern Florida during Hurricane Andrew, had wisely devoted considerable time to advance planning for the emergency that would someday arrive. The preparation left her free to make the many decisions that only she could make in the midst of the hurricane and communicate effectively with BellSouth's storm center in Birmingham, Alabama, and with people in the field. Managers tend to think of themselves as sponsors, team leaders, or internal consultants. They will deal with anyone necessary to get the job done, share information, and invite others into the decision-making process. In approaching the design of a new automobile with women in mind, Ford's Mimi Vandermolen first convinced top management that the best way to create a Probe would be to merge the interior and exterior design teams (mostly composed of men), which previously had reported to different managers, into a single, flexible design team under her charge.[20]

Effective managers will change the organization when that is necessary. Appointed director of the National Institutes of Health in 1991, the first woman to hold the position, Bernadine Healy plunged swiftly and decisively into the organizational overhaul necessary to orient people to the new goal of addressing women's health issues. Effective managers set the ethical standards of the organization. Levi Strauss plant manager Tommye Jo Daves rose to the top when she decided that telling people they were not ready for promotion was not enough. Fairness, she felt, required showing employees how to become qualified. She then designed a training and adult education program that enabled employees to qualify for promotion. It was so successful that Levi Strauss replicated it at all its U.S. plants. Effective managers demand and get results. Darla Moore, profiled in a 1997 *Fortune* article, was savvy and tough enough to oust corporate raider T. Boone Pickens from Mesa, a company he had originally founded, and take on the board of directors to remove Columbia/HCA CEO Rick Scott when the healthcare giant ran afoul of federal regulators investigating Medicare and Medicaid overcharges. [21]

LEADERSHIP, MANAGEMENT, AND GENDER

Researchers have found considerable support for the idea that women behave more democratically and men more autocratically in leadership situations. Women use interactive skills more frequently than men, place greater emphasis on maintaining effective relationships at work, and not only value cooperation and being responsible to others but are interested in achieving outcomes that address the concerns of all parties involved.[22] Harriett Mouchly-Weiss, a member of the Committee 200 and managing partner of Strategy XXI, a consulting firm in New York, has concluded that "in the beginning women tried to carbon-copy men, but it wasn't particularly successful. We have different ways of running things. We're consensus builders." She believes it is important for women to understand that their decision-making style and leadership approaches are effective and to have confidence in them.[23]

Power

Studies show that women are more likely to view power as related to the time and place in which it is employed and the people involved than as a structured process where subordinates carry out decisions handed down from above. Often uneasy about being or seeming aggressive and uncomfortable with motivating others through fear, women prefer to influence and change things by serving as a resource, sharing power, and encouraging others.[24] Gail Naughton's description of her firm's operations is a case study.

> Creating an environment where people can grow to be the best they can at that job—that's what I do. I make sure that people have the tools and a good working environment to stay creative but still able to work within the FDA and SEC regulations to achieve goals in a timely

fashion. Some days I feel my only job is being funny—days when people are so tense I walk around and make them laugh. That's my job that day. Other days I walk around with a two-by-four, in a nice way.

Does this mean there are female and male styles of leadership and management? Studies of culture suggest so. The argument is that the "female" style emerges from a socialization process that teaches women a set of "female" values. Boys are educated to seek and hold power; girls are told that acting powerfully is not feminine.[25] The image of a powerful man is expected; the image of a powerful woman can be disconcerting. As Elizabeth Kay has pointed out, images of first ladies and women government leaders provide a virtual Rorschach test for contemporary ambivalence about powerful women, and all reflect female stereotypes. There is the powerful spouse (Eleanor Roosevelt), the willful wife (Nancy Reagan), the honorary man (Margaret Thatcher), and so on.[26] As a person close to power and one to be reckoned with, Hillary Rodham Clinton was seen as a threat in the early years of Bill Clinton's first term. In the president's second term, as the wronged spouse conducting herself with great dignity—and not pursuing a policy agenda—her popularity soared. As she explored entry into the New York Senate race, and then as an active politician, the public discourse reflected the clashing images. Such stereotypes suggest that women managers face more difficulty because people are raised to expect male authority and female compliance.[27]

Workplace observations have reinforced ideas that gender and culture together program women and men to behave differently on the job. In a 1990 *Harvard Business Review* article entitled "Ways Women Lead," Judy Rosener, then a professor of management at the University of California, Irvine, argued that women often did not have the same access to formal power and, therefore, had learned to rely on personal power, influence, and teamwork and to employ an interactive style of leadership to get work accomplished. Women using this style, said Rosener, were distinguished by encouraging participation by others, sharing power and information, enhancing others' self-worth, and getting others excited about their work.[28]

There is no doubt that many female entrepreneurs operate in exactly this way. One is Katherine Kennedy, a former opera singer in

New York, and now the owner of Relocation Coordinates, Inc. In a focus interview she said,

> Yesterday I gave a Japanese American woman who works for me a new mission. In a three-minute meeting, which is what I like to have, I said, "I would like you to consider expanding what you're doing for the international services. These are the ways I see that you can do it, but I'm really open." She said, "Katherine, I've got it. I'll talk to you next week because I'm afraid." I thought later that maybe I had asked her to go too fast, and what was she afraid of, because there wasn't time to follow up. Last night at 12:00 I left her a voicemail that said, "I don't want to frighten you, but I just think you're more talented than maybe you think you are, and I will help you if you want to do this. If you don't, that's okay, too."

The appearance of Rosener's article was immediately followed by fierce debate between those wary of the potential disadvantages to women of celebrating gender differences—like creating ghettos in the marketplace or suggesting that a "feminine management" style indicated that women are not tough enough—and those who found the news little more than evidence that women do not have to follow male management models. The debate between the two points of view is not meaningless. Among other effects, as one woman business writer has noted, about half the "leadership seminars" for women are designed around a gender stereotype that before they can become leaders "women somehow need to fix themselves—to correct their career derailing defects." More recently, in a study of whether gender was a key career determinant, 60 percent of the members of the Financial Women's Association who were surveyed said "gender held back their careers and a much higher number said they believed gender had been a hurdle for other women in business."[29]

The problem with concluding that men and women are genetically or culturally programmed to manage differently is that it requires ignoring a considerable body of other evidence. No research study has found any differences between men and women in verbal, mathematical, or spatial abilities, moral character, or several other dimensions. No research study has found any gender-related differences among those who seek power, exercise power, and get anxious about exercising power or the style of leadership they exercise when in power. In fact, when women attain the leader's role, they tend to behave exactly the same way men do.[30] For example, though the idea is that new technology and a better-educated workforce have made the old command-and-control philosophy less efficient in harnessing the collective intelligence of the firm, not all successful female managers embrace the philosophy's most extreme elements. Says self-defined "reengineered manager" Jacky Seygorf,

> While some of the new management style may have some merit in some situations, in certain fields neither abandoning the hierarchical structure nor changing the soul of the company is always the right answer to business problems.[31]

What causes leadership styles to vary, as a review of the literature on how people negotiate tells us, is the situation in which people find themselves. People in powerful positions are more comfortable, competitive, and successful.[32] In these positions, women come to terms with their own approach to leadership and management styles. Maria L. Maccecchini, Bearsden Bio, Inc., learned what her leadership style was by default.

> I know exactly what style I use. I don't want to control. I want to be a leader by vision. I want to go there and I will tell you when I go there. If you tell me about your vision, I will let you pursue it. I am a very good boss for people who don't like bosses, I am a terrible boss for those who need direction. I absolutely can't stand to tell somebody that they have to put their name in the upper left-hand corner. If I have somebody who needs that who may be a good employee, I shuffle them under somebody else. It took me a while to figure out what my leadership style was. Those who have vision, I leave them totally alone. For the others, I have to find them a boss. I cannot micromanage.

This approach to leadership was shared by many of the entrepreneurs. Denise L. Devine, Devine Foods, Inc., says that she leads by commitment. "I never expect anything of employees that I don't expect of myself. I don't need another child. I have three of my own. I want people to set the direction and then go."

There is also the problem of being the first woman in the leadership role. Rebecca Smith was quick to realize the interactive component among the men in her construction company.

> One must realize that egos are fragile and male egos are the most fragile. You can alter the outcome of good management by inadvertently stepping on a person's ego. It is a very careful balance between managing and directing where management is correct and directing is perceived as dictatorial, thus causing an equal and opposite refusal and dissention. The older men in the company were not used to working with women in construction, let alone having one as their "boss." Most of the early employees of the company had worked with me at the other corporation so they knew that I understood construction and was effective in my job. The challenge to the relationship as they moved to A. D. Morgan was the transition from being their peer to being their leader. In the early days as an employee in another corporation I took great care to "blend in." There were issues of sensitivity. Soon I had earned their respect as part of *their* team. Later, I overheard comments to new arrivals like, "That's no girl, that's Rebecca." The key is not to overtly control them but to join them and influence their thinking to accomplish the task your way.

Transformational Leadership

Studies of women executives and interviews with female entrepreneurs reveal similar characteristics. Both groups see effective power as deriving from mastery rather than control.[33] Both move to integrate the personal and professional dimensions of their lives, as contrasted with the compartmentalization indicative of more traditional leadership approaches. Instead of being comfortable with the traditional perks and privileges that separate leaders from others in their organizations, women work to construct ties to individuals. Women "derive satisfaction and success from building relationships with customers and employees, having control of their own destiny, and doing something they consider worthwhile."[34]

Entrepreneurs have spoken of the caring and concern they feel toward their employees and their clients. Cathy M. Brienza, Waller-Sutton Management Group, Inc., notes, "My style of leadership tends to be somewhat maternal and I view myself as firm but guiding. I love to help people see ways to do things and yet I don't think I've ever said 'do it this way or don't do it,' but I certainly strongly and firmly guide them to the way I think is right." Some of this tendency can be attributed to any age differential among the owner and employees. Claire H. Irving, Investigative Consultants International, finds age to be a big factor in her approach to leadership. Many of the people who are helping her are in their twenties and thirties. They do not have extensive business experience. At times, she says, "It is difficult to make them understand that 'gray hair' does count for something."

One researcher has summed up women's leadership style by defining it as an "ethic of care," meaning managing with the respect that a person wishes for oneself. A former East Coast Entrepreneur of the Year expressed it this way, "I want everybody to be treated like I want to be treated. I think women do that more than men."[35] Gail Naughton's comments perhaps sum up the approach.

> I've been described by people in the company as a motivator and a nurturer and, quite frankly, I am because the mom in me comes out all the time. I'm not at all comfortable being a disciplinarian and I'm not at all comfortable being authoritarian. There are times when you feel you just have to say, "This is the way it is, thank you very much for your input, go away." I'm not comfortable with that, so I have to find other ways of getting it done. This is very much the personality of the company, too. I get to know everyone in the company as best as I can. I spend a part of every meeting asking about "you." "How did the soccer game go and did Joey win the hockey game last week?" Very different style. The men who had a lot of pharmaceutical background in the company said it would never occur to anyone normally, one on one, or in a meeting at Lilly or Schering Plough, to say, "And how was the ballet recital?" Or even remember there was a ballet recital. But that's important for me. I make a personal connection with people and they with me. They care about working here more because it's not just a paycheck, it's a family. On the downside, if somebody is not performing well, I have a tendency to say, "Oh, yeah, but you know, this person's mom is in the hospital for surgery and her teenager is being really difficult."

I make excuses, which, from a business standpoint, is not a good thing. For the business to work well, I've got to say, "I'm sorry you're having all these issues, but if you can't do the job, get out." I can't do that easily. So I'm primarily a motivator and a nurturer.

Old Styles and New Styles

An insight into such management practices has been found in comparative studies of the transactional and the transformational leader. The *transactional* (old style) leader focuses on short-term goals and stability, offering rewards for performance. The *transformational* (new style) leader articulates a vision of the firm that can be shared by peers and subordinates, empowers and encourages subordinates, models effective behavior, shows respect for individual differences among subordinates, and prefers effectiveness over efficiency. Recent research has promoted the transformational leader as the more successful model for leadership. Inherent in this model is the need for leaders to act as role models, motivating and empowering followers to become leaders.[36] Tara Stephenson, principal, The Woodward Group Ltd., believes that this style is most important for women entrepreneurs. Leading requires a "multifaceted approach. . . . As an entrepreneur you wear so many hats, not the least of which is the leadership visionary hat. But you must also show commitment and lead by example."

Female leaders more than males tend to utilize transformational behaviors. Some researchers have explained the highest amount of gender variance by coining a new term for leadership practiced by women: *innovative realism,* defined as flexible, innovative, action oriented, integrative, changing, and inspirational rather than emphasizing long-range formalized, strategic planning.[37] Rebecca Smith started her company at age twenty-nine. All of the men who worked with her were older, some much older.

They came from a different generation, one where women—let alone their boss—were not working in construction. However, on more than one occasion, at company functions, wives have come up to me and expressed such gratitude as they tell me that their husbands are so happy. One woman shared with me that her husband had planned to retire but decided to keep working because he was having so much fun. Our corporate culture is very free and very expressive with room for individuality. It is a little renegade when compared to other corporate cultures, but it is the natural energy resulting from the combined personalities required for an underdog company to succeed.

I was in the reception area one day when I overheard Lori, our receptionist, talking to one of the employees. She referred to the "A. D. Morgan family." I was a little uncomfortable with that phrase at first, thinking it sounded a little trite and somewhat cult-like, but then I thought about it. It was not a phrase that I had contrived to force a team environment, it was a phrase that the employees had come up with based on their sincere feelings of belonging to a corporate family, which I now refer to as our daytime family.

Rebecca is not unusual. Researchers have found that women and men make similar commitments to their enterprises and are equally interested in achievement, but women measure it differently. For women, it appears, achievement is wrapped up in self-image, and is often satisfied in areas larger than the business itself—families, communities, and the welfare of others.[38]

Interactive Leaders

The women entrepreneurs who employ the interactive leadership style share three distinguishing characteristics: they create a vision, frame a direction for their company, and inspire followers through personal communication and similar sources of power rather than by employing the techniques of traditional management.[39] In focus group discussions for this book, 90 percent of the entrepreneurs interviewed said they used an interactive leadership style and discussed specific ways they implemented it in their businesses.[40]

In a recent study examining the techniques of forty-three highly successful female executives, the style of leadership where the leader was concerned about subordinates doing their best dominated. Second most common was the style where the leader acted as a visionary. The combination of concern and vision may easily be the most important characteristic of female entrepreneurs. According to recent studies, women business owners give priority to retirement plans and are more likely to offer employees job sharing, flex time, profit sharing, and a wider range of investment options than are their male counterparts.[41] Women business owners also take on more volunteer activities in their communities and lead the way in employee benefits. Generally, this supportive leadership style results in higher employee job satisfaction, higher organizational commitment, and higher positive expectations among employees about their future with the company.[42]

Interactive leadership requires patience and thoughtful approaches. The challenge is often to communicate the vision of the firm and see that it is implemented. This was the case for Lisa Adkinson, a partner in the Strategic Eight Consulting Group of Greater Cincinnati. "I am always repeating the same things over and over. You can't move on until you have the last person on the train or you are forced to leave them behind," she points out. Renee Peyton of Atlanta adds, "I empowered my employees to do what they need to do. I didn't sit there saying, 'this is what we need you to do; you do it.'"[43] Carol E. Farren, Facility Management World Wide Ltd., says,

> I tell people what to do but not how to do it. I like to hire people who already know how to do project management. They may not do it exactly the way I do it, but as long as the job gets done on time and in budget and the clients are happy, my concerns are met. My role is more of a pioneer than a manager—I have to be involved in something where I am learning something new all the time.

Barbara Grogan, founder and president of Western Industrial Contractors in Denver, credits her success to making sure that information flows freely to all staff members. To ensure that it did, she constructed a 7,000-square-foot office building without any interior doors. Anita Rodick, owner of The Body Shop skin and hair care stores, works equally diligently to deconstruct the power trips that inevitably flow from lines of authority.[44] Another entrepreneur, the owner of an investment advisory firm facing a crossroads with an opportunity to grow significantly in the near future, tells employees, "In the beginning I set up the goals, but tomorrow we're all going to sit down. I'm going to say, 'We're getting more and more institutional clients. How are we going to do this, do it well, and make sure we meet the clients' needs as well as our own?'" Another businesswoman said of her employees, "They know exactly what they're doing. I've trained them. Now they're really good at it. And I'm not about to get in their way. . . . They don't need me to boss them. They come to me when they have a decision to make." The owner of a clothing design business defined her role as "creating an environment that encourages designers and artists to do something greater than they've ever done before." Evelyn Eskin, an entrepreneur who helps design more efficient medical offices, reports, "We work a lot with medical office managers and people who have never had an opportunity to think of themselves as change agents. We do a lot of teaching that they can change the environment rather than merely react to the situation."[45]

All of this does not mean that the new leadership approach for women puts an end to employee problems. Gail Naughton explains that in terms of her role as a mother.

> I've learned more about being a manager from my children than anywhere else in the world. First, I have three, and no matter how hard I try, at any time, two of them feel neglected. It's the same thing at work. The people you work with, whom you rely on, can never get everything they need. You have to balance, but also make sure they respect the time you're spending with others and know you'd give it to them if you could. But sometimes you have to deal with only the highest priorities. Dividing your time and energies and whatever else, you're never going to satisfy everybody.

It is not always possible to create an environment of contagious enthusiasm. As Katherine Kennedy points out,

> It is difficult to do because everybody is dragging unpaid bills, divorce, illness, and kids on drugs. They bring all that to the workplace, and unfortunately when we get on the phone with our clients we're dealing with people who are in various stages of relocating. These are trying times for people balancing marriages, children, expenses, and high emotions. Everybody is not going to Disneyland. So my people have to be that warm cup of coffee even though they're going through a difficult time themselves.

Katherine eventually had to hire someone to take over the interactive leadership role in her company so that she could take the tough stand. "I could be the inspiration, but I have to be the one who wears the black hat." It is Katherine's cohort who knows the employee birthdays and orders flowers and is the primary company nurturer.

Part of the equation is that being the boss means exercising power, and the popular image of women in power is both relatively new and disconcerting, even to some entrepreneurs. This can lead to operating difficulties. Linda Horn, a financial consultant from the Cincinnati area, wanted people to succeed so much that she found herself being too lenient, and it became a serious problem. "I recently let an employee go after two months," she said. "In the past I would have kept him at least six months. I consider this a major milestone for me." A Charleston entrepreneur who found she was getting tougher as she grew older and clearing out people who were not doing their jobs expressed a similar hardening of attitude. "I am sorry about the problems my employees have," she says, "but I have a business to run. You simply cannot get bogged down in their problems."[46] Maria Maccecchini says,

> As long as we reach our goals, it is easy for me to give up control. But when I feel things are not going well, I shake things up, pull them apart, see how they fall and change direction. So I do eventually take over if things don't work correctly.

The Hub Effect

By enhancing the attractiveness of what the firm does and appealing personally to others, female entrepreneurs have become effective leaders. At the base, the leadership and management approaches described earlier consist of a series of networks and direct personal relations that women in charge commonly forge. This female leadership style has been termed the *web approach*.[47] It suggests a management image much different from the traditional top-down organizational chart. A three-dimensional graphic of a business would be a sphere, with the owner at the center, connected directly to each management subordinate and individual employees on the surface by spokes. On the organizational surface, employees link to their neighbors and network to others. The owner or manager connects everywhere. It is the opposite of traditional, authoritarian management style. It is a style that encourages employee creativity.[48]

The contrast between the traditional organizational chart representing the company hierarchy and the spherical image of networking organizations more deftly managed by female entrepreneurs came across in the focus group interviews clearly and repeatedly. Says Rebecca Smith,

> In developing an outline for a large project analysis report, I sat with the team and asked them to consider how they would like to see the report formatted, assuming they were the client. I took notes, offered suggestions, and at the end of the meeting handed them an outline plan to deliver the report. The outline was influenced by my experience as a project manager but included my perspective as a president, one who reviewed many reports. The project team, however, had the opportunity to participate in drafting the outline while hearing immediate feedback on their ideas. It was a learning process for them and an opportunity for me to gauge their abilities. The resulting outline was my solution; however, the team process allowed learning instead of me taking obvious control. The project team left the meeting fully energized and focused on the next phase, which was to build each section of the report. It was very well received by the client.

Many of the entrepreneurs interviewed for this study contrasted their team-oriented approach with the management style that had predominated in their prior organization. "The definition of a corporate team player is doing the same thing, looking the same way, using the same language, and giving the same answers," said Susan Brown. "My definition is quite different. We don't all have to have soul bonding, but we have to have a common level of purpose." Ann Angel, the owner of a computer training company, works to create a teamwork environment with her employees. "If they have an obstacle, I remove it or fix it," she says. "If they need equipment, if they need me to smooth something through or help think something through, they come to me. . . . They are just as competent to make the decision as I am. And they have the power to do it."[49]

In operating your business you will encounter numerous management and leadership problems. Despite the proliferation of how-to-manage-it books that line the shelves, there is no quick-fix formula that fits all situations. When problems arise, it isn't useful to chase theories and fads. Grabbing the first cure-all that promises to work and then hopping to another will do more harm than good, advises Nancy Austin, coauthor (with Tom Peters) of *A Passion for Excellence*.[50] In addition to relying on your own experience and common sense, however, there are several useful suggestions. When faced with a tough decision that has to be made quickly, you might apply one of the 80/20 rules recommended by Andrew Grove; that is, 80 percent of the insights come from 20 percent of the participants, 80 percent of the insight is generated in 20 percent of the time making the decision, 80 percent of the vital information is discovered in the first 20 percent of the time investigating, and so on. [51] Adele Scheele suggests ten questions to ask about any major decision.

1. Do I have to make this decision alone?
2. What is the basic issue that I must address and resolve?
3. Do I have all the information I need?
4. Who, outside or inside my firm, can I consult?
5. How have I handled similar issues in the past? Would I do anything differently?
6. Do I have a track record of making poor decisions? If so, what has been responsible for it? Is it something I can change?
7. Do I rely too heavily—or not heavily enough—on experts' opinions?
8. If the stakes appear too high, is there a compromise that I can settle on as a safety net?
9. Whose style of decision making do I admire, and why?
10. If I were to set my alarm clock to ring in ten minutes, what would my immediate decision be?

In general, female entrepreneurs have found success using the transformational management style, serving as the core of their businesses, networking with employees, and relinquishing control to others who do things better. But again, no one style of leadership fits all situations or cures all problems.[53] There is ample room for individuality.

Exercise 9, Assessing Your Leadership Style, provides the opportunity for a self-evaluation of your leadership/management style across five dimensions: encouraging participation, sharing power and information, enhancing self-worth, energizing self and others, and boundaryless motivation. There are no right or wrong answers to this analysis. A high score for a cluster reflects a relatively strong behavioral orientation. A lower score may indicate a weaker orientation to the task. Many of the dimensions of interactive leadership here closely resemble the transformational style. [54]

Assessing Your Leadership Style

The questions below are grouped into five clusters. Circle the number indicating your response. Total your responses for each cluster. A high total suggests a tendency toward that leadership dimension, a low total the opposite.	Cluster Identification				
	Strongly Disagree		Neutral		Strongly Agree
	1	2	3	4	5
1. Unscheduled tasks and encounters provide me with opportunities to keep key relationships in good repair inside and outside the organization.	—	—	—	—	—
2. I welcome feedback from a wide spectrum of people and create clear paths for this to occur.	—	—	—	—	—
3. By sharing information, I encourage fuller participation in decisions among employees.	—	—	—	—	—
4. I seek information from a wide network in reaching decisions.	—	—	—	—	—
5. Negotiations are an important part of my decision making.	—	—	—	—	—
Cluster 1 Subtotal: Encouraging Participation					
6. I equate my success with empowering employees.	—	—	—	—	—
7. Teamwork is an important part of my operational style.	—	—	—	—	—
8. I make a habit of recognizing employees' achievements and successes publicly.	—	—	—	—	—
9. I see my role primarily as that of a facilitator at the center reaching out to peripheral links.	—	—	—	—	—
10. Negotiations are an important part of my business strategy.	—	—	—	—	—
Cluster 2 Subtotal: Sharing Power & Information					
11. I view my organization as a part of a larger environment which includes society at large.	—	—	—	—	—
12. I give credit to those who enable workplace accomplishments rather than taking it for myself.	—	—	—	—	—
13. I base rewards on objective criteria consistent with performance.	—	—	—	—	—
14. I take responsibility for the mistakes I make.	—	—	—	—	—
15. An important part of my job is assigning work, developing, appraising, and assisting.	—	—	—	—	—
Cluster 3 Subtotal: Enhancing Self-Worth					

Assessing Your Leadership Style *cont.*

The questions below are grouped into five clusters. Circle the number indicating your response. Total your responses for each cluster. A high total suggests a tendency toward that leadership dimension, a low total the opposite.	Cluster Identification				
	Strongly Disagree		Neutral		Strongly Agree
	1	2	3	4	5
16. I see my work role as separate and distinct from my private non-work life.	—	—	—	—	—
17. Creating and communicating a vision of my company's direction to others is a priority.	—	—	—	—	—
18. I make a positive personal difference in the lives of those working with me.	—	—	—	—	—
19. I value the flexibility to set my own hours.	—	—	—	—	—
20. I value the same kind of flexibility for those reporting to me and enable this to occur for them.	—	—	—	—	—
Cluster 4 Subtotal: Energizing Self & Others					
21. I am not prone to maintain the staus quo. I do not prefer stability and order to change.	—	—	—	—	—
22. I raise expectations, take people in new directions that may involve risk.	—	—	—	—	—
23. I generate enthusiasm through a sense of equity and empathy.	—	—	—	—	—
24. I work at a steady pace and feel driven to work long hours.	—	—	—	—	—
25. For me, accessing and employing power is related to time and place rather than attention to the organizational hierarchy.	—	—	—	—	—
Cluster 5 Subtotal: Boundaryless Motivation					

5. NEGOTIATION

Framing the negotiation is the art of defining issues in terms that are advantageous to you. Much like placing a painting in a frame helps to accentuate its features, making it easier to sell, framing your side of the issue in a negotiation makes it more marketable. Assume a beautiful painting done by an artist who is competent but not outstanding. The painting has been placed in an elegantly gilded frame and hung in the Louvre Museum with guards all around and precautions taken for its safety. Now think of that same painting in a beaten wooden frame hanging over a cold, darkened fireplace in a run-down tavern on a dirt road on the outskirts of Paris. Are the images anything alike? Does the painting have the same mystique and appeal in both settings? Whose frame is accepted as the foundation for the negotiation is critical to the outcome.

JAMIE L. MOORE

Negotiators are born. Each of us has to negotiate every day. In its various forms, negotiation is a common mechanism for resolving differences and allocating resources—a decision-making process among interdependent parties who see things differently. We develop negotiating skills throughout our lives. While some people have inherently stronger skills than others, everyone has skills. Some merely use these skills more effectively. The tools needed for successful negotiation are planning, information, experience, empathy, and the ability to remain firm, focused, and clear minded[1]

Negotiation may take place formally or informally. A well-developed, varied set of negotiation skills is needed to provide the flexibility to deal with an array of negotiator styles and personalities. As a general rule, your interest in negotiations is not just to reach an agreement, or even an agreement where you come out way ahead, but to reach an agreement that is desirable for both parties irrespective of the way each approaches the issues. Tomorrow is another day; you and the other party may do business again.

GENDER, POWER, AND NEGOTIATION

Historically, women have had little power in the workplace, as the managerial gender imbalance addressed in the previous chapter indicates. While women in power do not prove to be nicer, softer, or less effective negotiators than men, the sex-role stereotype of the American woman as passive and compliant can create a dilemma for women handling complex business negotiations.[2]

Numerous studies have attempted to differentiate male and female styles of negotiation. Few have found anything even remotely relating negotiating success to gender differences. The biggest difference, some research suggests, is that women tend to employ management styles that emphasize a relationship with the other party rather than the issue at hand, with possible effects in negotiations. The one negotiation study that showed that women tended to be more cooperative linked this to the fact that they generally had less power in organizational negotiation settings. Gender may have some indirect effects, however. Managerial women, for example, report feeling less confident about themselves as negotiators, despite the fact that they are as effective as men. There is also the possibility that a man negotiating with a woman with a low-key or cooperative management style assumes she is less capable and easier to manipulate because she is not overtly aggressive.[3]

ENTREPRENEURS AND NEGOTIATIONS

Successful negotiation requires knowledge, self-confidence, and perseverance. At the same time, it is important to know when to take advice or act on information provided by others and when to trust your judgment. In emotionally charged situations it can be important to back away before reaching a settlement, to take time to reflect on what is happening. Many female entrepreneurs have a fundamental desire to trust others. Important here is the understanding that while trust is at the heart of successful negotiations, negotiators who are not novices are making other moves—always seeking better deals.

Authors, actors, and athletes have agents. For much the same reason, entrepreneurs who have been very successful at running their business should not assume they are necessarily prepared for negotiating alone during the various stages of firm growth. At the same time, negotiations cannot be completely turned over to others. There is a delicate balance. Ruth Ann Menutis, owner of The Grove, describes the problem.

> Every day in a growing business you make decisions. You don't know if they are the right ones or the wrong ones. You really can't do it all yourself. You begin to believe what you are constantly told—that there are experts out there who can do it better than or as well as you. So you begin to turn this responsibility over to them. Then you take a less active role in the decision-making process. This often represents failure in many, many companies. You have backed off and people aren't making the decisions that they should be making because they don't have the same intensity that you have. Often I get accused of wanting to be involved in too many of the little decisions, but every time I back away and say, "No, you make the decision—as the new operations man, you tell them how to do it," I come back a month later to this disaster I have to pull together. Remaining involved and informed in all aspects of decision making is important.

Entrepreneurs negotiate daily. In external negotiations they interact with customers, suppliers, agents, and other businesses. Internally, they negotiate with a management team, employees, and a board of directors. Normally, negotiation includes some combination of compromise, collaboration, and possibly some forcing on vital issues.[4] For this reason, it is extremely important to keep in mind what is really important, like the financial side of the business and meeting commitments to clients.

Elements of Negotiation

For negotiation to be effective, a number of elements must be present. These include power, open communication, a focus on outcomes, a willingness to seek assistance, knowledge and skills, and research and planning.

Power

Power is the most important component in negotiation. Whoever has power and chooses to use it influences the outcome, even when the choice is to compromise or accommodate. A business owner has to balance her power and her interests. Rebecca Smith explains how she employs power.

> My challenge might be a little different in that my business is construction, and I find myself leading and managing men 99 percent of the time. Even some of our clerical staff are men. The men are of all different ages and intellectual levels. We have the guys in the field who supervise the subcontractors and laborers, and we have highly educated managers and executives as well as sophisticated clients. This is not a group of men who will all respond to the same style of management. To manage these guys you really have to pay attention. How do I do it? I think the key to my success is the fact that I don't ask them to do anything I wouldn't or couldn't do myself, and they know it. There is a tremendous power in knowing that you can walk out onto a job site and fire anyone in the company and do their job.
>
> I am not held hostage by any absence of knowledge. I had to learn this the hard way. I remember the lesson well. I had never really gotten involved in the accounting end of the business except as it directly related to project management. I would hand the details off

to the accounting department and then review their summary reports. The day-to-day accounting function was not an area that interested me. I had hired a young woman who was a CPA to handle our entire accounting operation. She was bright and worked very efficiently. I let her run the show. One day she announced to me that she had decided she didn't like construction accounting and wanted to go back to work for an accounting firm. So there I was. I didn't have a clue as to what she had developed in the day-to-day accounting operation. I was angry with myself because I was truly vulnerable. Accounting is very important to any business. How could I have been so foolish as to not learn it and instead trust someone else with such a key piece of my business—my life? I spent the next few months working seven days a week, twelve- to fourteen-hour days, teaching myself accounting. I did not hire a replacement until I knew what I was asking the replacement to do. It worked out in the long run, but it could have been disastrous.

My insistence and perseverance paid off years later. I had just arrived back in town from a business trip and was met at the door by one of the secretaries, who announced in a panic that the accounting clerk had gone into labor early and the payroll that was supposed to be mailed out that day wasn't done yet. She asked, "What are we going to do?" I responded very calmly, "I'll run the payroll." She exclaimed, "You mean you know how to do that?" I said, "Of course I know how to do that. I used to be the only one in this company." The payroll incident had allowed me to show the recently hired employees what the longtime employees had already learned: that they would never have the power of autonomy over me. It is one of the elements of power that need not be talked about—it is better understood if it exists at the base of our relationship.

Rebecca's management style illustrates two elements important to negotiations. The first is that having power is important. The second is that you do not need to display your power like a flag. Being effective means focusing on the issue on the table rather than concentrating just on winning. This is particularly true when dealing with employees, and almost necessary because people today are less likely to take orders passively compared with workers in previous generations.[5] In Rebecca's words,

I was twenty-nine when I started my company and the first men working with me were older, well seasoned, and field oriented. They were practical. If I had been this young whippersnapper telling them what to do all the time, they would have taken their tools and trucks and smiles and gone elsewhere. Why should they have to put up with that? So instead, I made decisions and gave direction on the basis of discussion and factual presentation. It worked because I had respect in the industry before I started my business. Many employees had joined the company because of the reputation of A. D. Morgan. There was never a need to be anything but professional. My approach to an issue would be, "The train is off the track, how are we going to fix this?" After listening to their suggestions, I would say, "Why don't we try this?" If they would hem and haw, I would go, "No, no, why don't we try this?" and about the fourth time, I'd say, "Let me show you how to do it." I tried to keep my comments related to the project and focused on straightening out problems that had emerged. Discussions were never about who they were, about their intellect or personal judgments in any regard. I deal strictly with the problem, not the personality.

Communication and Focus on Outcomes

Diane C. Harris, Hypotenuse Enterprises, is a veteran negotiator. She started with Bausch & Lomb right out of graduate school as a chemist, and spent half of her career, fourteen years, on the operating side and in the analytical instrument business, which got her into the solutions business. This got her into deal making. "It was kind of fun," she says. Her second fourteen years were spent as vice president of corporate development, reporting to the CEO. "I did 230 deals, including over 100 licensings," she remembers.

I survived because only 10 percent of my time was spent in the company and 90 percent outside. I was meeting all these company presidents, global players. Every project is new and you can go anywhere in the world you want. I had a lot of freedom. I was doing my own thing. You get measured by what you produce instead of by politics. If the deal gets done, the deal gets done, and most of the time I put the deals together. When I left, the *Wall Street Journal* interviewed me.

I was answering one of the questions usually asked by the guys: "After twenty-eight years, what makes you think you can be an entrepreneur?" My answer: "You're asking me the wrong question. You should be asking how somebody as entrepreneurial as I am could have survived for twenty-eight years inside a large corporation."

For a deal to result from negotiations, says Diane, a line of communications must be open.

Most CEOs think deal making is going to be more fun: "I'll see your million and I'll raise you a million." But the reality is 2 A.M. meetings and red-eye flights and sometimes tedious negotiations. What are the qualities of a good negotiator? Someone with personal credibility, intercultural skills, creativity, energy, and the ability to handle multiple tasks. The successful deal maker won't stop trying; she'll find the 101st way to make the deal. The negotiator has to find out what the other party really wants—the "hot buttons." In one acquisition, one key shareholder mandated that no one be let go for five years. Another wanted to make sure his son was taken care of after he sold the company.

Diane's negotiating skills included the critical ability to reach beyond the immediate issues to focus on ultimate outcomes and find ways to reach the important goals.[6] In a corporate cost reduction she was asked to fire a negotiator she had hired. She was unwilling to readily accept the decision of her superior. She knew it required two years of intensive training on her part to bring a negotiator up to par, and also that once the negotiator was gone not only would she not be able to readily replace him but her workload would double. Her boss insisted the company would not be able to do enough deals to support the second negotiator. So Diane told him,

"Look, if you really think we won't do enough deals, why don't you spin off the entire Corporate Development Department, give all my people severance, and give me start-up capital. I will start this business. Give me a contract to do Bausch & Lomb's deals and I'll credit the company with half my fees and pledge my own stock as collateral to pay back the start-up capital." Obviously this deal wasn't struck because it didn't match the corporate planning pattern.

Rather than give up her negotiator, Diane offered to take the money out of her salary and work a four-day week to pay him. To this her boss reluctantly agreed.

So for one month, I took Fridays off and got paid 80 percent of my former salary. I was later asked to come back full time and did, but I still never had to lay off the staff negotiator. In the meantime, the entrepreneurial bug had bitten. I had used my Fridays to do something creative and constructive. I started thinking I could do what I had proposed. I really could take these people and start my own business. Like a baby, the idea that I could do this started to grow inside of me. I incorporated at that point, and the result is the business I had proposed earlier.

Later, I got a new boss. On his first day on the job I walked in and said, "Bill, I have a deal for you." He said, "Diane, no deals yet, my first day." I said, "No, this is my deal, do you want to do it?" I thought, "I'm a negotiator for a living." I got everything I wanted. Inventing the package, I could not have asked for a better negotiation. I had already incorporated. My plans were written. I was talking to people. I was ready to go. There was a moment when you just snip it, like the umbilical cord, done. After twenty-eight years I had graduated from operating in a corporate environment to running a business of my own.

Outside Assistance

Entrepreneurs unskilled in negotiations may reach out for expert help. But it is difficult to know in advance who can help and whom to trust. Organizations have been formed to deal with just this problem. Susan Willett Bird founded one, the American Mediation Council, and is now president of Women.future, LLC. Her career also shows a series of fascinating changes, each successfully negotiated. She began her business career with IBM, where she not only was the first female computer "territory sales rep" but was cited as an outstanding regional marketing representative. She became an attorney and practiced law focusing on corporate litigation and representing corporate clients in various stages of growth. Susan later joined The Grubb & Ellis Company, where she led the company's investment division in dollar sales volume. She was promoted to the managing office of the northeastern United States, responsible for developing and implementing the firm's marketing strategy east of the Mississippi. In 1985, she founded her own real estate firm, S. W. Bird and Company, Inc., eventually employing sixty full-time professionals to pioneer her concept of focusing brokerage services on one side of the real estate transaction (trademarked "single side representation"). Susan later founded SMILE, Inc.™, a CD-ROM–based marketing company that obtained a patent in 1992 for its method of combining compressed color images and text in digital form. The company allied with Apple Computer to establish a leadership position in the field of interactive multimedia global marketing of real estate and related products and services.

Susan founded her present company in 1996. In 1991, she received the *Crain's New York Business* Award for Success and Excellence in Business, and the Life of the City Award from *New York Woman* magazine for her statewide efforts regarding disclosure laws addressing conflict of interest issues in the sale of real property. A founding member of the Committee 200, she has led the organization as chair for two terms and served as a director for numerous terms. She is also a founding member of the San Francisco Women's Forum, has served as a director of the New York Women's Forum, and is a member of the International Women's Forum.

Knowledge and Skills

Negotiations are inescapable. Learning something about the negotiation process is a must. This is true not only for entrepreneurs but also for people in large organizations. The changes in organizational structures over the last two decades removed layers of managerial authority. As the old reporting relationships disappeared, so did the buffers, rules, policies, and procedures that had kept the interactions structured in the organization. In the flatter organizations, managers find themselves dealing directly or through communications media with many other people in a variety of organizational positions at varying distances. Negotiating skills have become more important than ever.

Recent research suggests that it is advisable to enter into negotiations with a cooperative attitude because an approach that establishes elements of trust is more likely to resolve an issue than a more formal process. A research model suggests that conflict situations lie along a continuum, with increasing levels of skill necessary to resolve the conflict. Differences, disagreements, and dissonance are seen as being mutually inclusive, meaning they are amenable to being resolved by the negotiating parties through discussion, education, and compromise. Controversy, contention, and "war" are seen as mutually exclusive. These settings ordinarily require the intervention of a third party to mediate, arbitrate, or adjudicate. The model highlights both the alternatives available and negotiation limits.[7] The model also strongly suggests avoiding or ending conflict spirals because people have a tendency to respond to communications in kind, especially where issues are contentious. The recommended tactic is to refocus the negotiation by refusing to play the game of power communications and return to substantive issues, in the process providing clear signals that you are taking charge and are unwilling to follow the other party's lead into the contentious territory.[8]

Research and Planning

Whether the negotiation involves a one-time event or a long-term relationship, the interaction requires research. Without information about your side of the issue, it is difficult to create an action plan to realize the goal you have in mind. Without information about your opponent's side, you are left guessing about what might happen. You need to know what is most desired and also what may be acceptable, the available resources, the expected negotiation style, and the probable strategy and tactics that may be employed. You also need to know about the negotiating process itself, particularly if it can be derailed by something not readily apparent, such as an impasse, conflict, or competition from parties not originally involved. Contingency planning is necessary because, in addition to an ideal solution from your point of view, you need to establish two things. The first is an outcome that you will find acceptable if the pot of gold is out of reach. Second is the point at which, once you decide on the solution that is minimally acceptable to you, you will walk away rather than accept anything less. As Diane Harris advises, "Better to lose a deal than have a bad deal. It's as important to be able to walk away from a deal as to do a deal."

BUILDING THE PROFILE

Assume a negotiation important to your business is about to take place. Start with yourself. Identify what you need and want. List all the appropriate and available sources of information you have and any resources relevant to the negotiation: yourself, your networks, the other party and its networks, any previous interactions and history, public and financial records, media reports, customers, markets, locations (for negotiation), and related transactions. This listing should also cover any alternate sources of goods or services.

After you identify these sources of information, sort through them to establish a profile to work your side of the negotiation. Set your *target point* at the ideal outcome for the negotiation. Set your *reservation point* at the last acceptable outcome before you would walk away from the table. To identify your reservation point, select the alternatives to a negotiated agreement that you think are best. Consider whether options are available other than the current negotiation. Research and networks confer a competitive advantage here. An information base can identify substitute products or services, alternate vendors, other locations or markets, and the like.[9]

Researching your side of the negotiation is vital. While you want to enter into the negotiating process with a cooperative attitude, you should assume the worst, that conflict is inevitable. This requires you to consider some elements you might not otherwise think about. Have you set a firm walk-away or reservation point? Can you stick to it if the negotiations lead to an outcome you don't want to accept? Can you afford to walk away or not make the deal?

Never walk into an important negotiation without having done this homework. You are vulnerable if the other party is prepared and you are not. This is true whether you are negotiating for an increase in your salary or a promotion, to take on a client relationship, to parcel out part of your company, to merge with another firm, to complete a buyout or sellout, or anything else critical to your business.

WALKING IN THE OTHER PARTY'S SHOES

After profiling your position, identify the needs and desires of the other party. Make two analyses here. First, construct a view of the other party's situation from your vantage point. The other side is an important source of information because before or during a negotiation each party generally gives indications of the stand it will take, its strategy, and its targeted outcomes. Second, imagine your opponent's position. Building on what you have learned about the other party, its resources, past history, and possible strategy, construct a profile for negotiating its side of the situation.

With this research-based framework, you can now examine the arena for elements that could lead to a win-win negotiation outcome. The combined work of several researchers suggests the following approach.[10]

1. Seek a way to reach both your goal and the other party's.
2. View the other party as a partner.
3. Understand the situation.
4. Learn the personality of your partner.
5. Help the other party.
6. Develop and examine alternatives.
7. Accept other ways of doing things.
8. Finally, consider the act of negotiation as an ongoing process.

This is not easy. It takes careful planning and preparation, intense concentration during negotiating sessions, and the ability to remain clearheaded and cool.

FRAMING THE ISSUES

Entering a negotiation, each person brings business and personal goals into play. Strategies, the environment, allegiances, personal styles, preferences, and other factors influence outcomes. As a negotiator, you will need to alter your style to fit various situations. Sometimes it will be better to emphasize building the relationship with the other party, other times not. Sometimes the negotiations should focus on the task or issue at hand—on the practical and economic impacts—and at other times on emotional factors. At some times, you will want to maximize your share of the pie, while at other times your focus will be on creating a winning solution.[11]

As the quotation at the beginning of the chapter suggests, how issues are *framed* has powerful effects on bargaining and interpreting the outcomes. Framing can refer to how the task or issue is defined or it can refer to how people approach negotiation. Six cognitive frames in three scales can assist in identifying your value system and that of the other party and how these can change during a negotiation.[12] This sounds more complicated than it is.

The first four frames describe the personality of the individual in the negotiating process.

1. People in a *relationship frame* are focused mostly on the interactions with the other party. These individuals will key in on the tone of the conversation, the fairness of the process, the participation of all parties in the process, and the satisfaction of each party with the outcome.

2. People in a *task frame* are interested in the material details or substance of the interaction. They will focus on the agenda, key decision points, data, and feasible outcomes.

3. People in an *emotional frame* will focus on the feelings and emotions involved—how the process feels, how they feel they are being treated—the emotional content of the issues and outcome, and how the opponent feels about the outcome.

4. People in an *intellectual frame* are interested in the actions and behaviors involved in the interaction. Specifically, they are likely to focus on the logic of the process and outcomes, whether solutions are practical, and the most economically sensible outcome.

The last two frames deal with the approach individuals take during the negotiations.

5. In a *cooperative frame,* people concentrate on maximizing the outcome for both sides of the negotiation. These individuals will look for cooperation from the other party to determine the most important issues for each side and seek ways to achieve success jointly.

6. People with a *winning frame* are focused on creating the best outcome for their own side. These negotiators will look to gain the best possible outcome without significant regard for the desires of the other party.[13]

Understanding the frames can be a great help. You will deal one way in a negotiation if the other party displays an emotional and cooperative attitude, another way if the party is proceeding from an intellectual frame and focused on winning.

Gathering information on your tendencies and what you can glean of the other party is the first step toward identifying possible strategies for a successful negotiation. This information should be captured in your preparation profiles. The second step is to consider the different styles of negotiating each party can employ. It is important to remember that the frames discussed above may be directly related to the immediate events taking place and therefore can change. As a rule of thumb, during a negotiation, the greater the difference in how the parties to the dispute frame the issues, the more likely the two frames will converge.[14]

NEGOTIATING STYLES AND STRATEGIES

Researchers have set out a scale of conflict management that is commonly used to identify negotiation styles. Assertiveness lies at one end of the scale, cooperation at the other.[15]

1. The *competitive* approach to negotiation assumes or indicates that the individual feels he or she has enough leverage to get what he or she wants whether the other party cooperates or not.

2. Negotiators who are both assertive and cooperative, interested in satisfying the goals of all involved, are following a *collaborative* approach.

3. Negotiators with a moderate amount of assertiveness and medium interest in both parties' outcomes may end up sharing or *compromising*.

4. Unassertive and uncooperative negotiators, uninterested in the outcomes, are practicing *avoidance*.

A negotiation strategy may incorporate an array of these approaches.[16]

Applying the six cognitive frames to the three most important negotiation styles (avoidance is ignored here) points to three types of strategies. The choice of which is used does not always lie with either party. Resources, timeframes, relationships, and visibility of the outcome all influence negotiations.

In a **win-lose strategy,** the parties are negotiating over something finite. What one gains the other loses. This is referred to as a *distributive* negotiation. This strategy produces extra tension because dividing something both parties want introduces elements of human behavior driven as much by emotion as by logic. Popular advice about "separating the people from the problem," "getting to yes," and various similar suggestions may sound simplistic, but it is often difficult to execute. These ideas are, however, worth a try in negotiations.

In a **win-win strategy**, the parties are looking to satisfy both their needs and the other party's. This is referred to as *integrative bargaining*. Where both sides are collaborating, open communication, creativity, and good networks on both sides can help create options. Generally speaking, in a win-win situation, you want to look for issues that are more valuable to one party and less valuable to the other party and stock the negotiation with these so that both can leave with a slate of successes. Such negotiations are referred to as integrative because, ideally, the outcome leaves both parties satisfied.

A **mixed outcome strategy** depends on the willingness of both parties to follow an integrative approach to resolve a distributive negotiation, making it less competitive.

It is important to remember that the personality characteristics as well as the cognitive frame of the bargainer affect the integrative process and that there are definite benefits not only from increased communication but also from the ability to be an effective communicator.[17]

Joan B. Anderson, CEO, James H. Anderson, Inc., sole owner of the largest woman-owned heating, ventilating, air-conditioning, and design/building company in the United States, a recipient of the *Working Woman* Entrepreneurial Excellence Award for 1999 for regaining the competitive standing of her company within the industry, is a veteran negotiator. Early on Joan learned that it is either eat or be eaten in the competitive environment in which her company operates. She also valued and respected the relationships she established with her employees and thus established very good union and labor relations. With a company that is 90 percent union, she soon learned the value of going into a negotiation from a position of strength. She says it is important to "know your strengths and weaknesses and to always have a mental piece of paper in your pocket for your walk-away point." She illustrates this with the strategy that has worked best for her in negotiations.

> I knew what I wanted to pay. If we came close but it wasn't close enough, I learned the importance of walking away. In negotiating it is important to look at every day in your business life—it is better to talk about exchanges along the way so that when you get to the final negotiation there is not that much left at stake.
>
> If you know that you have a goal in mind, it is important to focus on how you will reach that goal. To me it is a series of negotiations. You can reach your goal without anybody ever knowing that's where you're going, and then it doesn't become a confrontation. The best way is to get someone to the point you want and then let him or her bring out the idea you wish to accomplish. I don't need the ego strokes because I am after a bigger piece of the apple.

Two basic temporal relationships influence negotiations. A *long-term* relationship is one that perhaps began before the present negotiation and will extend long after. One or both parties may have an interest in maintaining or even nurturing the relationship. This may require conceding on some issues. A negotiation with an important customer disputing a sale is a case in point. Keeping the customer who will make repeated purchases over time can make up for a one-time loss. *Short-term* relationships consist of one-time or limited contact between the parties. Here, one tries to make the best deal possible because it is not necessary to "build points" for a future deal. However, before moving to a distributive negotiation style, you might also consider whether the relationship is *pseudo short-term*. An example would be a situation where you have a customer from out of town who comes to your business to purchase an item. Is this is a one-time customer or a frequent traveler passing through, a person with contacts to constituencies important to you?[18]

The importance of timing in negotiations can be learned early and used successfully throughout life. Joan Anderson learned in high school what she considered the "saturation point" in negotiations. As an outstanding achiever, recipient of the highest honors, she was in high demand as a leader, and she worked hard. She set her mind on the goal she wanted to accomplish: more than anything else she wanted to be the prom queen. She developed her strategy early in the fall of her senior year when one more time she was asked to take on a major leadership role. And after careful thought, she said to herself: "People are going to say, 'well she has won all these awards, so we think the really big one (the one I really wanted) should go to someone else.' So I said no. I got the award I wanted. I have this philosophy that I will get there but not today. I will get there more successfully if I take these steps along the way."

This is the same strategy Joan used in electing to accept the vice presidential slot in the Parks and Recreation project over the presidential slot she was initially asked to take. She looked around the organization and realized that all the parts were not in place to be successful now in the presidential role. As the vice president she took on a less focused role and carefully worked to put all the parts in place to make her project a success. Then and only then was she willing to take on the role of president. It appears to be a theme that has emerged throughout her life. In the company, when she was a stockholder but was not allowed by her husband to participate in company onsite operations, she worked elsewhere. This did not appear to her to belittle her knowledge or position. The time simply was not right.

TYPES OF POWER

The ability to influence is a key skill for a negotiator. Influencing skills may be directly related to the types of leverage or power at your disposal. Power can be based on the ability to reward, punish, mentor, advise, sway, or charm another person. There are five bases of power.

1. Influence based on rewards that can be offered is *reward* power.

2. Influence based on punishments or threats in the event of noncompliance is called *coercive* power. Rewards and punishments can range from the tangible to the intangible. Money, goods, products, people, and other resources can be leveraged.

3. Power based on status, referrals, and vital interests is called *legitimate* power, usually manifested in the manager-employee relationship, but also seen in interactions between entrepreneurs and stockholders, on boards of directors, with critical suppliers, and in employees who are vital to the business.

4. *Referent* power is based on identification with, attraction to, or respect for the power holder. It is often found in charismatic leaders who have the ability to relate to and charm people. Referent power can also be gained through a track record of success or experience in a situation.

5. *Expert* power is based on the belief that the holder possesses superior skills and abilities and may be associated with greater experience, success, research, academic accomplishment, or exhibited ability.[19]

Assessing the power base of the negotiating parties will assist in identifying the style and cognitive frame most valuable to the negotiation. The selected power base depends on your relationship to the other party and fit with your negotiation profile. Suppose you are negotiating with your regular caterer for an important upcoming business event. It is unlikely that expert or referent power will be present. Depending on the amount of business you do with this caterer, you may have some legitimate power to exert. Most likely, you will use your power to reward or coerce. To determine which power base is most appropriate, you should review your profile and experience with this caterer.

Rebecca Smith's comments demonstrate how the bases of power come into play in operating a successful business.

> Dealing with the daily operational issues requires a different tack. We have a weekly Monday morning meeting where the managers report on their current project status. We mix weekend stories with business, which makes for an uplifting start to the week. We accomplish our business while enjoying the camaraderie. However, if a report is not complete or if someone can't respond to my inquiries, I have to shift from being a teammate to being his or her boss. I lean forward in my chair, look the person straight in the eye, and begin asking even more detailed questions. I pause, sit back in my chair, and ask for everyone's attention. I address the group and ask if they all understand their responsibilities as project managers. I turn back to the project manager who was initially addressed. "Let me ask the question again." The room is very quiet; the tone has changed. Without raising my voice and without excessive lecturing, the message is clear: enjoy your job, have fun and be yourself . . . but do your job and do it expertly. I will end the discussion with that project manager by asking for whatever information he or she did not have to be placed on my desk by a specific date and time. There are a few seconds of silence before we move on. This does not happen very often. The managers are generally very well prepared, partly to avoid being singled out like that in front of their peers.
>
> This low-key but serious style is very effective for me. I am a positive leader. I place such great emphasis on rewarding excellence and celebrating good work that a slight departure from that norm sends a clear message of dissatisfaction. I am generally upbeat and emotionally steady, moving around the office chatting and laughing while encouraging people and promoting their renegade spirits and innovations. My continuing message to them is that we have an agreement to each do our part of the job, which together makes a

successful team. If someone has not followed through with his or her responsibility to the team, I will not stand by and let the other members of the team suffer for a failure of one member to perform. I ask the person to give me all the details of the problem. After deciding how to correct the problem, I bring that individual into my office, explain what was done, and put him or her back on the project to take it forward from that point. I explain that I have confidence in his or her ability to carry out the task successfully, and we talk about what interrupted the effort.

ENTERING A NEGOTIATION

Before any important negotiation begins, completely research your personal profile and that of the other party. Use the information to establish an approach to the negotiation. In this process you will ask and answer the two most important questions: What is success in this negotiation? What is the best way to get there?

First impressions are hard to change. In a negotiation, the opening *tone* sets the stage for most of what follows. Starting with an antagonistic approach generally puts the other party on the defensive or gets him or her angry enough to respond in kind, often creating a spiraling effect. Identifying what tone is best depends on the situation, precedent, previous contact, and the tone used by the other party. *Situation* means the issues, the environment, and the people involved in the negotiation. *Precedent* refers to similar negotiations by other parties, industry or business standards, and any generally accepted rules of conduct understood beforehand by both parties. *Previous contact* with the other party gives you a baseline from which you can assess what tone is likely to be most acceptable and effective. It is important to remember that people react differently in new situations. The person you met with over drinks or shared a common interest with in a previous negotiation is not the same person you are facing on the other side of the table.[20]

Surprises occur during negotiations more often than not. People leave jobs, budgets get cut, businesses fail or are sold, alternate solutions become available, and projects and deals are abandoned for any number of reasons. The savvy negotiator assumes the unexpected. Invariably, the tone, style, strategy, process, or offers from the other party will cause you to change plans. This is why it is very helpful to prepare *contingency plans* and provide for some flexibility in your approach. Contingency plans can include changing your approach or offer to the other party, seeking alternate products or services to offer, or acting on your predetermined best alternative to a negotiated agreement. The rule here is that the more important the outcome of the negotiation is to you, the more important your best alternative becomes.

Entering a negotiation, you should understand that both the outcome and the process are under continuous negotiation. *Reframing* may be necessary. In a complex negotiation, new information, the other party's influence, any ineffectiveness of your strategy, a change in style by the opponent, or any number of other things can require you to reevaluate. If the original frame is not working, review and reevaluate.

In engaging the other party, building a relationship is critical regardless of whether this is a one-time relationship or a continuing one. To create a functional relationship, it is necessary to establish an understanding and some common ground, and to set boundaries for interaction. In essence, you need to set guidelines for when, where, and how you will interact and what or whom you are bargaining for. Depending on the situation, there may already be precedents or standing agreements for a number of these guidelines. You will want to be aware of or inquire about these from more experienced parties. There are various guidelines, expectations, agendas, and goals you need to consider in the process. These include any verbal or written agendas for the negotiation, boundaries for discussion (what you're negotiating), methods of contact, a timetable for making decisions and taking breaks, discussing alternative approaches, and involving outside parties.

There are a number of issues to consider when you are discussing guidelines and parameters for a negotiation. Learning the preferred medium, method, timing, and style of communication is integral to building trust and creating a foundation to understand the needs of each party. Having developed an understanding of how to communicate most effectively, the negotiating parties will want to agree on how and when they will check the process and goals. It is important to set up a method for reevaluating goals or expectations based on new information or resources. It can be useful to agree on a method for researching or creating alternate solutions to "expand the pie." You may also wish to identify parts of the negotiation that might require mediation from an outside party, such as contracts, legal issues, or situations when the involved parties reach impasse—that is, you are not able to come to a solution but realize you must find one.

STICKING TO THE RESERVATION POINT

One of the common pitfalls in a negotiation is agreeing to an outcome that is not as valuable as your best alternative. Knowing and understanding your reservation or walk-away point is important. Acting on your reservation point is critical. Again, planning will be the key factor in determining whether a position on the table represents a successful agreement, an acceptable agreement, or an option to be rejected. While there are situations when you will need to reevaluate or even change your reservation point based on new information, as a general rule, a reservation point based on solid research should dictate when you leave the negotiation without a settlement. It is important to know when to take charge and lead the negotiation into new territory and when to dismantle it all together.[21]

DON'T BURN YOUR BRIDGES

In a distributive (win-lose) negotiation where you have ample coercive power, it may seem obvious that a no-holds-barred approach will bring the maximum rewards at no cost, and you can act without restraint. However, beware of situations where it seems that nothing can stop you from getting your own way. A true family story, half a century old, illustrates this point.

Shortly after the end of World War II, two bright young men with extensive corporate managerial experience in the grocery business and a remarkable strategy for selling fruits and vegetables went out on their own and established a consulting firm. What they had to offer was a combination sales, merchandising, and marketing strategy. They put on programs and training sessions for produce wholesalers and food chains, charging a prearranged fee based on the number of people attending the sessions. Their consulting business was extremely successful. One day a produce wholesaler from the Southwest attended one of the sessions. He was impressed with what he saw. But rather than signing up his own people and paying the fee, he had his representatives take copious notes on the program. He then used his political contacts to suggest to a government official that a government agency should distribute the seminar information for free, and he handed over the notes that had been taken. The federal agency set up an information program. The resulting product was nowhere near as good as the program given by the consultants, but it cost the participants nothing, and soon the consulting firm was out of business. One of the consultants took a position as a vice president of a large midwestern grocery chain. Years later, this chain purchased a smaller chain of stores in the Southwest. When the consultant-turned-vice president toured the area, he was surprised to be enthusiastically greeted by the same produce wholesaler. It seemed that the wholesaler's business depended almost entirely on the stores the VP's chain had acquired. The VP smiled, was cordial, returned to his Midwest headquarters—and the next day gave orders that no one was ever again to purchase anything from the produce wholesaler. Then he called his former partner in the consulting business and said, "Guess what I did today?"

Employees, Performance Management, and Negotiations

Day-to-day performance management—that is, the entire spectrum of personnel decisions from hiring to rewarding to promoting to disciplinary action—requires good negotiation techniques. Approaches can be tailored according to your management system, but the basics are always the same. You want the best people, and you want them to give their best efforts in your business. You also want to avoid running afoul of state and federal laws and regulations governing hiring and employee relations. You understand this requires that you treat employees fairly and also that they understand their treatment is fair. Achieving this requires a system.

The first step in your personnel system is to always assess performance based on established criteria that deal with *performance-related behavior.* When hiring or reviewing employees, at the beginning discuss and set expectations. This requires you to assess the strengths and weaknesses of each employee, identify performance goals, and get employee agreement. In performance reviews, this may also require pinpointing specific employee behaviors that need to be changed to meet the agreed-upon goals. If problems have cropped up, explain your objective reaction to the employee's past performance, make requests for future performance so the employee understands, and describe benefits to the employee for meeting these requests. It is a good idea to keep written records and communicate in memos or letters so that what is discussed is not later forgotten or misinterpreted.

The approach incorporates *management by objectives.* This way of addressing people allows for some flexibility. For example, assume a longtime employee made a major business decision while filling in for you when you were out of town. On returning, you didn't like the decision. How did you handle this situation? Chastisement? On the one hand, you really did not like what was done. On the other hand, you don't want to outlaw employee initiative. If you do, in the future, if you are not available for counsel, employees might avoid making any decisions important to the business.

DEVELOPING SKILLS

While negotiations often appear to be instinctive, they are not, and skills are developed through research, preparation, and practice. For example, a customer walks into your business to return a product.

You see nothing wrong with the product. You have two options. You can choose to replace the product or refund the customer's money and thus preserve the relationship. Or you can decide that you can't do this for every customer, and that losing this one isn't important compared with the wider consequences. Making the choice in this simple situation requires a very quick assessment of what you have at stake, and is easily handled. However, in a business so large that you can't deal with every customer, the situation becomes more complex. Now you have to make rules. Are the rules to be followed in every case? If there is to be flexibility, what is flexible? Who can decide this?

Keep in mind that in negotiations it is always wise to maintain a rational and emotion-free tone, at least in the beginning. Finding a rational solution in the midst of chaos and in emotional situations requires a high level of skill. A delivery person for Company X is rude and abusive to your staff. Your original reaction may be to stop doing business with this company. You could, however, negotiate by bringing this person's behavior to the attention of the company, requesting a new delivery person, and asking for some reparation.

In more serious cases, even if the issues have spiraled beyond ready repair, there are some steps you can still try. You might want to simply schedule a break in the negotiations. This would give both parties some distance and time to cool off. You might want to reanalyze the situation. Most important, unless you are positively ready to kill the prospective deal, leave the other party a way out. A face-saving strategy can be a very important feature in successful negotiations. You might expand the options by offering incentives for a negotiated settlement that was not readily apparent at the beginning of the discussion.

Curiously enough, demonstrating rationality—an approach to the other party that is logical, open, and fair—may not always be in your best interest. Assume an issue where the stakes are high. The other side has dealt with you before. Because you have always been calm, cool, rational, and interested in the most cost-effective outcomes in prior negotiations, your opponent decides to make a less than desirable offer. The logic is that you will not reject it because that would cost you more than accepting it. You have become too predictable. You would be better off if your opponent carried a seed of doubt in his or her mind about just what you might do. Though it sounds absurd, understand that the most rational thing you can do as a negotiator is to make the other party aware that you are capable of behaving irrationally. An attorney, an experienced negotiator, offers this thought: Most people are risk adverse. They like certainty. In a negotiation, you are always trying to minimize your areas of uncertainty and maximize your opponent's.

Keep in mind that both sides may not wish to resolve the conflict in a satisfactory way. If all negotiation approaches fail but the issue cannot remain unresolved (a labor dispute, for example), you may wish to hire a mediator. The mediator must be credible to both parties. Mediators open up communications by setting guidelines and structuring discussions—key factors in the negotiation process.

While we live in a high-tech world of rapid communication through e-mail, faxes, conference calls, videoconferencing, and the Internet, face-to-face communication still is the most effective medium. The concept of "when in Rome" may seem not to hold when we can go to Rome without leaving our house, but we miss a great deal—the beauty of the countryside, the ambience of the people, and the sensation of viewing the art in the Sistine Chapel, for example. The most effective mode of communication is in person. All the other forms are poor substitutes. Keep this in mind in negotiations, particularly when the stakes are high and subtleties are important.

CORPORATE LIVING

For people in corporate life, salary negotiations are important. The basics, summarized by Joseph Byrnes, are

1. Never ask for something you don't want or can't justify.
2. Separate the issue of trust from the negotiating process.
3. Protect yourself from unethical and abusive negotiators.
4. Remember to view negotiations as a problem-solving process, not a contest of wills.[22]

No one should prepare for a salary negotiation without knowing what the comparable salaries are for the same work. Check with all your sources—friends, family, placement offices, trade journals, and other sources that provide annual salary survey data. Adjust these data to reflect the job level that concerns you. The research is critical. Having at hand the information that in applying for jobs men B.A.s and MBAs ask for salaries 16.5 percent higher than women and then acting on the information can begin to level a playing field instantly.[23] Your greatest leverage is an accurate assessment of your skill level in terms of your ability to meet the demands of the job. This places you in the position of being able to show why you are worth the salary and benefits you are requesting. Your leverage increases if you can walk away if the offer doesn't meet your needs—that is, if you have a couple of job offers or are already holding a position. In job application negotiations, avoid the trap of naming a specific salary you will accept. The figure might be too low or place you in the position of saying you can't accept less.[24] Instead, say you would find it difficult to accept the terms first offered. Keep in mind while negotiating an entry-level salary, a promotional raise, or another type of strategic decision, your interest is in the long-term package. Can alternative benefits be brought into the discussions? an earlier promotion? a signing bonus? a better job title? special training sessions? fringe benefits leading to tax breaks? reimbursements for child or elder care?[25] Above all, remember that the base salary, annual bonuses, and other company perks may not be the key elements. Does this job move you forward or give you the tools you need to advance your career?

After you have been on the job for a while, you begin thinking about lateral moves for career advancement. Here, you may find the negotiation strategy developed by Stephen M. Pollan and Mark Levine (1996) helpful. Target the position that you want. Once you have it firmly in mind, assemble the skills to show you have developed the necessary expertise to handle that job. Specifically, show how you would contribute to the bottom line. If there is an important project coming up, work up a memo outlining how you'd handle it. If the boss is waffling, however, push for a trial run. If you sense hard-core resistance, end the meeting by asking for another shot at a future date.[26]

CONFLICT SKILLS AND STRATEGIES

This chapter has introduced you to the foundation for developing your skills as a successful negotiator and has provided a number of examples of how you can use a successful negotiation strategy to your advantage. Now it is time to assess your skills and strategies for dealing with conflict, which is an inevitable part of the negotiation process. Many approaches are used to resolve and cope with conflict. To develop the most effective strategy it is important to understand your style. Exercise 10 will help you discover which conflict coping strategy you use most often and why others react to you the way they do while you are negotiating for something you want. Knowing where you stand—whether you have a tendency to be avoidance driven, an accommodater, a compromiser, or a competitor, or have a clear preference to develop a collaborative strategy—will serve you well in developing the key skills needed as a successful negotiator. After you have developed a score for the self-assessment and examined your negotiation conflict profile you may wish to read the chapter again or refer to the notes to learn about additional books you can use in becoming an even more effective negotiator.[28]

Strategies for Coping with Conflict

For each item below, select a number from 1 to 5 as a measure of how frequently you apply this approach in attempting to reach a solution.	Rarely Use 1	2	3	4	Almost Always Use 5
1. I know that my side of the issue is right.	—	—	—	—	—
2. I try to put the needs of others above what I want.	—	—	—	—	—
3. I try to arrive at a position both sides can accept.	—	—	—	—	—
4. I don't like to get involved in conflicts.	—	—	—	—	—
5. I am interested in working with the other person to find a solution.	—	—	—	—	—
6. I look for faults in my opponent's position.	—	—	—	—	—
7. I seek harmony without disruptions as the important consideration.	—	—	—	—	—
8. I want to walk away with a portion of what I have proposed.	—	—	—	—	—
9. I don't want to be involved in controversial issues.	—	—	—	—	—
10. I want to gain the commitment of the other parties involved.	—	—	—	—	—
11. I meet every steamroller head-on.	—	—	—	—	—
12. The issue is more important to the other party than it is to me.	—	—	—	—	—
13. Realizing that we are equal, I seek middle-ground solutions.	—	—	—	—	—
14. I see no chance of getting what I want.	—	—	—	—	—
15. I encourage open dialogue in sharing concerns.	—	—	—	—	—
16. I don't get bothered if the other party feels defeated.	—	—	—	—	—
17. I discovered in the middle of the negotiation that I was wrong.	—	—	—	—	—
18. My goals are somewhat important but not worth a bigger fight.	—	—	—	—	—
19. I feel emotional about this issue. Others can handle this problem better.	—	—	—	—	—
20. I try not to tie my position to my personal feelings.	—	—	—	—	—

continued

EXERCISE 10 *Strategies for Coping with Conflict* continued

Scoring		Score
High scores on questions 4, 9, 14, and 19 suggest an approach to negotiation that fails to address conflict. This is not to be interpreted in a negative light. However, over time, it will be easy for the competitive side to gain the upper hand in the negotiation because the pattern of behavior may become predictable. The style places the bargainer in a position of always showing his or her hand as if playing a poker game. To change from this strategy, it is important to recognize that conflict is a necessary condition of reaching solutions and should not be interpreted as good or bad.	Avoidance 4 9 14 19 Total	
High scores on questions 2, 7, 12, and 17 suggest an accommodating style. Sometimes it appears more worthwhile to sacrifice some of the desired outcomes in order to achieve a smooth working relationship. To avoid a "wimp" syndrome, consider when it is valuable to your long-run strategy to give up something now for a better relationship in the future.	Accommodation 2 7 12 17 Total	
High scores on questions 3, 8, 13, and 18 indicate a willingness to compromise. This strategy applies when only partial satisfaction can occur for both parties. It requires willingness to be flexible and the realization that you will not win the whole pie. For example, take a situation in which both parties are equally committed, yet a settlement must be reached that satisfies the needs of both or both will lose. You both need to reach an agreement to move on to business that is more important.	Compromise 3 8 13 18 Total	
High scores on questions 1, 6, 11, and 16 indicate you are in a power game in which you consider what you are after more important than what your opponent wants. The approach is win-lose rather than win-win. If the stakes are high in terms of building long-range relationships, careful consideration of why you are using this approach is important. Losers usually make ripples. In a competitive arena you may take on the reputation of a bully. However, toughness is not always bad and is sometimes very necessary.	Competition 1 6 11 16 Total	
High scores on questions 5, 10, 15, and 20 indicate a collaborative negotiation style. At the outset you realize that when you walk out the door it is not the end of the relationship with the person. You would like this to be a win-win situation where you both walk away satisfied with the bargain you have struck. This can be done by examining the underlying concerns and attempting to address those, and in the process developing a sense of sharing—which leads to the best negotiation decision for all involved. Trust and commitment are important ingredients in an approach where neither party wants to have full responsbility for the outcome.	Collaboration or Integration 5 10 15 20 Total	

This diagnostic tool is based on the review of the literature in the chapter (see notes) and formatted on the basis of the work of Whetten & Cameron (1998), pp. 319–320, 562. See also Johnson & Johnson (1994).

6. GROWTH, TRANSITIONS, AND SUCCESS

How do we know when we are successful? We know. There is no one to pull the curtain up and down and to hold up the cards for applause. Entrepreneurship is the joy of challenge, putting ourselves on the line again and again.

DEBORAH SZEKELY

A s the previous chapters have indicated, career growth often begins with the accumulation of experiences in organizations. The movement to entrepreneurship is often a transitional process in which former organizational incubators, business ownership, and other roles take on important functions. Once the decision is reached to found a business venture, one can then examine the entrepreneurial career in terms of growth, transitions, and success.

GROWTH

Founding, establishing, and expanding the business involves the critical tasks of defining markets, developing products, and bringing the two together. Important in the inception of a new venture is having a realistic understanding of what it takes to succeed; assembling the business plan, financing, and other start-up tools; developing a strategy; managing the fear that accompanies a leap into the future; and committing to hard work. A person coming to entrepreneurship from an incubator organization has often been accustomed to the protections afforded by working while someone else has been at risk. The most common pitfalls in starting a business, according to the Online Women's Business Center of the Small Business Administration, are the dramatic change in one's routine, the difficulties of balancing career and home life, recognizing undeveloped business skills and doing something about the lack, and constantly reexamining the basic business concept. According to the experts, the founding stage of a business lasts until annual sales reach approximately $1 million.[1]

As the sketches in Chapter 1 show, an array of approaches have been used to launch business ventures. A new idea is usually the reason a business is founded, according to Catalyst and the National Foundation for Women Business Owners, who recently reported that half of their random sample of 650 women and 150 men with previous work experience started businesses because they had thought of something new.[2] By itself, however, the idea isn't enough. It is "about 5 percent of the success equation," says William Dunn, associate director of the Sol C. Snider Entrepreneurial Center at the University of Pennsylvania's Wharton School. The rest of the equation is made up of business skill, an internal drive, a strong work ethic, and, if not the ability to do it all, certainly the ability to see that it all gets done. As an SBA publication notes, "You have a great idea . . . but is it a business?"

The common advice of consultants and college business experts in entrepreneurial centers is to plan and prepare carefully before launching a business. This places you in good stead in avoiding common myths, identified by many writers. [3]

- I'm smart, I can just wing it.
- I can do it on a shoestring.
- No sweat, I have a great idea.
- I've got nothing better to do.
- Starting a business will help my personal relationships.
- With all my experience, starting a business should be easy.

• A bad economy will mean fewer competitors.

• A good economy will ensure success.

• I'm mad as hell and I'm not going to take it anymore.

A well thought out plan backed by experience is almost always necessary. Evelyn Reis Perry, CEO of Carolina Sound Communications, Inc., and Sound Communications, Inc., both headquartered in Charleston, South Carolina, is a graduate of the University of Wisconsin at Madison and a transplanted New Yorker. Both of her companies are sound, video, and systems contractors that design, install, and service a variety of systems. Before starting her own business, Evelyn worked in a number of executive management and consulting positions: for the city of Raleigh; for the state of North Carolina, in the governor's office; in the White House in Washington, D.C.; in the Peace Corps in Colombia and Washington, D.C.; for the Olympics in Mexico City; and for a number of private firms. She brought to her business considerable experience in turning around a floundering or poorly performing organization and then handing it off and moving on to the next exciting challenge. She was elected to head the South Carolina delegation to the White House Conference on Small Business in 1995. She has chaired the South Carolina National Federation of Independent Business Leadership Council for five years. Most recently, she founded the Lowcountry Chapter of the National Association of Women Business Owners.

A veteran successful entrepreneur of fifteen years, Evelyn reflects on the endless challenges involved in starting and continuing a successful business: "In the beginning the entrepreneurial god created a multitude of short-term demands and long-term plans and goals." She says, "It is the start that stops most people." She recalls her early days when she did everything from begging the bankers to sweeping out the warehouse. Operational headquarters was her Queen Anne desk in the warehouse. "The true challenge," she says, "becomes one of avoiding burnout from the daily operations and keeping the entrepreneurial spirit that drove one into business alive and well." Success is "handling the transitions as they occur, not forgetting the importance of each of your customers, and maintaining the passion of the beginning."

The critical tasks necessary for success during the start-up stage are defining markets and developing products. There are a number of approaches, but having a novel idea and knowing how to package the product and market it are usually important ingredients. Mary Feldman, owner of Aunt Mary's, Inc., and a public relations company, Creative Public Relations, in Charleston, South Carolina, started not with a dream, a market, or a product, but with a desire to help her three-year-old nephew chase away "ghosts." Little did Mary, the holder of a B.A. in philosophy from the College of St. Catherine in St. Paul, Minnesota, realize that her previous organizational skills—learned in an array of rich backgrounds, from Director of Public Relations for the Breakers in Palm Beach and appointment secretary to U.S. Senator David F. Durenberger in Washington, D.C., to special assistant to First Lady Nancy Reagan in the East Wing of the White House—would transfer so readily into getting her new product off the ground. Her business idea was born when Petey, her nephew, needed to get ghosts and the other things that go bump in the night out from under his bed and out of the closet. Mary designed Ghost Away, a sure-fire ghost repellent in a spray can, and then used her considerable public relations experience to market "Aunt Mary's" product.[4]

Numerous other approaches have been employed to launch a venture, including the precarious steps taken by Nikki Hardin, founder and owner of *SKIRT!*, a regional newspaper in Charleston, South Carolina. Nikki just jumped right in. In a recent presentation she explained how her businesses started.

> As soon as I agreed to participate in this evening, I remembered that I hate to speak in public. And to make things worse, I realized that anyone who attended was probably going to expect to hear my "plan" for success—a carefully thought out strategy—tactics I developed to ensure *SKIRT!*'s market penetration. That's when I had the sinking feeling that my portion of this discussion should probably be titled "How to Succeed in Business in Spite of Yourself."
>
> Being undercapitalized was just one of the mistakes I made. I didn't have a business plan. I didn't own a suit. I didn't know what an editorial plan was. What I did have was this idea and a few devoted

friends who believed in it or me. Which is good because I was often too shy to tell people about my idea and ask them to get involved.

Not only did Nikki defy the odds in starting her business the way she did, but she launched *SKIRT!* as a women's publication with a clearly feminist viewpoint in Charleston, the heart of the South. Colleagues thought the idea was, at best, misguided. As Nikki reflects back, her early days appear almost mystical.

> We moved to a new office in downtown Charleston last year. A month later the building next door was torn down and on the side of our building was revealed a sign that had been hidden for decades, a sign that read "Skirt Factory" in big bold black letters. As it turned out, this building that I'd waited for months to become available had been an actual skirt factory in the early 1900s. I have to admit I feel that it was a sign from the cosmos, that we were destined for that building, and that my path was meant to cross with those of the people who have been crucial to the success of *SKIRT!*

Bren Norris, winner of Vice President Gore's Hammer Award for innovative contributions to technology, is a San Francisco–based entrepreneur who used a series of organizations as incubators to cultivate the skills and contacts she would need to open her dream business.[5] She had gained expertise as a stockbroker with Paine Webber and a rich corporate background in the information systems industry, working for such corporations as Xerox and Pitney Bowes. Each of these experiences provided her with the background for the development of a market niche in the previously male-dominated business sector. Bren Norris Associates, Inc., and Bren International provide global personalized information technology services. One of her first clients was the president of Toshiba. He told her, "You can manage your business alone with no one else, until you reach $100 million."

During its first year, Bren Norris Associates doubled in size and profits tripled, yielding, among other things, an enormous and unforeseen tax consequence. With no plan to deal with this kind of success, Bren had to adjust to get the right management systems in place, reach out for professional assistance, and move key employees into the right strategic locations. Critical transition issues had to be faced. Employees who set their own work schedules were producing the results that made the company successful. Opening a "virtual office" where she would meet with employees at a hotel, in someone's home, or in her own home would save on office rent and responsibility and keep employees closer to clients by not having to fly in and out of a central office. But taking the step was, Bren says, "one of the most frightening decisions I made." She believes the reason is that it was a sense of possibly losing control. In her second year of operation, Bren opened an international office. In the third year, her company continued to grow and expand. A tribute to the importance of establishing high-quality service goals is the fact that Charles Schwab, her first client, is still a regular and loyal client in Bren's eleventh year of business.

TRANSITIONS

Among the greatest challenges entrepreneurs face are those involved in moving a business from one stage to another. Planning and launching the firm comes first. Maneuvering successfully through the start-up phase follows. Then come the problems of growth. The only constant is continuing change. One of the most difficult problems arises when a business is very successful: knowing when to hand over some or all of its management.

Founders and Management

One of the most difficult entrepreneurial dilemmas is dealing with the overwhelming sense of being continually tired, of always having to work hard, of being a one-person band. As a number of entrepreneurs interviewed for this book cautioned, never believe that the "experts" know more than you do about the business you developed. And don't relinquish control until you are sure your managers know as much as you do about your business. The dilemma, called reaching the threshold management stage, comes at the point in the business when you must decide whether to hire a professional manager, employ a team, or remain the founder-manager of your company. It is a difficult decision because there is much at stake. A founder may successfully establish a business, but continued growth and successful operation are not assured if things continue to be done in the same way. Perhaps the small business has prospered amid an informality that made it possible to operate without well-defined plans, goals, responsibilities, or controls, but now has grown to a point where informality must give way to a more formal structure. Perhaps a transition to professional management may be called for because organizational growth and more complex operations require time and skills independent of entrepreneurial creativity. [6]

Evelyn Reis Perry faces this decision. She has been careful not to grow her business too fast or try to be all things to all people, but now, in her fifteenth year of operation, she says, her business is "in its adolescent stage, no 'mom and pop' but certainly no IBM either." She can no longer keep track of everything but remembers the days when she walked through the warehouse and knew exactly what the inventory was; she could put her hands out and touch it. Now the warehouse is too large and everything is inventoried on bar codes on the computer. The best thing to do to ensure further growth and performance is not clear. "It is difficult," Evelyn says, "to let go—to delegate and bite your lip when you see it being done, perhaps not wrong, but not the way you would have done it." Evelyn and her business have reached a threshold.[7]

Research offers no clear guidance in individual cases as to whether the solution for Evelyn and others with businesses at this stage of growth is to employ professional management or to continue running the daily operations themselves. An abundance of research shows both courses have been successful. What appears clear is that the owner-manager must make important changes in the way the business is being run to remain successful. But changing the entire operating system may be neither wise nor necessary. Recent research suggests profits do not always suffer when the founder remains the CEO instead of turning operations over to a professional manager once the threshold stage is reached.[8]

Difficult Passages

Transition issues are not easy to resolve. They involve the company, ego and self-esteem, how one defines oneself, questions of separating from the daily blueprint of company operations, and expectations for the future. Transition questions may appear in early growth, later growth, or stability stages of a business. At stake may be the key issue of whether the owner can give up the management role and at the same time remain a vital link in the successful operation of the business. A transition period may be marked by delegation or leadership crises. When the firm requires a larger management team but the founder is unwilling to give up control over important decisions, a delegation crisis has been reached. A leadership crisis arises when the founder is unable or unwilling to develop the new skills necessary for leading a larger management team. In the worst case, a threshold dilemma decision that requires CEO adaptation or succession goes unrecognized, causing grave problems for the firm and founder.[9]

Entrepreneurs are probably approaching a major transition when they find themselves wrestling with the crucial decision of whether to separate from daily operations. The owner knows how hard she works, how important each customer is, how she wants her customers to be treated, and what it means to put all the pieces together. She is not sure she can turn over the operation to someone else and get the same results or satisfaction. But she also knows that she can't keep operating in the same way. Will the new professional manager or team share her vision or be as interested in the bottom line as she is? This is an important question and there is no magical formula, nowhere in the research to turn to find agreement on the best course of action.[10]

Audrey Smaltz, owner of The Ground Crew™, New York, and a very hands-on manager, turned over the transition and management of her company to her niece because she had other things she wanted to accomplish. The decision to walk away was very difficult. Audrey says,

> It required getting in the position to let go. It is fabulous. It's so refreshing, you are so free. My clients call and say, "So and so is in this show and who is in that show?" and I respond, "I don't know anything about any fashion shows." "Well, how many shows are you doing?" "I respond, "You will have to talk with April" (April Brookins, vice president of The Ground Crew). "Well, who is working this?" My response, "I don't know, talk to April." "Well, don't

you want to take this information down?" "No," I say, "I don't do it right anymore. April has her own system." It is fabulous to just let it all go and still know that you are making money and you don't know every little detail about where this money is coming from, but the checks just keep rolling in. This is a whole new experience.

Rebecca Smith is facing a threshold decision as the result of a growth spurt. Her construction company works throughout Florida and her Wireless Communication Division is working its way up the southeastern United States. Her main office is in Tampa, with a second office located directly across the state on the East Coast in Melbourne near Cocoa Beach. Her company has just been awarded an $18 million contract from the Department of Corrections, adding to more than $52 million in current backlogged work. It is, she says, "truly a tremendous opportunity to be in an industry that moves quickly with interesting people."

Going public is a threshold decision with special challenges. Gail K. Naughton recalls the course of Advanced Tissues.

> When the company went public, we brought in a president, a CEO, and a chair. I became president two years ago and have developed a succession plan for this job in the next twelve to eighteen months. I had to bring in my potential successor.
>
> Over the last year and a half I have brought in people who would run the company with the same vision, spirit, and passion that I would. For the first time in my life I didn't know how I would feel. It is kind of like giving up a baby but also knowing that your child is going to be taken care of regardless. So I am looking toward the new challenges of taking on the CEO role. It is a wonderful relief to know that even if I weren't part of the company, it would go on without me.
>
> If I had known when I started what I know now, I would not have gone public so early. My dream would be to start a nonprofit company that would be able to get organs, tissues, and medical information to those who need it, but would not be a public enterprise. The transitions in the size of the company have provided special challenges. It was difficult to maintain the excitement about the business, to keep that entrepreneurial spirit in full force, and to try to have

that personal interaction with people, especially as the company moved from five employees, where everyone knows everything in the company, to two hundred, where you can't know everything and there's a lot of trust involved. This is especially true for the people who started the company. They want to still be at the center, part of that team that knows everything. But often the people you start with aren't the people running the company ten years later. They're in the company, but they're no longer in love with their work. To retain people and keep them motivated is a very big challenge. To maintain that entrepreneurial environment with increasing numbers is difficult.

For other entrepreneurs, transition has meant expansion into broader international markets and mergers. Maria-Luisa Maccecchini, president and CEO, Bearsden Bio, Inc., has formed a merger with a pharmaceutical company for research, developing drugs, and producing drugs in Glasgow, Scotland. The merger and expansion has included purchase offers to two companies and raising $10 million to carry out the acquisitions and grow them. "The goal is to go public in two to three years for about $200 million."

For some entrepreneurs, transition means opening a business completely unrelated to the one that pays the bills. Building on her past skills as creator of the foremost spas in the country, Golden Door and Rancho La Puerta, Deborah Szekely founded Eureka Communities, which is her full-time passion. In 1940, when she and her husband founded the first-ever destination resort devoted to fitness, they charged $17.50 a week and asked guests to bring their own tent. After ten years of long days and faith in their dreams, they were able to rent the small cabins they had built for $25 a week. In case you are thinking of rushing out and making a reservation, the Rancho now costs between $1,645 and $2,580 a week (depending on accommodation) and Golden Door is $5,250. Both have perpetual waiting lists. Today, at seventy-seven, Deborah is on her seventh full career, which is her most satisfying. Says Deborah,

The movement from one career to the next involves seeing a need and how it might be fulfilled. It all begins in the way we value and measure the finite amount of time that we each have. It is the dictum of the manager to "multiply thyself." In order to be free, one has to grow people. In the end, the vision is what counts.

SUCCESS

From discussions with many successful entrepreneurs it seems clear that success is a moving target, a goal that changes with times and conditions. One cannot define entrepreneurial success on the basis of a set of characteristics; it would be too narrow a frame.

Corporate Success

In their prior corporate lives, many of the women entrepreneurs interviewed for this book had measured success in salary increases, the size of their bonus, perks, and how much autonomy and power they had. Carol A. Vincie, New Era Consulting, recalls the difference in her outlook when she worked for a large corporation.

> Most of the time I couldn't remember what my salary was. It was important because it was a relative measure of position—a scorecard if you will. But what I really remember is all the people from the janitor on up who always felt that they could come by my office—it was such a curiosity for them that I had such a large office as a woman manager in the company. This is something they didn't do with the male executives.

Reflecting back to her corporate experience, Denise L. Devine, president of Devine Foods, Inc., noted that money had been the measuring stick of success. She believes that because she was not happy with the way she was contributing to the world, the size of her paycheck took on a greater meaning.

Entrepreneurs and Success

As an entrepreneur, success takes on a very different meaning. At the beginning of the business, success is meeting the payroll, breaking even, or making a small profit. As the business becomes established, success can be associated with market position, niche, or continuing demand for the product. Suzy Spafford, CEO of Suzy's Zoo, says,

> The concrete evidence of my success is that people actually buy my product and year after year they choose this over other things—this gives me a reason to continue doing the things I do year after year. The other side to success is the warm and fuzzy, the ability to make people happy. Irrespective of where the sales fall as I project ahead I will feel successful because we are making children's books. Success is growth and opportunity and the ability to get into new markets.

In operational terms, success means learning to organize and manage resources, employees, and technologies and the capacity to deal with markets, financial backers, and customers. In the middle stages of a business, success can mean the understanding that you are in charge of keeping things going and that what you are doing matters in ways that go beyond profits. To Elise E. McCullough, Staffing Solution, success means the happiness of one's life measured in "enjoying what you do." Competitive, she has found that success is also wrapped up in challenges and trying to get ahead, in "being the best that I can be, making sure the people around me are happy and we're kind of working as a team." Says Jackie Jennings, Johnson & Jennings,

> It isn't being there, it's getting there and continuing. It is a refreshing reminder to consider oneself unemployable and therefore in the driver's seat, responsible to make this work. I analyze success in the image I have with my children. It's clear they know what I do. My daughter thinks that all moms are contractors.

"Success is always something on that horizon," adds Margaret M. Larkin, Larkin Pension Services, Inc. "Once you are successful you just keep going forward and looking for more."

According to recent surveys by the National Foundation for Women Entrepreneurs, business goals are clearly important to success. Optimistic about increased revenues and profits, 80 percent of the owners surveyed cited business growth, finding and keeping qualified employees, staying abreast of new technology, and controlling labor costs as key ingredients.[11] However, underneath it all is a continual struggle that becomes an important part of understanding the challenge of being an entrepreneur. This struggle has taken on an entirely different dimension for the woman entrepreneur than it had in the previous corporate environment. There is a high or thrill in the process. For Joan Anderson, whose personal accomplishments in the company she turned around at the age of fifty-five placed her business in *Crain's* top twenty-five list of Chicago's largest women-owned firms and garnered her nomination by her employees as the best employer in 1999, the road to success has been filled with struggle. "There were days when I would sit outside my building and feel that I had to move the building literally one brick at a time to bring the changes needed to make it a productive environment." To Joan, "corporate success is not good or bad, it is a choice that we make, free of barriers to what can be achieved in life and age limits to when it can be achieved." She measures the business elements of success in three ways:

1. Dollars and the bottom line

2. Meeting the internal and external competitive challenges in considering whether "to eat or be eaten—the corporate quandary embedded in the inherent matter of weeding the corporate garden"

3. Building a survival strategy not caught up in the status quo

But ultimately success is measured in

> the opportunities you can give your employees if you have money, the teams you build, and your ability to share and give credit. You must spread the credit around. A company is people made up of families and relationships. All money and success can do for you is keep that going and make you realize the responsibility that creates for an owner. That is the power of feeling success.

The Moving Target

Ruth Ann Menutis, The Grove, has built three previous successful companies and is currently expanding into a partnership with a large corporation.

> I had to be successful. I think that I've tackled many things that could have been failures, but I just didn't allow them to become failures. I worked all the extra hours that were necessary to make them a success, but you have to continuously become a moving target, whatever

you're into. We were the first to go into airports and open our little nut stands. And then along came a huge corporate competitor, starting exactly what we were doing in a whole slew of airports. I could have thrown up my hands and said, "Well, I can't compete with them. They're too big." But I had the idea that I was the moving target—that they were trying to get my business. I wasn't going to let them. I had to develop a strategy that would be more successful than theirs. I knew that this meant we had to personalize everything we did and give extremely good customer service. We put lots of extra training into developing this plan. It had taken me ten years to open ten airport nut shops. My competitor opened ten airports in one year. Our drive for quality and service made it necessary for them to close all ten within five years. You are a moving target. Measuring success is a continuous process. You measure by saying, "What did they do wrong and what did I do right? What do I have to keep doing to continue growing this business?

For both Joan and Ruth Ann, as well as for many other women entrepreneurs, there was a feeling that success was the only option. Joan remembers the driving feeling that "I never thought I could possibly fail. I had everything riding on the success of the firm because I knew that with each of the employees in the company I had a responsibility not only to them as individuals but to their entire families. I simply had to find a way—it meant the survival of the company." Joan also attributes her success to the support she received from both of her daughters. At the critical start of her business she sold all her cars, the house, and the silver teapots, then said to them, "'this is what I have to do to try to make it' and they fully supported what I did. They were always there to back me and to encourage me along the way. Literally they understood what it meant when I said, 'I have to go to the teapot for this.'" So to both Joan and Ruth Ann success means survival, moving forward, and never being content with the status quo. And for both, personal success is simpler—it is measured and satisfied from within.

Jeanette Scollard Hester, Hester Foods, summarized general agreement among entrepreneurs about the relative place of money in the success equation.

It has very little interest to me personally. It is not what drives me, but there is the realization that you can't be in business if you are not making a profit. The true satisfaction comes from building the company and having the business connected with the employees.

Identifying Success

How do we know when we are successful? There is no clear answer. For Barbara Bry, Proflowers.com and ATCOM/INFO, success means making it through an array of transitions and at each stage witnessing the triumphs. Ultimately, it is measured in terms of the combination of personal and business success. As Barbara puts it,

> I achieved more in my life than I ever expected to. I've had lots of careers. I started out as a schoolteacher. I got an MBA at Harvard, became a business writer for the *Los Angeles Times,* got married, dropped out of the labor force to spend valuable time with my children while working half-time, and, after a divorce, have started two companies in the last three years. I feel very good about my life at this moment. I'd like some more financial success, and that's coming.

To some, success consists of recognizing their dream as a reality. "One of the things I would like to do," says Maria-Luisa Maccecchini, "is to work part-time, to have time for travel and still be involved."

Entrepreneurs measure success by personal growth, business growth, and handling the risks. Jeanette Scollard Hester, chair of Hester Foods and a member of the Committee 200, has founded several businesses. She is also the author of several books on women in the business world, including *Risk to Win—A Woman's Guide to Success.* She has been a groundbreaker for women in organizations. In 1978, she was named the first woman vice president in the hundred-year history of Chesebrough-Pond's. Jeanette equates success with the ability to take risks, a skill that is not innate but cultivated. "A risk taker faces life head-on, with the ability to develop strengths and meet challenges with resolve, determination, passion, and a sense of honor. Creativity and charm in dealing with others also help. The greatest challenge one faces on the way to becoming successful," she says, "is to compete against yourself and win." [12]

For Marian V. Marchese, Virtu, Inc., success means complete financial independence. This is a recent realization.

Five to six years ago I would get calls from younger women who would say, "I know you are a successful businesswoman and I would like to know how I can get involved in this business." I would say, "You made a mistake. I am not successful." To me, success meant you didn't have to struggle. And when you have your own business you struggle every day, every hour, every minute. I kept thinking they had called the wrong person.

New Goals, Different Goals

While women entrepreneurs appear to always sense that success hasn't yet arrived, it may be because they keep setting new goals. Carol Farren, Facility Management Worldwide Ltd., constantly seeks new challenges and says she gets bored if she is not doing something new and different. "I have something that I would really like to do, but I haven't been able to get funding for it," she says. "I would like to build environmentally conscious, quality-of-life retirement communities with new concepts to guarantee independence in northern climates." She is presently finishing a revision of her book on planning and managing interior design projects.[13]

Conversations with entrepreneurs reflected the considerable support found in published research for the idea that women heading businesses associate success not wth high growth rates and profits but with the strong driving forces of personal accomplishment, freedom, and self-respect. Beyond this is an underlying struggle for the recognition they feel their work richly deserves. There is also the desire to make a positive impact on the lives of others. From New York to California, women mostly wanted to make a difference, to add value to our world.[14]

For Patti Roscoe, president of PRA Destination Management, success is wrapped up in franchising her idea and teaching others methods that have worked in her companies. She feels it is important to reach out to women everywhere to provide a role model of what drive and ambition can accomplish.

I started with nothing. Success was having my own money, not having to look at a price tag, gaining recognition within my industry. I have really enjoyed watching the young people in our organization grow and mature. Several of our management team members started as college interns. I am chairing a drive to fund a four-year degree program in hospitality and tourism management at San Diego State University. We are going to work hard to provide scholarships for young people who may not have the finances to matriculate into college. I'm also working with the YWCA on the second annual In the Company of Women program, a fundraiser for battered women and children's shelters. Last year we raised over $120,000 in just an hour and a half.

Women have to learn how to be philanthropic. Writing checks for nonprofit agencies is not something we're trained to do. If women's organizations and women politicians are to succeed, it will be the women who make it so. Women are learning to give, and I hope I can be part of that teaching process. As those of us who may be nearing retirement look around, we know there will be young and vibrant women to whom we can pass the baton. It's a real high being at the top of your career, and I want other women to share in that exhilarating feeling.

Just as common a characteristic among potential women entrepreneurs is the drive to be their own bosses. As a successful businesswoman the interest is focused more on giving something back and less on making money. As Aliza Sherman, Cybergrrl, Inc., says,

I just want to feel good about myself and happy and healthy. I want to know that the things I do impact other people's lives in positive ways. My validation is getting that e-mail from some woman somewhere across the country that illustrates that my services have made a difference in her personal life.

For many, their sense of success changed as their careers evolved. Susan Bird, Women.future, summarizes it like this:

Others, my outside sources, originally set my definition of success. I sort of collected achievements because that was the way it was done in my family and that's certainly the way it was done in the circles in which I moved. So I just did that better than everybody else. I went to Harvard Business School and Stanford Law School. Now I am sitting here with this conversation sort of spinning through me. I just came from a funeral, from a memorial service.

That always makes you think. It sends a special wake-up call. It was for a highly successful businesswoman who was also regarded as a source of love by everybody around her. Somebody said they never heard her say anything negative about anybody else. She was really a fantastic person, an inspiration to all of us. It reminded me of my old days at IBM where they used to always say, you never have to say anything negative about the competitor because we have such great products. We just need to talk about what we are doing. I'm not sure that, being trained as a litigator, I always remember that. I ran a company with a view that it was my way or the highway, and I won most of the time. And now I'm a business mediator, which probably confirms that you teach what you're supposed to learn.

For Carol A. Vincie, New Era Consulting, success is, along with the good life, being free to help—understanding that because of the assistance you provided, others will be able to meet a special business challenge.

One of my clients this summer raised several million dollars for her business. That's very satisfying. I give 10 percent of all revenue from employee assessment tools to Building Women, a Habitat for Humanity project in Westchester County. I was one of the people who launched the project. Building Women is specifically oriented to providing women with construction skills to qualify for job opportunities and to become self-sufficient in their own homes. To me, success means being able to ski twenty to thirty days a year—being able to get on an airplane when Alta has had four feet of fresh powder. Having built a business that can sustain itself and having enough money to indulge my passions is success.

Says Audrey Smaltz, The Ground Crew, New York:

I do not want to be the richest person anywhere. I am not greedy. I love sharing. I don't need a lot of money to be happy. Success has nothing to do with how much money you earn, success is what you are doing for someone else. I'm interested in the success of all the young people who've worked for me all through the years—once a Ground Crewer, always a Ground Crewer. If you see them successful, then I'll know I'm successful.

Cathy M. Brienza, Waller-Sutton Management Group, Inc., notes that of course we have to make a living, but success is measured beyond that—not by the dollars that roll in but rather "in the psychological satisfaction of a job well done, a project completed, the respect of my peers and other people, and my integrity. It is important to have time in my life for my family and my business. I believe that if one does the job that one loves well, the money follows along."

For Denise L. Devine, Devine Foods, success is wrapped up in building a business—not just any business, but one "of value to society. I want something tangible that I have a hand in creating that is a useful product and ultimately a financial success, which will allow me to continue creating the product and making a contribution to society."

For many entrepreneurs, the desire to be successful encompasses much more than the bottom line. Bren Norris wants to be a positive role model for women in high tech. We will know when women have really arrived, she says, "when we begin seeing company names with the name of the female entrepreneur and daughters (i.e., Bren and Daughters)." Recalling her childhood and background, she reflected on how many women of her generation were not brought up to be powerful businesswomen and/or owners and how many talented women are out there now who are leaving the corporate world and are available to help you in your company.

> My mother worked in a factory for fifty years at piece rate, sewing whatever they asked her to sew and working long days. My father worked as a day laborer. My parents had seventh- and eighth-grade educations. What they transferred to me was a strong work ethic, a strong sense of honesty and integrity, an insurmountable drive to succeed. This was great training for building the strong business relationships I have today. What you have in business is all built on your relationships with customers. I can get a higher price because of the relationships I have built with my clients. They depend on me, they know I am there to take care of their needs, and they can call on me personally. Success is all about relationship building— keep them good, keep them strong, and remember to be truthful with yourself. I will measure my success by how I can help women in technology break through the barriers.

Like other successful women entrepreneurs Bren has enacted her dream of success by reaching out to expand her interest in making an improvement in her high-tech field for others. In 1995, she was an elected delegate to the White House Conference on Small Business where she worked on issues and recommendations to Congress on intellectual property law. She has since worked with the National Performance Review (NPR) working with focus groups on the Internet site U.S. Business Advisor (www.business.gov). In August 1997, Bren and her NPR team were awarded the prestigious Hammer Award for their outstanding work in technology by Vice President Al Gore.

In Gail K. Naughton's public company, Advanced Tissue Sciences, shareholders measure success in terms of profitability. Because it takes eight years to meet all the FDA-regulated animal and clinical trial tests from the time you have a product idea until you hit the market, she is planning new launches now for the year 2008. For a public company, planning for profitability is the measure of success because without the profit the company cannot continue to make the new products. At a personal level, however, Gail measures her success very differently. She asks herself

> Did I make a difference in the world today? If I weren't around today would it be not as good a place to be? Because we make products that help patients with severe burns, including many child abuse cases, it's easy to feel good about what we do. There is no recipe for this. If I get this product to more people who need it, this does translate into sales. But the impact it has on the personal lives of those we help makes me feel successful. The more people we help, the more successful we feel. What we do is creative, but we mimic nature. We are burdened by public pressure and every day is a challenge. But I don't measure my personal success by the dollars, nor do I measure my success by the stock price because stock prices rarely indicate how successful you are. When you have creative passion and a group of compassionate people working for you and something doesn't go well, the morale dips. They take it very personally. They beat themselves up because they feel like they are failing the patients, they're not getting this product out to the people who need it. I don't think there's a person in the company who is driven solely by a paycheck, by the stock price, or by how much we sell.

In a 1994 study, the National Foundation for Women Business Owners found that women "derive satisfaction and success from building relationships with customers and employees, having control of their own destiny, and doing something they consider worthwhile"[15] The finding clearly is reestablished here. As Rebecca Smith says, "success is self-esteem driven from a feeling of pride of accomplishment all wrapped up in fulfilling the ultimate challenge. It is so much more than money."

What is success? The entrepreneurs interviewed for this study provided many answers: witnessing the triumphs, making dreams a reality, growing a business and growing as a person, handling the risks and succeeding, and personal things—finding financial independence, a sense of freedom, and enhanced self-respect. But as they talked seriously, something even greater came through. They had the desire to make a positive impact on others, to add value to the world, to be a role model to family and young women and—most of all—to make a difference.

7. DEVELOPMENT AND ENTREPRENEURSHIP

When I would come up with a new idea in business, the first question was, "Who else is doing this?" I told this story to a friend, a male venture capitalist: A female entrepreneur is walking down the street and there's a $100 bill lying on the sidewalk. The female entrepreneur says, "Look at that, there's a $100 bill." The male venture capitalist says, "Couldn't be. If there were, somebody would have picked it up by now."

DIANE HARRIS

With a few exceptions, the entrepreneurs interviewed for this book all had worked in organizations owned by someone else prior to launching their own businesses. They considered the experience they had gained, the level of expertise they had acquired, and their transferable skills to be invaluable. But because they sought something more, they opted to create their own environments. In them, rewards and success could be more directly related to performance. They could take control of their personal and professional lives. The entrepreneurial environments they created enabled them to "make a difference and to become a role model for other women."

They all had to ask themselves important questions:

- What kind of situation is best for me?

- How can I play from my strengths and mitigate my weaknesses?

- Have I reviewed all my internal options objectively?

- How can I play from my strengths and mitigate my weaknesses?

- If I leave this organization and go to another will it just be more of the same?

- Do I have what it takes to go out on my own?

- What kind of entrepreneur will I be?

- Have I accumulated the set of skills I need to make it on my own?

- Do I have the personal, technological, financial, marketing, management, and other contacts I will need?

- Have I arranged a personal financial package to take me through the most rugged initiation stages of the business?

- Have I planned a business strategy to place me in a strong competitive market position?

- Have I developed strong communication links to keep me on top of the cutting-edge developments in my field?

When their personal assessment was complete and they had taken time to develop a full analysis of their situation based on objective criteria, they were ready to make the leap onto the road they had carefully mapped out. As with any trip, they realized that the map would not necessarily match the highway, that there would be detours and delays, and they developed contingency plans to deal with these.

Are you ready to continue the planning process to determine whether you can best advance your career by starting a business venture? If so, here are some pointers to assist in the development of the best personal plan for you. Most of all, it will be important to remember to not burn any bridges and to continue developing the very best relationships possible for future liaison opportunities. When the business you left cannot handle one of its major contracts, it would be great to have it recommend your business. You might even want to suggest taking a part of the business in which your previous company is not making a profit and turning it around. Many of the entrepreneurs in this book were asked to come back to their former organizations because of their high level of expertise, to troubleshoot a particular problem or take over a more prestigious role than the one they left behind. The options are endless.

If you decide that you do not like the entrepreneurial route and you have developed a successful entrepreneurial venture, you can be assured that someone in a corporate environment will consider you a great asset. You may be in a transition stage just ready to seek a new challenge when the corporate environment is seeking someone with your talents. Marjorie Alfus found herself in exactly this position. She had already established herself in the Italian knit business, earned a law degree to be able to more fully deal with the complexities of the international market, and then sold her business when she was first approached by the Kmart Corporation. As noted in the section on Mavericks in Chapter 1, the corporate environment offered Marjorie the new challenges she was ready to pursue. But in accepting this new challenge, she relied upon a tried-and-true approach that had served her well in her previous corporate and entrepreneurial transitions. Describing her early venture into television, she says,

> I made no mention of all my degrees, passed a typing test, and took a job as a receptionist at the local TV station owned by the *New York Daily News*. It was my intent to learn the business as quickly as possible and find a niche for myself. I spent eighteen hours a day there. I hung around everyone, particularly with a young woman who was producing the *Gloria Swanson Hour*. When that was over, I persuaded her to join me in forming an independent production company called Woman's World Television. We put together assorted women-oriented daytime shows on beauty, fashion, home sewing, and so on. I went out and solicited sponsors, and when I had enough to cover two hours of programming I went to NBC and they gave us the airtime. The business flourished.[1]

At Kmart, she had accepted a job offer from a friend who was chairman of the apparel division to be in-house counsel for a salary of $12,000 a year and shared office space. The friendship provided access and special projects, and that catapulted her into making presentations to the board of directors. With both access and visibility, she continually floated ideas to senior management, and that led to a top executive position in the presidency of Kmart's in-house manufacturing subsidiary. She never stopped being a Careerpreneur.[2]

The entrepreneurs in this book reflect similar characteristics. For them, learning and growth became a lifelong process. Early in their careers they established reputations for candor and trustworthiness. When Marjorie participated in executive sessions with senior management at Kmart, including CEO and president Joe Antonini, she not only was considered "highly intelligent, well-read, tough, and imperious," she was also "someone who hadn't been sucked into the Kmart corporate culture." Superiors found her "willing to give frank critiques of company policies and decisions."[3]

The underlying hallmark of success for many of the entrepreneurs here was the tenacity for learning. Before they became entrepreneurs they dove into the training programs offered by their companies. Many acquired advanced degrees because they recognized a need to fill a void in their personal skill set or area of expertise. They took on new, creative challenges and tasks not directly related to the job they were doing. The accumulation of experiences became a resource to make their businesses competitive and strong. They were professional at all times in their business dealings. They understood that professionalism includes not just expertise, keeping commitments, and exercising integrity, but also demeanor and how you respond to those around you. Joan Anderson took over a business that was in crisis. She also understood that "I had a responsibility not only to each of the employees but to their entire families. They were counting on me."

ASSESSING YOUR ENTREPRENEURIAL READINESS

Women contemplating starting a business, acquiring a franchise, or expanding a current operation would be well advised to consider several important factors. As Katherine Kennedy, Relocation Coordinates, Inc., points out, you have to have a deep, burning passion to carry you through all the ups and downs. "You've got to have that, and you've got to arm yourself. If you do that, and believe in what you have, you can do it."

The first step is to make an objective evaluation of the strength of your motivation and your sustaining power. Examine carefully your real reasons for considering the transition. If you're thinking of going into business for yourself, ask if you're willing to

- Do a lot of everything
- Sell yourself and the business constantly
- Be involved in nonstop networking
- If necessary, wait for success

You also need to ask yourself, "How do I react to continuous pressure?"

There may be no downtime during or after the transition. You will bring your concerns home at night and pack them with you on vacations, if you are fortunate enough to have them. You will soon learn that the day's concerns don't end when you lock the door the way they do when you are working for someone else and it is their capital or reputation on the line. Can you balance this pressure with a healthy lifestyle? It may not appear possible in the early days, but later it will be important to remember that there is more to life than the business, the expansion, or the increased growth.

According to the American Women's Economic Development Corporation, the personalities of most entrepreneurs differ from those of other people, not just in creativity but also in risk taking, vision, and courage. Entrepreneurs tend to be just a bit "offbeat."[4] Gail K. Naughton provides this testimonial and advice:

> I usually tell people if you believe in what you want to do, what others think doesn't matter. I augment that with a story that actually happened to me while I was a postdoctoral fellow at NYU. One of the key papers I sent out for publication in a dermatology journal was rejected. The first sentence in the letter from this journal said, "Publication of this paper would be a disservice to dermatology." I was crushed. I lived for research. My boss and mentor said, "It doesn't matter what he said. Your work is good, you believe in it, and it doesn't matter what the reviewer said." I replied, "Well, they're the experts." A month later I received an acceptance from a better journal. I was so pleased, I took the letter to my boss. He said, "Your competition must have been the reviewer for the last journal. The work was good and is now accepted. You have to believe in your work and learn from each lesson." What I learned has served me well all of my professional life. It doesn't matter what people think—if you're doing what you believe in and think it is right, sooner or later they'll come around.

If you are seriously thinking about leaving the corporate environment to start a business of your own, there is a 40 percent chance you will actually do so within a year, according to a pioneering ten-country study led by researchers at Babson College, Wellesley, Massachusetts, and London Business School.[5] Intention, whether latent or long range, appears to be a good predictor of starting a business. Whether the business will be successful or not is something else. A 1993 study using data from the National Longitudinal Survey of Labor Market Experience, which followed a national sample of women entrepreneurs from 1967 to 1984, found that approximately two-thirds of women who started businesses left them after about three years, although a substantial number might return to self-employment.[6] One reason for failure is that people jump into new business fields. Darlene Thomas founded Thomas Travel and Cruise in 1994 in Houston and later moved the business to New Orleans. Before that, she was the CEO of Watts & Company, a Houston-based law firm. Skills learned there helped her start her own business. She advises,

> If you're looking for a business to operate, you need to make sure you have experience before you leap ahead. You work for someone, gain the necessary information, or get the necessary training so you will avoid the perils and pitfalls that will surely come. That's called homework. You lessen the chance for failure if you do your homework first.

Entrepreneur or Small Business Owner?

Being an entrepreneur and owning a small business are not exactly the same. A small business owner, in contrast to an entrepreneur, travels a familiar path, often replicating the pattern of other small businesses in the industry group. To be an entrepreneur is to focus on a new product or idea—something that has not been on the market or the revival of an old product or idea in a new market. Being entrepreneurial means spotting opportunities that others miss. The California gold rush made paupers of thousands, but Levi Strauss saw gold in supplying rugged jeans to the prospectors.[7] Obvious, but only in retrospect.

While the verdict is still out on pre-ownership experience, there is sufficient case data to suggest that entrepreneurs have a much better chance of survival if they get into a familiar business field.

Katherine Kennedy, Relocation Coordinates, Inc., noted that this would have made a big difference in the initiation of her business.

> The three things I would say about starting a business and becoming an entrepreneur are these. First, how much do you believe in what you're getting ready to do, because you need the passion to fire all the other engines. Second, prepare yourself by learning as much about what you're getting ready to embark upon as possible—everything you can learn about it. I didn't do that. It took me more years because I didn't. I would have charted a different road map with the necessary preparation. And third, I would align myself earlier with people—experts, CPA, an accountant, and a business friend. Be sure to align yourself with a business mentor who is a friend. Somebody you can just throw up your hands to and say, "I'm a mess. I don't know what I'm doing. What am I doing wrong?" You can't get that in tech groups and CEO roundtables. But it's different when you're one on one with somebody with whom you don't have an emotional history, like with your spouse or your significant other. You can just say it all. The business friends, the experts, I think are critical. If you're thinking of being in business, you've got to have that guidance.

Education and Training

How prepared are you? Part of the self-assessment calls for you to evaluate your education and experience. Acquiring the needed education, training, and skills is extremely important. As noted in earlier chapters, according to the most recent (1994-1995) figures, nationwide 69 percent of all associate's degrees and 48 percent of all bachelor's degrees in business and marketing were awarded to women. But women earned only 37 percent of the faster-track master's degrees and 27 percent of the doctorates. The significance? The higher up you go, the more you will stand out. In making plans for higher education, it is important to check colleges and universities carefully. Most important, make sure the program is one of the select 392 worldwide programs accredited by the International Association for Management Education.[8]

Women focused on career advancement are attaining everhigher levels of education.[9] Women who aspire to become entrepreneurs are getting the same levels of education as men and in the same fields.[10] Though the case cannot be made that the education level and sales are directly related, there is a strong suggestion that skills learned in the educational programs are very important for business ownership. A recent report of the National Foundation for Women Business Owners indicates that women owning firms with $1 million or more in sales are likely to have a graduate degree.[11] You should assess your educational background and skills carefully before making a career change. You can determine strengths and weaknesses and identify programs and courses of action to meet your operational needs prior to going into business. Once in business, you will most likely not have enough time to gain the necessary skills and expertise.

Your education does not have to be in a practical or business field. Marian Marchese is president and CEO of VirTu, Inc., an Internet company in Philadelphia, which she cofounded. The firm specializes in Internet strategic planning, marketing, and development for major corporate clients. She did not start off planning to be in business for herself. Her college degree is in German, but she had little interest in teaching. Her first job was as a receptionist in an advertising agency. She chose that position because she needed to work right away and believed advertising would give her a lot of exposure. On the job, she was immediately asked if she could write. She became a copywriter and later even acquired a position with this title in another agency. Still later,

> I wound up in an agency run by a man. It was a very specialized advertising agency, and his method of maintaining costs was that once someone rose to a certain salary level he would fire them and bring in a younger person. Once I got to be vice president of account services and was making what the owner thought was too much money. I walked in one day and had my personal effects from my office handed to me. I had just bought a house and had scraped together every penny I could, and I literally was out on the street in Philadelphia. I resolved at that moment that I would never allow anyone to do this to me again. All around me people were starting businesses. I thought, how hard could it be? I started my own ad agency. Obviously, I knew very little about the business because you need to have people who can write and do art and take photographs

to start an advertising business. I joined forces with another person from my former agency and we were very successful very quickly.

Difficulties soon plagued the partnership, and for many years Marian ran the business alone. In 1995, she entered into a new partnership. Realizing that the Internet was going to make a major difference in the way the world operated, she and her partner started a separate Internet company called VirTu. Within eight months it was more profitable than the ad agency had been in eleven years. Merging the firms, they created VirTu, Inc., a new media company. "In the last six months," Marian recounts, "we have been approached by so many venture capital firms and other companies to go public, merge, or do something with the company."

Being Professional

Be prepared to adopt a professional demeanor in business relationships and appearance. Says Rebecca Smith:

> Focus on your business presence, focus on independence. The wisdom I try to share with women who ask how to be successful in a nontraditional field is simple: A woman's sexuality is part of who she is as a person; it should not be part of who she is as a businessperson. If the roles begin to overlap in business, my experience in dealing with men has proven that they begin to concentrate more on the woman and less on the business. I have learned this by watching behaviors and having discussions with my male peers. I don't want to imply that you cannot be a woman in your business role because you can. I am. There is a distinct line, which cannot be crossed. You cannot date the men you work with, and you cannot afford to be emotional under stress, and you cannot act like a "girl." If you exhibit these behaviors, the men will not be able to help but revert to treating you like the women in their personal lives. They all had mothers and they all have wives or girlfriends. They can get confused between their perception of their role as a man and their role as a teammate or employee. I know some very capable women who have undermined their own careers because they confused their role as a businessperson with their presence as a woman.

The issues of being a woman versus being nonsexual are more subtle than issues of appearance. If a woman approaches me with questions about being successful, the first thing I do is look at her appearance. If she has a basically strong presence and seems to be articulate with reasonably good command, then I might comment on a few simple things like clothing and jewelry. If she doesn't have the basics, I don't bother commenting on the details. There are some characteristics that are absolutely essential to success in a nontraditional field. The same skills a man must possess to be a leader must be exhibited by a woman, with even more refinement.

One either appears professional or not. Observes professional writer Joanne Gallucci, "It's funny how the ultracasual look hasn't extended to male newcomers to the office. When was the last time a young man—or any man, for that matter—showed up for a meeting in a muscle shirt?"

Last summer, as I sat across from an Ivy League graduate ten years my junior who was revealing cleavage as deep as the Great Divide, I couldn't help but wonder why. A low salary or $20,000 in tuition bills might be an excuse for an inadequate wardrobe, but where was the brain that rewarded her with such a prestigious degree?[12]

In the realm of professional dress, it can take some work to find the right clothes. Someday, someone in the high-quality end of the women's fashion industry is going to make a mint marketing professional business attire for women—probably by catalog or over the Internet—that is not centered around the mini or knee-length skirt and shoes with heels so high they appear designed to keep women in captivity. A woman in a business meeting with a skirt unavoidably slid halfway up her thigh or teetering on her toes with a misaligned spinal column is not on the same professional level as a man dressed in a business suit.

In her book *Risk to Win—A Woman's Guide to Success,* Jeanette Scollard Hester, chair of Hester Foods, provides additional good advice. Prepare for every meeting. Arrive at least two minutes early. Have your materials so organized that one reach inside the briefcase makes it possible to retrieve professional-looking documents. Be positive. Don't say, "I think it is." Say, "it is." Regarding accessories, "carry an expensive-looking writing pen, wear brilliant colors and/or black and white, bold costume jewelry or the real McCoy, and all rings should be the real McCoy."[13] Answer all messages promptly, even when you are ill. Develop a positive relationship with your assistant or secretary. Keep up with current events. Under no circumstances resort to tears or introduce your personal business into the work environment. Project confidence in all business relationships. Avoid expressions of surprise; they signal a lack of confidence.

> If you are soliciting a contract for a project that is really more than you can imagine, you should never let on that you don't expect to get it. You walk in and make your pitch as though you are convinced you will get it. And when you get it, you show no surprise, but merely comment how wise they were to award you the project. You shake hands, walk briskly out to your car, get in, and roll up the windows. Then, and only then, do you permit yourself to scream with delight.[14]

Making the Change

The next step is to examine the change you intend to make in terms of the product or service offered, the creativity of the underlying concept, and your capacity to execute it. Key to this assessment is the understanding that you will need staying power. Probably there will be no regular paycheck in the beginning and perhaps for some time, and no structural support except what you provide. The transition is often very difficult for people used to corporate life, who are ill prepared to suddenly find there is no fancy copier down the hall, no secretary or assistant to run the errands, and no technical expert available for consultation. If the decisions you made went wrong in the corporate environment, there probably were no personal financial costs; now there certainly will be. In moving to her consulting practice, to her surprise, K. Shelly Porges discovered that her self-esteem and orientation to work were completely tied to the company she had worked for and that she depended on myriad corporate services. She had to change her entire modus operandus in a hurry.[15] In business for yourself, you pay the cost of training programs, all travel expenses, and anything else you need. As one business owner says, "We multitask. Here, everything is yours. We're the legal department, we're the marketing department, and that's exhilarating."[16]

Selecting the right business does not mean just selecting a business you are interested in; it also means seeing that the business you select will have a future. You need to be sure that you have not only the necessary information and experience to build a business that meets a market need but some assurance that the market will continue to exist. This is perhaps one of the reasons so many women who leave corporate life start out in consulting. Marion Gold, a thirteen-year employee at a Chicago medical education firm, realized that she would never advance in the organization despite her key role in building it into a powerhouse with more than $10 million in annual billings. But she didn't want to jump to join a competitor.[17]

Personal Planning

Personal planning goes beyond assessing your personal strengths, your staying power, and the market potential for the business that best suits your entrepreneurial profile. These come first, but once they are completed you are ready to complete one of the more important aspects of determining whether you can be a successful business owner. This assessment will start with an analysis of current income and expenses, which will allow you to project financial needs for a year or more down the road. Don't underestimate the difficulties of getting started. Says an entrepreneur in the Deep South, beginning entrepreneurs "should be able to support themselves for at least twelve months . . . there are at least a hundred things you've never thought of." A Chicago entrepreneur advises an even longer perspective. "I would make sure that I had enough income from all resources to survive for at least two years," she says, "If you have to make money during those two years starting out on your own you probably are not going to make it." Suzan Kotler, a certified financial planner in Cincinnati, advises, "You need resources for those days when you are not making any money. You must be able to survive."[18]

At a minimum, you will need at least six months of savings during the start-up phase of your business. The Women in New Development, Bemidji, Minnesota, and the North Texas Women's Business

Center, Dallas, have developed a four-step plan to analyze the financial feasibility of your starting a business.[19]

1. Identify and write down your fixed expenses for each month for the next year—for example, insurance, home and other property obligations, car payments, utilities, and savings.

2. Identify your discretionary expenses. These include such things as food (including dining in restaurants), clothing and personal care, entertainment, transportation, and the like.

3. Consider what you've spent in previous months and anticipate changes.

4. Subtract your total fixed and discretionary expenses from your expected monthly and annual income.

Constructing this important personal financial operating profile allows you to evaluate the essentials in your daily life and separate them from everything else. The assessment also makes you look in a very realistic way at just how important venture creation is to you. This step provides a critical reality check. The odds are you may not be profitable during your first five years in business, and, if you do not have the resources to stay afloat, the only thing all your sacrifices may get you is experience. Assume that your income may be half that in your old job in the corporate environment. This is one reason that many women, 24 percent according to the National Association of Female Executives, start their new businesses while still working full time. Women of color might want to consider the following statistics. While solid majorities of Asian, Caucasian, Hispanic, and Native American/Alaska Native women (78 percent, 78 percent, 65 percent, and 62 percent, respectively) all started their firms on a full-time basis, this was true for only 52 percent of black women. The majority of Asian, Caucasian, Hispanic, and Native American/Alaska Native women (61 percent, 59 percent, 71 percent, and 55 percent, respectively) started their firms with one or more business partners. But fully 65 percent of black women business owners start their firms without any partner.[20]

The Business Plan

As you begin thinking seriously about going into business for yourself you should formulate a business plan. This comprises two types of planning: *strategic planning* (What business am I in? What products or services are involved? Who are my competitors? What competitive advantages do I have?) and *operational planning* (finance, marketing, production, scheduling, and all the other nuts and bolts of running a business). The planning process involves developing a strategy, assessing ways you can differentiate yourself from your competitors, examining sales potential, setting a timeline for achieving your organizational goals, and making important budgeting decisions. The implementation process moves you to examine the location, size, and shape of your business and decide on the amount of capital you need and how to acquire it.

Formal Planning

The formal, written plan, one expert suggests, should include the following items: an executive summary of the plan; a description of the business and its field or industry and the uniqueness of your products and services; your company goals; identification of the target market and possible competitors; the research that went into designing the product or service; the location of your business; how your firm will be managed and how the management will be compensated; an assessment of any critical risks; a financial forecast; and milestones to be reached in the first few years of the business.[21] A carefully thought out business plan will be critical if you seek financial backing. The United States Small Business Administration, through its Online Women's Business Center, has a wealth of information available, including descriptions of the planning process, worksheets, and answers to frequently asked questions about management, marketing, finance, and procurement.[22] The SBA's Office of Women's Business Ownership provides one of the most comprehensive service centers for women in the nation.[23] The Women's Business Enterprise National Council (WBENC) also works to enhance the opportunities for women by providing access to a national standard of certification. WBENC provides information through an Internet database.[24]

Professional Advice

Getting the right information is important. One of the best places to start is with professionals. Good advice will give you a broader perspective on your business concept and methods of implementing it. Information can be acquired on all facets of a business start-up.[25] A 1997 study by the National Foundation for Women Business Owners found that female entrepreneurs who have ten or more employees consult with a wider variety of sources than do male business owners in making financial decisions.[26] The online women's business center provides a host of services that you can use in-house or online and also has helpful contacts with a number of reputable agencies. The Ohio Women's Business Resource Network suggests the following list:

1. Insurance agents who can help with auto, liability, fire, theft, life, and other types of insurance

2. An accountant to help with setting up your bookkeeping structure, tax planning strategy, and payroll

3. Attorneys for help with contracts, incorporating, lease review, and so on

4. Business counselors for planning, loan applications, and referrals to other professionals

If you are already working with a women's business center, Service Corps of Retired Executives (SCORE) volunteers, or a small business development center, their counselors can probably steer you to someone who is familiar with your type of business or resources and databases to explore for assistance.[27]

In addition to identifying the battery of service supports needed to make a successful launch, it is also important to think about a number of points when working with a professional.

- Can you easily talk to the professional?
- Did you develop a clear and concise way to get your questions answered by the professional—that is, did you ask for the most convenient method of contact, via fax, e-mail, or regular mail?
- Did you check the billing rates and payment process, fines, and/or penalties for which the professional is willing to take responsibility?

- Did you carefully review the major points in the meeting prior to leaving to avoid misunderstandings and unmet expectations later on services to be provided?

- Did you follow up on your commitments and completion dates?

- Did you make a record in your calendar and follow the meeting with a memo covering the understanding you had reached with the service provider?

FINANCING AND CAPITAL

A recurring problem for all entrepreneurs is financing the business. Only slightly more than half of all business owners (52 percent for women and 59 percent for men) obtain bank financing.[28] A 1998 North Carolina survey found that more than half of women- and minority-owned firms were operated by undercapitalized first-time business owners who had gotten no outside assistance before starting up.[29] A 1997 Federal Reserve study showed that nearly one-third of women business owners financed their business growth with personal savings and one in four with personal credit cards. In a 1998 Federal Reserve study, 29 percent of the female respondents reported they had had a negative experience while seeking financial assistance.[30] The difficulties for women exist despite statistics showing that women's businesses are at a lower risk of loan delinquency than firms in general and are no more likely to go out of business or be less successful than those owned by men.[31] Refreshed attention has been directed to this concern by Aida Alvarez, SBA administrator, who notes that "last year, nearly two thousand companies received venture capital; of those, only 2 percent—just thirty firms—were women-owned." She further cites the recognition of this problem by Alan Greenspan, chairman of the Federal Reserve, who recently said, "We need to make further progress in establishing business relationships between the financial services sector and the rapidly growing number of minority- and women-owned businesses."[32]

Among the reasons that women, relative to men, face difficulty in obtaining capital is that they generally come to the table with fewer assets and unproven track records. Female entrepreneurs also tend to be more conservative than men when borrowing money, so many unwisely liquidate assets and go through their credit cards before approaching the bank for help. There are also the traditional objections lenders have used to deny women entrepreneurs credit. In a 1996 Sacramento study, these included stepping outside the stereotypical areas of female business ownership (restaurants, catering, and retail), joint collateral tied up in spousal ownership, and the perception that the business was a hobby rather than a venture.[33] Bankers also tend to hold women to higher standards than men in assessing loan requests, according to a 1993 study, particularly in the level of educational attainment.[34]

The problem is most acute for women of color, who operate one in eight of the nearly eight million women-owned businesses in the United States. They are less likely to have capital or bank credit, and are more likely to have been turned down for a loan when starting their businesses.[35] Not surprisingly, nearly three-quarters say that access to capital for current business needs is a very important issue to them, compared to 60 percent or fewer of other women business owners."[36]

There is little doubt from recent studies that accessing credit is a major concern for many women entrepreneurs. The difficulty women have in accessing capital helps explain why they use it differently from male entrepreneurs. Women use outside capital primarily for growth and expansion, men to smooth out cash flow and consolidate debt.[37]

Having the capital to grow and expand the business is directly related to business success.[38] Starting up an underfinanced business is a huge risk, as two sisters who recently closed a museum shop in Victoria note: "It's great to be your own boss—it really is—but make sure you go into it with enough resources. . . . We had just enough to get started, but not enough to carry us through the slow times. . . . We were literally scraping to pay the rent. . . . It was a beautiful shop, but how long can you go on?"[39] True, there are the success stories that suggest that strength of will alone can overcome the lack of capital. Terri Bowersock started with enthusiasm, creativity, and a $2,000 loan from her grandmother. Terri's Consign & Design Furnishings, in Phoenix, grew to become the largest chain of upscale furniture consignment stores nationwide, with 187 employees and sales over $14 million, and Terri received an Avon Products, Inc., Women of Enterprise Award in 1998.[40] But her experience is not the norm.

Lending barriers are being overcome, but slowly. The growing realization that women's businesses are not more likely to fail or to be less successful than those owned by men helps, as do studies that show that businesses headed by men and women show similar growth rates and return on assets.[41] A recent report published by the National Foundation for Women Business Owners and Dun & Bradstreet says that women-owned firms are at a lower risk of loan delinquency than firms in general. Examination of the credit and financial records of a broad spectrum of American businesses shows that women not only pay their bills on time—they pay early.[42] And of the women entrepreneurs who quit business, only one in seven leaves unpaid obligations behind, according to the U.S. Small Business Administration.[43]

Researchers have observed that more than half of women entrepreneurs seek financing from only one financial institution and slightly fewer than one in four approach two institutions.[44] Part of the problem is in the lack of knowledge of what it takes to get a loan. That gap is being bridged. The Women's Business Development Center in Chicago, codirected by S. Carol Dougal and Hedy M. Ratner, seeks to "graduate" borrowers to traditional lending sources.[45] The center has developed an intensive evaluation system to help women determine if they need equity and where they can turn for support. An example is Sonyini Walton, who developed the idea for a consulting firm while serving as an engineer at IBM. She needed only $3,500 to get started and the training in operating and running a business that she received from this program.[46]

The Small Business Administration's Women's Prequalification Loan Program enables loan guarantees for women prior to going to a bank. The pilot program is now available nationwide. The SBA also has the new Low Documentation (LowDoc) and SBAExpress programs, which cut the application form for loans under $150,000 from an inch-thick document to a single page and include a commitment for thirty-six-hour turnaround. Now available through electronic applications, these programs are targeted to provide more than $1 billion in hard-to-get small loans.[47] The SBA also provides a resource guide of important comparative tips on acquiring capital and making sound borrowing decisions.[48] For those in economically distressed areas, since 1994 the SBA has offered the "One-Stop Capital Shops," partnerships between the SBA and a local community designed to offer small businesses comprehensive assistance from one location. Presently the SBA has these shops in seventeen states.[49]

The new women-owned, women-directed small business investment companies (SBICs) are another capital resource. These companies are SBA-leveraged, private sector operations that make equity capital available to businesses needing up to $5 million in financing. The SBICs are focusing their efforts on women-owned businesses, which means at least $50 million is now available for women-owned firms.[50] The Online Women's Business Center (a joint venture by SBA's Office of Women's Business Ownership, the North Texas Women's Business Development Center, and SBA Women's Business Centers across America) offers information necessary for a woman to succeed in business free of charge on its interactive web site. Included is information on best business principles and practices, management techniques, networking, industry news, and market research. The web site also has immediate access to the network of women's business owner representatives in every district office, more than a hundred mentoring roundtables, lists of women-owned venture capital companies, and more than eighty women's business centers in forty-seven states, Puerto Rico, the District of Columbia, and the Virgin Islands. In addition, there are links to SCORE resources and counseling, small business development centers, business information centers, and Procurement Pro-Net, along with information on an array of lending programs and services to help women succeed in business.[51]

Financial networks where women can turn for insider information on capital access are springing up around the country. One such program has been developed by Elizabeth Pap, assistant vice president at M & T Bank and chair of the steering committee developing the guide *Women Entrepreneurs: Access to Capital and Educational Services.* The guide, a first of its kind, has evolved on the basis of recommendations made in a workshop held by the National Association of Women Business Owners Council, the Federal Reserve Bank, and the Small Business Administration and will include listings and resources for fourteen counties in western New York and Rochester.[52] Iris Newman has been involved in this important effort. Earlier Iris, along with a group of female founders and executive officers, established the Women's Investment Network in Philadelphia to create greater visibility for women in high-growth and high-tech businesses and to enhance awareness in the financial community that women's enterprises, like those of men, are not always focused in a cottage industry or a business needing to raise only $5,000 to $10,000.

Financing is available through venture capital, initial public offerings (IPOs), and other mechanisms. In 1996, $71.7 billion was raised by IPOs in the United States and $10 billion was raised in venture capital.[53] In 1998, reports the National Venture Capital Association's research arm, Venture Economics Information Services, venture capital investments rose to $16.02 billion.[54] Women entrepreneurs have been extremely hesitant to seek venture capital, with only 2 percent of them actually doing so, according to an SBA study. This is partly because women traditionally go into business for themselves to gain control and autonomy and are thus reluctant to include the venture capitalist in the business operation, and partly because venture capital companies, like banks, have traditionally lent to men.[55]

The Women's Business Development Center in Chicago has developed an intensive evaluation system to help you determine where you should turn for support and potential sources if you need equity. They identify investment services in terms of the size of equity investments, suggesting that one would approach private investors such as Ace-Net (a new SBA computer matching service for investors and business owners) for equity under $500,000 and small business investment corporations for larger amounts. People like Cathy M. Brienza (described in Chapter 1), a principal of Waller-Sutton Media Partners, New York, a private equity fund that focuses on the media and communications business, are out looking for investments in private companies. She and her partner/ husband use their business contacts and experience in raising equity capital to invest in other companies, helping other people become entrepreneurs.

For really large investments, those exceeding $1 million, entrepreneurs turn to venture capitalists. The process of negotiating arrangements may be lengthy and expensive, with investors interested in high profit margins, market appeal, prospects for rapid expansion, and a high potential for a significant return on investment through an exit strategy such as going public or acquisition by a larger corporation. Factoring, the process of "selling" invoices to receive your money today, instead of waiting 30, 60, or 90 days to be paid, also provides a source of funding and might be considered.[56]

A number of venture capitalists have recently taken on an array of partnerships to provide capital to women business owners. Nina Brown, president of Women's Collateral Worldwide, a Philadelphia-based venture capital firm and the SBA's first small business investment corporation (SBIC), will collect private dollars to be matched up to $40 million by the SBA dedicated to funding women-owned businesses.[57] Three other SBA-backed venture capital companies are listed at the SBA site. Whitney Johns, a board member of NAWBO, founded Capital Across America (CXA), located in Nashville, Tennessee, the first women-oriented venture funds company to be licensed as a small business investment company by the SBA. It targets companies in need of growth capital. These funds specifically provide second-round financing (mezzanine capital) to growing companies (with proven management teams) that have passed the early stages of business development. The advantage of using mezzanine financing is that the "goal of the lender is to have the borrower repay the obligation and retain control and ownership of the company."[58] To pass the Dequity® test for Capital Across America, your company's profile must show three years in operation, growth at an annual rate of 15 percent, profit, and experienced management team. If you meet these criteria you could be considered for a loan that ranges between $250,000 and $1.5 million over a five-year period. Other SBA-backed venture capital companies owned by women include Patty Abramson's Women's Growth Capital Fund in Washington, D.C., and Christine Cordaro's Viridian Capital in San Francisco.[59]

Equity injections, provided through private investors, make up the "angel market." This market is usually looking for investments in the range of $50,000 to $500,000. Sources are difficult to find because they are fragmented and disorganized and have traditionally been part of the "old boys' network"[60] Before seeking venture capital, it is always advisable to check with a random sample of clients to determine the satisfaction level with the management style of the venture capitalist.[61]

In every state the Small Business Administration provides a resource guide of important comparative tips on acquiring capital and making sound borrowing decisions.[62] For example, the *South Carolina Small Business Resource Guide—1998 Edition* (U.S. Small Business Administration) provides tips on getting started, acquiring assistance, complying with regulations, and financing (a comparative analysis of methods) and is an invaluable resource for all entrepreneurs at every stage of business development. The key initial question: Does your business need equity, debt, or alternative financing?[63]

The Ohio Women's Business Resource Network in Columbus advises entrepreneurs to make a quick phone call to a professional before making any important business decision. This is good advice and there are a host of professionals to contact, after you have carefully assessed your needs and their credentials. Advice can be obtained from the SBA's Online Women's Business Center or SCORE and from the analysis of Jade Knapp.[64]

Finally, the big banks have developed strong programs. Citibank of New York, the first bank to gain approval for the SBA's capital access program, allows more flexible lending criteria for businesses over a year old. Chase Manhattan, New York, will consider loans up to $50,000 with little or no collateral to business owners or start-ups with a good credit history and a strong business plan. The Wells Fargo/National Association of Women Business Owners Women's Lending Program has a loan fund for women entrepreneurs with firms in business for two or more years or women who have equivalent experience, good personal and business credit, and an established bank account. Women Inc./The Money Store, by arrangement with the Bank of America, provides a loan pool for members of Women Inc. who have a business plan and a good credit rating.

While there are increased opportunities available, there are a number of women who believe it is very important to establish their business free of debt. They value their experience as shoestring operators and point to the potential long-term benefits. Claudette Weber, who has employed a strict no-debt policy in the male-dominated world of construction, worked on and off at construction companies while starting four small businesses. Rather than borrowing, she took a second job doing part-time financial management while her own venture got under way. Keep it simple, she recommends. "You don't spend any more than you have coming in."[65]

Like nearly everything else involved in a small business, there are a few basic principles (assess your motivation, draw up a good business plan) but no fixed formulas to guide one to a successful business launch or growth period. The best rule of thumb is to remember that your objective research into the business prospect will cost you little beyond your investment of time, and can save you from a bad decision. The key word here is *objective*. It is all right to fall in love with an idea and pursue it. It is a very different thing to fall in love with the idea of being in love—or being in business.

ACKNOWLEDGMENT AND APPRECIATION

I appreciate the assistance of the following centers and individuals for the use of their facilities.

Resource Conference Centers and Research Facilitators

American Women's Economic Development Corporation (AWED), New York. The association, a premier national not-for-profit organization, is committed to helping entrepreneurial women start and grow their own businesses. Based in New York City, AWED also has offices in southern California, Connecticut, and Washington, D.C. It has served over 150,000 women entrepreneurs through courses, conferences, seminars, and one-on-one counseling provided by a faculty of expert executives and entrepreneurs.

Roseanne Antonucci, director

Catalyst, New York. The national nonprofit research and advisory organization founded in 1962 has a dual mission: (1) to help women in business and the professions achieve their maximum potential and (2) to help employers capitalize on the talents of women. Under the leadership of Sheila W. Wellington, president, the library resources on women at 120 Wall Street were made available for background research on women entrepreneurs for this book.

Those especially helpful at the center were:
Dr. Mary Mattis, vice president of research
Jennifer W. Allyn, senior associate

The National Association of Women Business Owners (NAWBO), Washington, D.C. The association propels women entrepreneurs into economic, social, and political spheres of power worldwide. NAWBO offers assistance in securing access to financial opportunities; opportunities to meet, exchange ideas, and establish business ventures; educational programs, seminars, and leadership training; chapter programs, regional meetings, and national conferences; discounts on products and services; an international network of business contacts; visibility and clout in political arenas; and procurement opportunities.

Regional and national offices assisted in research. My special thanks go to the Chicago, Lexington, Philadelphia, and San Diego chapters.

The Women's Business Development Center (WBDC), a not-for-profit organization in Chicago, is a full-service business resource that helps entrepreneurs start and expand their businesses. The WBDC provides entrepreneurial services including management, financial and marketing assistance, entrepreneurial training, vendor development, WBE certification, subsidized employment programs, major conferences, and advocacy.

S. Carol Dougal and Hedy M. Ratner, codirectors

University of South Carolina Small Business Development Center, North Charleston, South Carolina

John Clarkin, Darlene Gauer, Bill Pointer

Center for Women, Charleston, South Carolina, is a private, nonprofit organization dedicated to empowering and enriching women in their private and public lives.

Women Entrepreneurs, Inc., Cincinnati, Ohio, seeks to promote self-employment as a viable alternative to achieving financial self-sufficiency through training, technical assistance, one-on-one counseling, networking, personal development, and assistance with access to financing. The organization is particularly designed to address barriers to the low-income community and women.

Charleston County Public Library: Thanks to Susan Wolf Neilson for facilitating data collection on women's networks.

Conference Rooms and Business/University Facilities and Facilitators

University of New Orleans School of Business

Dr. Kenneth Lacho, professor of management and marketing and director of entrepreneurship, gave encouragement and support that were instrumental in the identification of successful entrepreneurs in New Orleans.

New York University Leonard N. Stern School of Business, Berkley Center for Entrepreneurial Studies, Management Education Center

> Daniel A. Nathanson, clinical professor
> Loretta Poole, special assistance
> Dr. Greg Udell, former director of center

University of California, San Diego, Dean's Conference Room, Extension Complex

> Dr. Mary Lindenstein Walshok, academic vice chancellor, extended studies and public programs

> Deborah Szekely, founder and president of Eureka Communities and chairman of the National Board of Trustees

> Deborah and Mary both helped identify a number of successful entrepreneurs in San Diego to participate in focus sessions for this research.

Patricia L. Roscoe, CITE, chairman of PRA Destination Management Company, and Patti Roscoe and Associates, Inc., gave support in the identification of successful entrepreneurs in the San Diego Bay Area.

Iris R. Newman, president and chief executive officer of Veritas Medical Services Inc., Philadelphia, and a major contributor to the founding of the Women's Investment Network, gave assistance with focus sessions in the New York and Philadelphia areas.

Diane C. Harris, founder and president of Hypotenuse Enterprises, Inc., Rochester, New York, gave assistance in identifying successful entrepreneurs.

Teresa A. Taylor, executive business editor, Business Review, *The Post and Courier,* Charleston, South Carolina, is instrumental in supporting women-owned businesses. She publishes a monthly column on the concerns of women business owners in the "Business Major" section.

Biographical Sketches of Entrepreneurs, 1998–2000 Focus and Interview Sessions

Marjorie Alfus is president of Alfus Family Limited Partnerships and creator of "Golfer's Gizmos," an e-commerce business venture with the mission of "Products for profit and profit for philanthropy," from which funds will go to her charitable foundations. A former Kmart executive, her background has spanned the corporate and entrepreneurial worlds, with a law degree sandwiched in between. Marjorie has been a writer of popular science articles, an editor at McGraw-Hill, producer of science and fashion shows, and the creator of Alberto Imports, a high-fashion knitwear manufacturing and import business in Italy. One of the first women members of the Young Presidents Organization (YPO), she is presently on the Foundation of Committee 200 and on the board of NFWBO. At her initiation and seed funding, the Harvard Business School is preparing case studies featuring women as protagonists

Joan B. Anderson, sole owner of James H. Anderson, Inc., the country's largest woman-owned heating, ventilating, air-conditioning, and design/build company, is also founder of Advanced Cleanroom Technologies LLC. She is the 1999 recipient of the *Working Woman* Entrepreneurial Excellence Award, ranked by *Crain's Chicago Business* as second among Chicago's largest women-owned firms, and a member of the Committee 200. Among her numerous other accomplishments, she founded the Joan B. Anderson Fine Arts and Community Center in Villa Park, Illinois.

Cathy M. Brienza is principal of Waller-Sutton Media Partners, New York, a private equity fund that focuses on the media and communications business, a new venture looking for investments in private companies. Previously, she spent more than twenty years as co-owner of Sutton Capital, an investment management firm in cable television and cellular telephone businesses and related industries. Prior to cofounding Sutton, she was a member of the Corporate Finance Department of a Wall Street investment bank. Cathy received her MBA degree in finance-investments at NYU.

Barbara Bry, vice president of marketing and business development, Proflowers.com, is cofounder and director of ATCOM/INFO, the leading provider of home-away-from-home Internet and e-mail services in public locations such as hotels, airports, and convention centers. Barbara has spent several years as executive producer and moderator for *The CONNECT TV Show*, which is devoted to issues impacting technology companies around the nation. She is part-time executive director of Athena/UCSD CONNECT, and has served on numerous boards. She has been recognized as one of the "Who's Who" in San Diego, among other awards.

Bink Cook, MPA, founder and owner of *The Brighter Side,* is a certified mastectomy fitter and a breast cancer survivor. The first executive director of The Wellness Community in San Diego, Bink worked with cancer patients and their families there and elsewhere over a five-year period. She was recognized as the Woman of Distinction in 1997 by the Salvation Army and as Local Hero by the Komen Foundation Drive for a Cure in 1997. She received the Women Who Mean Business Retail Award for 1998 and was recognized as Advocate of the

Year by the local chapter of the National Association of Women Business Owners.

Denise L. Devine is founder and CEO of Nutripharm, Inc., and its operating subsidiary Devine Foods, Inc., Philadelphia. Her achievements have been recognized by business publications such as *Entrepreneurial Edge* (Rising Entrepreneur of 1993), *Business Philadelphia* (Twenty-five Companies to Watch and Women to Watch), and *Working Woman* (Women to Watch). In 1999 she was named one of Pennsylvania's Best Fifty Women in Business. She is a leader in professional organizations such as the Forum of Executive Women, the AICPA Governing Council, and the Pennsylvania State Board of Accountancy. She holds an MBA degree from Wharton and an M.S. degree in taxation from Villanova Law School.

Carol E. Farren, CFM, IFMA Fellow, is president of Facility Management Worldwide Ltd., a New York City–based firm that provides facility and administrative management consulting services. The former director of facilities at Time-Warner, Inc., she has more than thirty years of experience in interior project management. She is the author of *Planning and Managing Interior Projects,* 2nd ed., and numerous other design publications. She is a graduate of Cornell University and holds an MBA degree from NYU Stern School of Business. She is the recipient of numerous awards and a member of numerous advisory boards including Cornell University's Design and Environmental Analysis Department.

Mary Elizabeth Feldman is the owner of Aunt Mary's, Inc., and her own public relations company, Creative Public Relations. Formerly she was a director of public relations for The Breakers in Palm Beach, Florida, a special assistant to First Lady Nancy Reagan, and appointment secretary to United States Senator David F. Durenberger in Washington, D.C. Mary holds a B.A. in philosophy from the College of St. Catherine in St. Paul, Minnesota.

Nikki Hardin is founder and editor of *Skirt!* magazine, a monthly print publication and web site for women. A native Kentuckian, she left home at seventeen to elope with her high school boyfriend. Divorced with three children ten years later, she started college at the age of twenty-nine. She received a B.A. degree from American University and, prior to moving to Charleston, South Carolina, she was a senior editor with a subsidiary of Prentice-Hall Publishing Company.

Diane C. Harris is founder and president of Hypotenuse Enterprises, Inc., Rochester, New York, a mergers and acquisitions advisory business specializing in corporate development outsourcing and consulting. She is a Phi Beta Kappa graduate of Catholic University, holds an M.S. degree from Rensselaer Polytechnic Institute, and has been listed twice in *Business Week*'s "Top Fifty Women in Corporate America." In 1995 she was awarded the President's Twenty-first Century Leadership Award of the National Women's Hall of Fame. She is a director of Flowserve Corporation and has served as president of the Association for Corporate Growth.

Linda R. Horn is owner and initiator of Capital Concepts, Inc., Harrison, Ohio, an internationally recognized, fully integrated Financial Planning Organization, now in its sixteenth year with gross sales in excess of $6 million annually. She has supported, mentored and counseled hundreds of entrepreneurs, frequently on a purely voluntary basis. Linda's triumphs over personal tragedy and professional challenges have created great demand for her as a local, regional, and national speaker. Among her numerous awards, Linda received the Entrepreneurial Excellence Award from *Working Woman* in 1999, is listed among Twelve Women of Enterprise by the SBA/Avon Corporation, and has received the Greater Cincinnati and Northern Kentucky Woman Entrepreneur of the Year Award.

Claire H. Irving, founder and principal of Investigative Consultants International LLC, is a licensed private investigator with more than twenty-five years of senior management and business experience in the investigations field. Her experience includes: Chase Manhattan Bank, Arthur Andersen & Co., Ernst & Whinney, Lepercq, de Neuflize & Co., and Bankers Trust. Her 100 percent women-owned firm does corporate investigative work. She has personally led investigations dealing with complex corporate takeovers, defense issues, competitive intelligence, external fraud, due diligence, and asset searches for a cross-section of international clients.

Jackie Jennings is president and cofounder of Johnson & Jennings, one of the top ten women-majority-owned businesses in San Diego. A graduate of San Diego State University, she serves as chief financial officer and heads up the company's marketing efforts. Her business is among the leading commercial tenant improvement firms in southern California. Before opening her business she had twenty years of experience in real estate marketing and sales. Jackie is a member of the Regional Economic Task Force, Commercial Real Estate Women, and the Board of Directors for St. Vincent de Paul.

Phyllis Jordan is owner and founder of PJ's Coffee and Tea Company, New Orleans, a leader in the specialty coffee industry. PJ's Coffee and Tea has gone from relative obscurity to fourth ranking among twelve coffee franchises in the United States and Canada, with operations in twenty-six locations across the southeastern United States. Franchisees opened the first of four planned cafes in the New Orleans airport in January 1999, and further expansion is planned in Denver, Las Vegas, and

Atlanta. Phyllis is active in community, civic, and public service organizations, having served as president of the board of WRBH, Radio for the Blind and Print Handicapped. She has served as president of the Specialty Coffee Association of America and on the advisory board of Coffee Kids, an industry group seeking to improve the quality of life for families and children in coffee-growing areas.

Katherine Kennedy, founder and president of Relocation Coordinates, Inc., an independent relocation consulting firm, serves on a number of corporate and public sector boards. Started in 1982, her company brings top-level, highly skilled individuals to San Diego and provides relocation counseling, cost-of-living comparisons, and housing and school search consulting for newly hired employees. She is founder of the San Diego Relocation Council, an association dedicated to educating corporations on trends in recruiting and relocation. She is heavily involved in community activities from LEAD, San Diego, to local political campaigns, and has received numerous awards.

Carolyn Smith Konow is a co-owner of and consultant with Framan & Smith Communications, with offices in San Diego, Los Angeles, and Albuquerque. She is also a co-owner and president of California Alternative Medicinal Center in San Diego. Carolyn is president of the San Diego chapter of NAWBO and has been an entrepreneur for over twenty years. She previously founded and managed a highly successful graphics and printing firm, which specialized in cutting-edge design and high-quality lithography.

Margaret M. Larkin is president and owner of Larkin Pension Services, a firm specializing in the design and administration of qualified retirement plans in San Diego. She is a 1996 recipient of the San Diego Women Who Mean Business Award for financial services and two additional awards given by The Work and Family Coalition of San Diego for excellence in employee benefits. Margaret is engaged in numerous professional boards and organizations and has taken on key leadership and service roles in civic and community activities.

Maria-Luisa Maccecchini, Ph.D., continued her studies with two postdoctoral fellowships at the Roche Institute of Immunology in Basel and the California Institute of Technology. She received special training in business and patent law, economics, and general and project management from Indiana State University. She followed this with a corporate finance degree at Wharton. Maria-Luisa is founder, president, and CEO of Bearsden Bio, Inc., in Aston, Pennsylvania. With more than twenty years of experience in science and biotechnology, she has made a successful transition from scientist to executive. She serves on many boards, including the Ben Franklin Technology Center Board, is the holder of numerous patents and awards, and has published many papers.

Marian V. Marchese is president and CEO of VirTu, Inc., a Philadelphia-based Internet company, and cofounder of Marchese & Barone Advertising, Inc. She is an eighteen-year veteran of the Philadelphia advertising and marketing community. Among other civic activities, she is on the boards of the Boy Scouts of America and the United Way of Southeastern Pennsylvania. Marian is a past president of Philadelphia Business Executives and is now president of the Forum of Executive Women in Philadelphia. She received the 1996 Pennsylvania Honor Roll of Women Award and the 1998 Who's Who in Technology Award from the *Philadelphia Business Journal.*

Elise E. McCullough, president and founder of Staffing Solution, has nearly a decade of experience with two of the largest national professional recruiting organizations in New Orleans. She has successfully completed job assignments in temporary and permanent placements of office personnel ranging from receptionists to CFOs for major corporations and smaller firms throughout Louisiana and Mississippi. Previously she served five years as a corporate controller.

Ruth Ann Menutis is president and founder of Natural Energy Unlimited, Inc., The Grove, a natural snack retail and wholesale business headquartered in New Orleans with more than $20 million in annual sales, operating in eighteen major airports in the United States. She has built three successful companies. Ruth Ann has served as Louisiana chairperson to the National White House Conference on Small Business and as president of the French Market Corporation. She is a recipient of the Chamber of Commerce Person of the Year award and the Louisiana Small Businessperson of the Year award.

Gail K. Naughton, Ph.D., president and CEO of Advanced Tissue Sciences, Inc., a world leader in tissue engineering, is director, cofounder, and coinventor of the company's core technology. She received her M.S. and Ph.D. degrees from the New York University Medical Center in dermatology and served as an assistant professor of research at NYUMC for two years before moving to the City University of New York in 1985. She holds numerous issued patents and has been extensively published in the field of tissue engineering. Her advisory board service includes Johns Hopkins University, The Georgia Institute of Technology, the University of California, Massachusetts Institute of Technology, and the University of Washington.

Iris R. Newman is president and CEO of Veritas Medical Services, Inc., Philadelphia, and winner of the 1998 Ben Franklin Emerging Business Award for the most innovative service (for computerized credentials verification for physicians). She previously founded InConcepts, Inc., a consulting firm that specialized in developing and implementing strategic business, marketing, and public relations plans. She was instrumental in creating Women's Investment Network in Philadelphia and is a driving force behind attracting corporate sponsors to assist women who have started businesses with high growth potential.

Bren Norris, founder and owner of Bren Norris Associates, Inc., and Bren International, provides technical expertise on a contract basis worldwide. In 1995 she was an elected delegate to the White House Conference on Small Business, and in 1997 she received Vice President Al Gore's Hammer Award for her work on the web site U.S. Business Advisor, May We Assist You? (www.business.gov). She continues to work with this administration in technology and intellectual property law. She is also a professional speaker.

Evelyn Reis Perry, CEO of Carolina Sound Communications, Inc., and Sound Communications, Inc., both headquartered in Charleston, South Carolina, is a graduate of the University of Wisconsin at Madison. She was the elected head of the South Carolina Delegation to the White House Conference on Small Business in 1995, chaired the South Carolina National Federation of Independent Business Leadership Council for five years, and most recently founded the Lowcountry Chapter of the National Association of Women Business Owners.

Patricia L. Roscoe, CITE, chairman of PRA Destination Management Company, with offices in San Diego, Orange County, Los Angeles County, Palm Springs, and Santa Barbara, also owns Patti Roscoe and Associates, Inc., a national franchising operation. The Greater San Diego Chamber of Commerce named her the 1998 Entrepreneurial Spirit. In 1999 she was named by *San Diego Magazine* as "one of fifty people to watch." She has been a delegate to the White House and named as the Woman of the Year by the Irish Congress of Southern California. Her community, civic, and board involvement is vast, including the City of San Diego Commission on the Status of Women commissioner.

Aliza Sherman is president of Cybergrrl, Inc., a new media company empowering women through technology, and is an Internet thought leader, speaking worldwide about the Internet for women. She created Cybergrrl® in January 1995 and founded Webgrrls®, a networking group for women interested in the Internet, which has over 100 chapters worldwide. She is also the author of *Cybergrrl: A Woman's Guide to the World Wide Web.* She was named one of the Most Powerful People in Their Twenties by *Swing* magazine in 1997 and one of the Top Fifty People Who Matter Most on the Internet by *Newsweek.*

Audrey Smaltz is founder and CEO of The Ground Crew. She is also a fashion authority and has been named three times to the International Best Dressed List. In 1998 she received a *Crain's* award as one of New York's top six entrepreneurs. She combined her knowledge of fashion and modeling with her head for figures from an array of corporate experiences (including recognition as the unforgettable commentator for 800 Ebony Fashion Fair shows) into the expertise behind her present business.

Rebecca Smith, a Class A certified general contractor, is founder and president of A. D. Morgan Corporation, a commercial general construction company with offices in Tampa and Melbourne, Florida. Her firm is widely recognized as the fastest-growing company in Tampa Bay. In 1998 she received Ernst & Young's Entrepreneur of the Year Award for Florida and the Tampa Chamber of Commerce Small Business Award. She has received numerous other awards and is very active in civic and business activities in her community and state. She is the present chair of the Governor's Council for Women and Minority Business and Economic Growth and a recognized advocate and supporter of women and minority business owners, often making national presentations.

Loretta G. Soloway, owner of a fashion agency in the Carlisle group, began her career working between two companies for about eight years. Among other corporate experiences, she worked at Manhattan Industries where she was in charge of the Anne Klein Scarf line and was very successful because of her eye for color and design. Later, prior to starting her own business, she also freelanced for Barr & Beards, who handled the Bill Blass line.

Suzy Spafford is CEO of Suzy's Zoo. Product lines include two children's books, *Alphabetical Soup* and *Witzy and Zoom Zoom*. She has more than 900 designs on the market with export and licensing arrangements worldwide. Her stationery products are translated into eleven languages. Her art is licensed to more than sixteen major U.S. companies, including Gerber Baby Products. In 1996, she was the winner in the Greeting Card Division of the National Cartoonist Society. Winner of many other awards, she serves on a number of boards and in civic activities.

Tara Stephenson, president of The Woodward Group, Ltd., Media, Pennsylvania, an advisory services company for mergers and acquisitions, raising capital valuations, and pre-transaction services, previously headed investment banking for a regional investment/merchant bank and was a founding principal of Berwind Financial Group. She is a member of several boards, was named to the Pennsylvania Honor Roll of Women, was awarded the *Philadelphia Business Journal* Forty under Forty designation in 1996, and was named one of *Business Philadelphia*'s 1997 Women to Watch. She holds the Master of Management degree with distinction from Northwestern.

Deborah Szekely, founder of Rancho La Puerta and the Golden Door, gained important network access through participation on dozens of boards over a span of forty years. Building on her past skills as creator of the foremost spas in the country, she founded Eureka Communities, a 501-C-3, which is her full-time passion. She is now chair of the national board of trustees. Eureka, a national organization created to assist disadvantaged children, youth, and families, works directly with leaders of community-based organizations and is centered in San Diego, Los Angeles, Detroit, the San Francisco Bay Area, and Boston. Among her many activities, Deborah is a member of the Committee 200, the International Women's Forum, and the Women's Forum of Washington. She served as the U.S. delegate to the Organization of American States, Inter-American Commission on Women.

Darlene Thomas, owner and operator of Thomas Travel and Cruise, a leisure travel agency that she founded in 1994 in Houston and later moved to New Orleans, is a graduate of the University of Houston. Formerly, she was CEO of Watts & Company, a Houston-based law firm. She is involved in many civic and community activities, including membership on the board of directors of the Chamber-New Orleans and River Region. She also serves on the Chamber's Small Business Executive Committee.

Carol A. Vincie, president and owner of New Era Consulting, turns products and services into a business and connects businesses with money. She works with companies with revenue between $2 million and $10 million that are looking to move to the next level. She firmly believes that hiring the right person for each position at every level is essential to the long-term success of all businesses. Her website tells the story: www.artofsmarthiring.com.

Mary Lindenstein Walshok, associate vice chancellor, Extended Studies and Public Programs of the University of California, San Diego, has been the driving force behind the expansion and outreach programs of UCSD. She oversees a staff of 200 and an annual budget of $24 million. Among her numerous scholarly activities are her two published books, *Blue Collar Women,* and *Knowledge Without Boundaries: What America's Research Universities Can Do for the Economy, the Workplace, and the Community.* She serves on numerous boards at the regional, state, and national level, and is the recipient of numerous awards.

Biographical Sketches of Cited Entrepreneurs in Initial Focus Sessions[1]

Lisa B. Adkinson, a former CEO of Inner Applications, an office interiors firm, is presently a partner in the Strategic Eight Planning Process and works as a strategist serving more than 200 companies. She has served as president and board chair of Women Entrepreneurs, Inc. (WEI), and received the 1992 Entrepreneur of the Year award. In 1994 she was selected as one of the area's top forty business leaders under age forty.

She has served on Ohio's Small Business and Entrepreneurship Council since 1994. She has been featured in *Small Business Journal*'s issue on Women in Business, and Inner Applications has been listed among the top twenty women-owned businesses in Cincinnati.

Ann Shelton Angel was president for thirteen years of Technologies Training of the Triad, Inc. (TTT), a computer training and consulting company in Winston-Salem, North Carolina. Under her leadership TTT served large companies including Wachovia Bank and Thomasville Furniture as well as over 250 small businesses. Ann served as a delegate to the 1995 White House Conference on Small Business in Washington, D.C. At the close of 1999, she sold her business and has just released a book entitled *Calculated Risk Taking*. Ann's present career focus is on speaking and writing.

Lorena M. Blonsky, president and owner of LMB, a Chicago-based executive/professional search firm, specializes in information systems recruitment. Lorena has placed professionals in a variety of systems roles. For the last twelve years she has been a member of the University of Chicago Women's Business Group, serving on the board of directors from 1987 to 1991 and as president in 1990.

Patty M. Breeze has an insurance practice, Mass Mutual, The Kentucky-West Virginia Agency, in Lexington. She works with professionals and business owners in the areas of life, health, and disability insurance, annuitie, and mutual funds. She is a charter member and past president of the Lexington Chapter of the National Association of Women Business Owners.

Susan O'Connor Brown, The Avalon Consulting Group, Rosemont, Pennsylvania, spent eighteen years in the financial services arena as a senior executive managing growth and change. She formed her own consulting firm in 1991 and consults to organizations and executives primarily in the areas of strategic planning, change management, and leadership development.

Rebecca Carney, owner of BECCA et al., a Philadelphia-based company, is an experienced professional in the fields of sales, marketing, and management. After more than twenty-five years in the corporate world, in 1989 she started BECCA et al., which provides gifts, promotional products, premiums, and incentives to local and multinational companies. Since 1995, BECCA et al. has been in the industry's Multi Million Dollar Roundtable.

Alice Collier Cochran, The Cochran Group, San Rafael, California, is a planning process and meeting facilitator who helps organizations manage change successfully through collaborative approaches. She is working on a book to "feminize" business meetings, *Roberta's Rules of Order.*

Sherie A. Conrad, president of Conrad Consulting Group, New Orleans, is a human resource and small business management expert specializing in contingency and retained searches, temporary and contract technical staffing, customized training and seminar production, development of business and marketing plans, outsourced staffing services including evaluation/assessment, needs forecasting, and job analysis. Sherie's corporate background includes sixteen years as owner and president of Pembo & Associates, an employment agency, ten years as president of Common Sense Consulting, and the 1999 founder of The Women's Resource Center, a nonprofit organization dedicated to the education and economic mainstreaming of women in business.

Ethel Cook, owner of Corporate Improvement Group, Bedford, Massachusetts, consults, writes, and speaks on creating dynamic and productive work environments. She works with her clients to help them improve the relationships and systems that enable them to get things done on time and on budget.

Eileen Duignan-Woods, P.E., E.D.W. Associates, Inc., an engineering and construction consulting firm based in Chicago and North Carolina, has successfully owned and operated her own business for many years. A licensed professional engineer in five states, she received her B.S. degree in mechanical and aerospace engineering from the Illinois Institute of Technology. She has published articles, lectured extensively, and held seminars on mechanical systems in buildings and the construction business.

Evelyn Eskin is president of Health Power Associates, Inc., Philadelphia. Founded in 1987, the firm provides practice management, educational, and planning services to physicians, hospitals, academic health centers, and other health care organizations with commitments to physician practice success. She is a frequent speaker and writer for pharmaceutical companies, health care systems, universities, medical and other professional societies, and health care journals.

Jill Martin Fugaro is the San Francisco Bay Area designer for the Jill Martin label, acquired by Mariall Apparel, Inc., in 1989. The line of clothing is sold in better stores in major cities across the United States. A Michigan State University Honors College graduate in retailing and communication arts, she later headed the merchandise and fashion division of Levi Strauss in San Francisco.

Patricia A. Gallagher, owner of Evergreen Supply Company in Chicago, started selling electrical supplies out of the basement of her home in 1986. Patricia did everything. Her customers knew her in a suit, as well as in a hard hat. She now has a sales volume of $7 million annually, employs close to twenty people, and recently started a second company that recycles fluorescent bulbs and ballasts.

Wendy Ginn is an authority in the field of intuition in business. As a professional Intuitive Business Consultant, she offers training and individual counseling in this important new field for executives, managers, and entrepreneurs. Her practice combines groundbreaking work in the fields of personal integrity, humanistic business policies, and mind/body/spirit integration with her comprehensive business experience. Wendy spent twelve years in operations and marketing management at Xerox Corporation and twelve years as founder and CEO of Convert! Inc., a high-tech company in San Francisco. She is a staff instructor at the Academy of Intuitive Studies where she is enrolled in the doctoral program for Intuition Medicine.

Janet Goldman, owner of Fragments, New York, manufactures a private label of jewelry for Banana Republic, Ann Taylor, and other clients and has a retail store in Soho, New York. Her mission as owner is discovering new talent and bringing it to a high-end market—for example, Saks Fifth Avenue and Neiman Marcus. In 1996 she graduated from the O.P.M. Program at Harvard University.

Diane C. Hanson has been president of Creative Resource Development, West Chester, Pennsylvania, for more than fifteen years. The firm specializes in training, team development, organizational change, and creating innovation in organizations. Prior to starting her own business, Diane was a pioneering female in pharmaceutical sales, reaching the level of district manager.

Vickie L. Henry, chairman and CEO of Feedback Plus, Inc., known as "America's Mystery Shopper," is a pioneer in the customer service industry. Now celebrating its twenty-eighth year, her company was named Small Business of the Year in 1994. Author of two books, *Feedback on Sales* and *Feedback on Calls,* she has served as president of Executive Women of Dallas and as a member of the executive board of International Just-Say-No, and is an active member of the John C. Ford Program to benefit low-income individuals and businesses. She was a nominee for two distinguished awards in 1999: the Merrill Lynch Entrepreneur of the Year and the Trailblazer Award. She is a professor at the Entrepreneurship.com University.

Joan M. Holliday is one of four partners of Women in Process Consulting, Chadds Ford, Pennsylvania, founded in 1988. Women in Process is a developmental organization dedicated to helping make systems more effective through the use of a holistic approach. The organization works to improve diversity, enable strategic processes, and encourage authentic leadership toward a fuller expression of potential for the individual and the system.

Lisa Jacobson founded Stanford Coaching, Inc., a one-on-one private SAT-preparation firm based in Manhattan. She is a member of the

Executive Committee of the American Women's Economic Development Corporation and has appeared on the *Today Show, NBC Nightly News,* CNBC, and in the *Wall Street Journal,* the *New York Times,* and *Inc.*

Karen Kline is president of Accent Chicago, Inc., which she launched in 1979 and has now grown to six stores plus an advertising specialty distributorship, Accent Promotions, and a wholesale distributorship, Sunburst Souvenirs. She is active on several boards, including the Lutheran School of Theology at Chicago. She received the Chicago Woman Business Owner of the Year award in 1992 and served as Governor of Rotary International District 6440 in 1996–1997.

Dale Leach works as Systems Redesign Coordinator/Change Management at Zale Lipshy University Hospital in Dallas, Texas. Her passion comes from beauty and spirit visible in her art, writing, travel, and nature. Dleach@zluh.org.

Susie Marshall is owner of CompuTactics, Inc., a Dallas firm that designs and develops computerized management information systems, with particular emphasis on Internet web sites. Her new company, Technology Interchange Resources, is establishing an Electronic Commerce Resource Center in Dallas to teach businesspeople how to do business electronically and assist them in conducting electronic commerce.

Laurie Moore-Moore is a partner in Real Trends, a Dallas-based communications and publishing company serving the residential real estate industry. In addition to producing a monthly subscription newsletter and an e-mail newsletter, the firm publishes industry research, runs CEO brainstorming groups, and hosts national CEO conferences. Laurie speaks to about 100 audiences annually.

Elizabeth Morris is a consulting economist specializing in economic development issues. She is CEO and founder of Insight Research Corporation, the largest economic research firm in the nation, which is located outside of Washington, D.C. Insight provides economic, employment, tax impact, and cost/benefit analyses for public and private sector clients. Insight now performs approximately 300 such analyses each year, and has contributed to location decisions affecting the workplaces of more than 1.7 million workers. Every day in North America, an Insight research project is front-page news.

Terri Parker-Halpin, principal consultant/trainer in International ISO Group, Cincinnati, is the author of more than 100 technical books and numerous technical articles, and has spoken nationally on technical writing and documentation management. She is cofounder of the Cincinnati Chapter of the National ISO 9000 User Support Group. To date, all of her clients have achieved registration on their first attempt.

Sudha Pennathur, a California designer of jewelry, accessories, gifts, and other objets d'art, is president of the House of Pennathur. A native of New Delhi, she holds an M.B.A. degree from the University of Washington. She served in senior management at Levi Strauss, Carter Hawley Hale, and Allied Stores. Her firm fashions an India-inspired jewelry line incorporating designs from the merger of two cultures and works exclusively with award-winning artisans of the Indian subcontinent.

Susan L. Pickman, president of The Pickman Group, Inc., Orlando, Florida, is a management consultant and licensed private investigator. For the last fourteen years, she has owned Tuscawalla Travel. In 1994, she ran for the Florida legislature.

Joanne Pratt is president of Joanne H. Pratt Associates, a virtual company specializing in helping both public and private organizations implement telework. She is a recognized futurist and an authority on home-based work, including business impacts, transportation implications, family issues, and corporate work patterns. She is the author of *Telecommuting—Checking into It* and *Myths and Realities of Working at Home.* Her new research study, *Homebased Business: The Hidden Economy,* a report from 125,000 women, men, black, Hispanic and other minority entrepreneurs, has just been released by the U.S. Small Business Administration. Joannepratt@post.harvard.edu.

Anne Sadovsky, CEO of Anne Sadovsky & Company, a Dallas-based marketing consulting and seminar firm, provides counseling, training, and speeches to a variety of industries. *Mirabella* has listed her as one of the top 1,000 women of the 1990s. Her books, *101 Thoughts to Make You Think* and *101 Thoughts for Becoming the Real You,* can be found in bookstores nationally.

Linda Sahagian founded Sahagian & Associates, Inc., in 1971, in Oak Park, Illinois. The firm manufactures specialty snack foods and confections under its own brand name and private labels. Her trademark packaging and designs, "The Whole 9 Yards," features A YARD OF and A FOOT OF Sahagian's manufactured edibles, which are sold throughout the United States and internationally.

Carol A. Scarano established Helping Hands Network, Inc., New York, in 1990. The multifaceted human resource, financial, and marketing firm consults to small and start-up companies to establish administrative and accounting support departments.

Kris Schaeffer, founder of Kris Schaeffer & Associates, San Francisco, has had twenty-six years of professionally challenging responsibilities. She has built entire training departments from scratch and has developed a long list of "first evers," including sales training, product

knowledge training, and plant supervisor training and team building. For fourteen years, her company has provided comprehensive
human resource programs for a wide number of industries, and it is
currently doing a lot of work in call centers and e-commerce.

Dianne Semingson, owner of DLS International, Inc., and its affiliate,
New Source Management, in Philadelphia, provides business devel-
opment, marketing, community relations, and corporate philan-
thropy consulting services to businesses and foundations, including
Bell Atlantic, Watts & Wyatt, Data Systems Analysts, Inc., The Barnes
Foundation, and the William Penn Foundation. Prior to founding
DLS International, she served as a member of the mayor of
Philadelphia's cabinet and as U.S. Department of Commerce
Regional Director for the Mid-Atlantic States.

Honi Stempler, N.D., M. H., of Atlanta, Georgia, is a doctor of natural medicine and a certified Holistic Health Practitioner with the American
Association of Drugless Practitioners. She also practices kinesiology,
the science of energy balancing, and specializes in pain and stress relief.
She has over twenty years of writing and production experience.

Mary Louise Stott, Bioplans, Inc., Winston-Salem, North Carolina, is a
Chartered Financial Consultant (ChFC). She began her career in
insurance sales in 1982. Bioplans assists small businesses and individuals
in putting together their life, medical, and disability insurance packages.

Julie Coulter Thomas of Thomas & Thomas Architects, Ltd., Evanston,
Illinois, is a licensed architect and interior designer whose work has
been featured in *Art by Architects*. Winner of the Charlotte Danstrom
Woman of Achievement National and Regional Award in 1993, she
has served as a role model for the annual Futures Unlimited Conference, which encourages young women to pursue careers in math and
science. She received second place in the Burnham Prize competition
in 1985 and first place in the "Late Entries to the Sears Tower."

Janee Tucker, president and COO, Tucker & Associates (TAI), and vice
president of Integrated Logistical Support, Inc. (ILSI), New Orleans,
is a specialist in marketing, planning, and financial systems. She has
received numerous awards for success as a business owner and for service to the community, including the New Orleans Woman Business
Owner of the Year, Best of Black Business Award, National Council of
Negro Women/Quaker Oats as Community Leader, and Employer of
the Year by the Business and Professional Women's organization. She is
included in 1996/97 Strathmore's *Who's Who Registry of Business Leaders*.

Susan Weiner of West Newton, Massachusetts, is editor of the leading
weekly trade publication on the mutual fund business. She formerly

designed and led customized training programs for Americans on "How to Do Business with the Japanese." She has also managed Japanese business development and marketing communications for an investment management firm.

Catherine Friend White, FinArc LLC, Lexington, Masachusetts, manages stock, bond, and mutual fund portfolios for individuals and institutions on a fee-only basis. The firm offers social screening of investments and solutions to clients' financial problems.

Gale P. Wise, B.C.S.W., Center for Change, Inc., a clinical social worker in New Orleans, has nineteen years of experience in the specialty areas of child abuse, sexual abuse, and domestic violence. She received her M.S.W. degree from Atlanta University's School of Social Work.

Pauline Yeats is a designer of "home couture" and interiors. Her collection of furniture and fabrics is sold at Pauline Yeats' Interior Design Shop in New York and through architects and designers nationally and internationally.

Participants Who Elected to Be Acknowledged by Name

Babineaux, Michele Janet. Proprietor, MICHAUL'S on St. Charles, New Orleans

Bensu, Janet. BENSU, Inc., San Francisco

Clesi, Marie M. State Farm Insurance Agency, Kenner, Louisiana

Coates, Andrea. ChiroCare Plus, Brookline, Massachusetts

Coury, Lillian. Pineapple Printing, Inc., New York

Drake, Darlene. President, Fitness Pro Health & Exercise Equipment, Lexington, Kentucky

Droppelman, Patricia A., CPN. President, Pediatric Nursing Care, Inc., Cincinnati

Gerla, Barbara Ullman. Attorney at law, Cincinnati

Gibbons, Jo Anne. President, The Gibbons Group, Cincinnati

Green, L. Elaine. President, Video Features, Inc., Cincinnati

Griffith, Jackie. General manager, Hunter Management Group, Inc., Lexington, Kentucky

Harris, Gloriann. C.P.A., Northbrook, Illinois

Hecht, Carol, CLA. President, BarriCorp, Inc., Dallas

Hueppeler, Deborah. Financial Consultant, Dallas

Hill, Hattie. CEO, Hattie Hill Enterprises, Dallas

Johnson (Raglin), Fran. Elite Travel Services, Cincinnati

Kelley, Roberta Gose. Jim Kelley Associates, Atlanta

Kotler, Suzan B. Certified Financial Planner, Money Concepts, Cincinnati

Levine, Saralyn. Delectable Dining, Chamblee, Georgia

McCann, Janet. Interior designer, Wilmette, Illinois

Marrs, Catherine L. Liaison, Inc., Dallas

Peyton, Renee. Atlanta

Porco, Anita L. President, Nurses Today, Inc., Dallas

Pizel, Pamela (Pam). Pizel & Associates Commercial Real Estate, Dallas

Rust, Debra. President, Alpha Communications Technologies, Inc., Warrenville, Illinois

Sayre, Patricia S. Fiber-Seal, Cincinnati

Schwaller, Shirley F. Owner, Horizon Communications Group, Dallas

Sifford, Marilyn O. Marilyn Sifford Organizational Change, Philadelphia

Smerz, Nancy. President, Air Comfort Corporation, Broadview, Illinois

Stange, Deborah. President, West Fuels, Inc., Westchester, Illinois

Tighe, Jeanne P. Blue Grass Advertising Specialties, Lexington, Kentucky

Verdich, Lauren. President, Lauren's Catering, Inc., Chicago

Wise, Gale P. M.S.W., B.C.S.W., Center for Change, Inc., Counseling & Psychotherapy Associates, New Orleans

Special thanks go to another group of successful women entrepreneurs who have been cited throughout the book but requested to remain anonymous.

Centers and Individuals Contributing to Earlier Focus Sessions

Accent Chicago, Inc.: Karen Kline, president

Alumnae Resources (AR), San Francisco: Alice Cochran and Linda deMello, facilitators

Charleston Trident Chamber of Commerce: Ginger Norvell

City of Charleston, South Carolina, Office of the Mayor: Joe Riley

DePaul University Department of Management

EBC Conference Center, Atlanta Financial Center: furnished by Tom Dye, president; arranged by Bernie Mercer

Female and Minority Business Incubator, Cincinnati, Ohio: Cassandra Middleton

Just Brakes Corporation, Dallas: Deborah Hueppeler

Louisiana Small Business Development Center, Loyola University, New Orleans: Professor Ronald Schroeder

Massachusetts Mutual Life Insurance Company, Lexington, Kentucky: Patty M. Breeze

Bernie Mercer & Company, Atlanta: Bernie Mercer, president,

MICHAUL'S Live Cajun Music Restaurant: Michele Jacob-Babineaux

NAWBO:

>Lexington, Kentucky: Melinda Duncan facilitated focus sessions

>New Orleans: Patricia Ann (Patty) Habeeb facilitated focus sessions

>San Francisco: Jill Martin Fugaro facilitated focus sessions

Nurses Today, Inc., Dallas: Anita Porco

Pizel & Associates Commercial Real Estate: Pam Pizel, owner

San Francisco Renaissance Entrepreneurship Center: Claudia Vieke, executive director

Senator Strom Thurmond's and Fritz Holling's offices: Phil Black, business assistant

Swinson's Communications, Dallas: Mary Swinson

Women Entrepreneurs, Inc., of Cincinnati

The Women's Business Development Center (WBDC), Chicago

The Citadel, Department of Business Administration

University of Cincinnati Small Business Development Center: Nancy Rogers

University of New Orleans, Small Business Development Center: Michael Cusack and Alice Kennedy

---

[1] Entrepreneurs who participated in focus sessions conducted specifically for the coauthored work *Women Entrepreneurs—Moving Beyond the Glass Ceiling* are listed here in appreciation. Quotes by these entrepreneurs are cited to the previous work. These entrepreneurs were asked to provide an updated biosketch for this book, and the updates received are included.

Notes

....

Preface

1. Council of Economic Advisors. (1998). Table B-40; Lynch, M., & Post, K. (1996). What glass ceiling? *The Public Interest, 124,* 27–37. Htt://web7.searchbank.com/info-tra... (pp. 5–6 on web site). Statistics also based on recent releases of information from National Foundation for Women Business Owners, Catalyst, United States Department of Labor, and the *Chronicle of Higher Education.*

2. National Foundation for Women Business Owners, NFWBO Research Summary. (1999, May 11). Facts of the Week, May 11, 1999. [http://www.nfwbo.org]. As noted in the SBA Office of Advocacy, Economic Statistics and Research on Small Business, Women in Business (1998, October), A report on statistical information about women-owned businesses prepared by the U.S. Small Business Administration's Office of Advocacy, p. 4, the federal government collects and disseminates the most comprehensive federal statistics under a special program of the Census Bureau's Economic Censuses, the Census of Women-Owned Business (WOB). The most recent data available, released in 1997, are for 1992 and are the only federal data that cover all women-owned businesses. Data at: http://www.sba.gov/ADVO/stats/wib.html.

3. Kaye, E. (1993, October). The face of power. *Working Woman,* pp. 50–54, citing Elizabeth Kendall's book *The Runaway Bride.*

4. Moore, D. P. (1999). Women entrepreneurs: Approaching a new millennium. In G. N. Powell (Ed.), *Handbook of Gender and Work* (pp. 371–390). Thousand Oaks, CA: Sage.

5. Gregg, G. (1985). Women entrepreneurs: The second generation. *Across the Board,* pp. 10–18; Hisrich, R. D., & O'Brien, M. (1982). The woman entrepreneur as a reflection of the type of business. In K. Vesper (Ed.), *Frontiers of Entrepreneurship Research* (pp. 54–67). Wellesley, MA: Center for Entrepreneurial Studies, Babson College; Moore, D. P. (1990). An examination of present research on the female entrepreneur—suggested research strategies for the 1990s. *Journal of Business Ethics, 9*(4/5), 275–281; Devine, T. J. (1994). Characteristics of self-employed women in the United States. *Monthly Labor Review, 117*(3), 20–34.

6. Moore, D. P. (1987). First- and second-generation female entrepreneurs—Identifying the needs and differences. In D. F. Ray (Ed.), *Southern Management Association Proceedings* (pp. 175–177). Mississippi State: Mississippi State University; Moore, An examination of present research on the female entrepreneur.

7. Bureau of the Census, Current Population Reports Series P-23, No. 146 (1986); Birley, S. (1989). Female entrepreneurs: Are they really any different? *Journal of Small Business Management, 27*(1), 32–37; Hisrich, R., & Brush, C. (1987). Women entrepreneurs: A longitudinal study. In N. C. Churchill, J. A. Hornaday, B. A. Kirchoff, O. J. Krasner, & K. H. Vesper (Eds.), *Frontiers of Entrepreneurship Research* (pp. 187–199). Wellesley, MA; Center for Entrepreneurial Studies, Babson College; Kalleberg, A. L., & Leicht, K. T. (1991). Gender and organizational performance: Determinants of small business survival and success. *Academy of Management Journal, 34*(1), 131–161.

Chapter 1

1. Hall, D. T. (1996). Protean careers of the 21st century. *Academy of Management Executive, 10*(4), 8–16.

2. Kanter, R. M. (1989). Careers and the wealth of nations: A macro-perspective on the structure and implications of career forms. In M. B. Arthur, D. T. Hall, & B. S. Lawrence, *Handbook of Career Theory* (pp. 506–521). Cambridge, England: Cambridge University Press; Cox, C., & Jennings, R. (1995). The foundations of success: The development and characteristics of British entrepreneurs and intrapreneurs. *Leadership and Organization Development Journal, 16*(7), 4–10.

3. Kanter, Careers and the wealth of nations; Cox & Jennings, The foundations of success; Sullivan, S., Carden, W. A., & Martin, D. F. (1998). Careers in the next millennium: Directions for future research. *Human Resource Management Review, 8*(2), 165–185.

4. Gartner, W. B., Bird, B. J., & Starr, J. A. (1992, Spring). Acting as if: Differentiating entrepreneurial from organizational behavior. *Entrepreneurship Theory and Practice,* pp. 13–27.

5. Schein, E. H. (1996). Career anchors revisited: Implications for career development in the twenty-first Century. *Academy of Management Executive, 10*(4), 80–88; Hall, Protean careers of the 21st century.

6. Sullivan, S. E. (1999). The changing nature of careers: A review and research agenda. *Journal of Management, 25*(3), 457–484.

7. Arthur, M. B., & Rousseau, D. M. (1996). A career lexicon for the twenty-first century. *Academy of Management Executive, 10*(4), 28–39.

8. London, M. (1998). *Career Barriers: How People Experience, Overcome, and Avoid Failure.* Mahwah, NJ: Erlbaum (see chapter 8).

9. Drucker, P. (1999, March–April). Managing oneself. *Harvard Business Review,* pp. 64–74.

10. Arthur & Rousseau, A career lexicon for the twenty-first century; Rousseau, D. M., & Arthur, M. B. (Eds.) (1996). *The Boundaryless Career: A New Employment Principle for a New Organizational Era.* New York: Oxford University Press,

11. Bird, B. J. (1992). The operation of intentions in time: The emergence of the new venture. *Entrepreneurship Theory and Practice, 17*(1), 11–20; Bird, B. J., & Jelinek, M. (1988). The operation of entrepreneurial intentions. *Entrepreneurship Theory and Practice,* 13(2), 21–29; Hansen, E. L., & Wortman, M. S. (1989). Entrepreneurial networks: The organization in vitro. In F. Hoy (Ed.), *Academy of Management Best Paper Proceedings: 49th meeting* (pp. 69–73). Atlanta: Darby; Katz, J., & Gartner, W. B. (1988). Properties of emerging organizations. *Academy of Management*

Review, 13(3), 429–441; Katz, J. (1994). Modeling entrepreneurial career progressions: Concepts and considerations. *Entrepreneurship Theory and Practice, 19*(2), 23–39; Shapero, A. (1982). Social dimensions of entrepreneurship. In C. A. Kent, D. L. Sexton, & K. H. Vesper (Eds.), *Encyclopedia of Entrepreneurship* (pp. 72–90). Upper Saddle River, NJ: Prentice Hall.

12. Schein, E. H. (1990). *Career Anchors: Discovering Your Real Values* (rev. ed.). San Diego, CA: Pfeiffer; Moore, D. (1999). Women entrepreneurs: Approaching a new millennium. In G. Powell (Ed.), *Handbook of Gender and Work* (pp. 371–390). Thousand Oaks, London & New Delhi: Sage.

13. Moore, D. P., & Moore, J. L. (1999) Networking: An interactive approach to threshold management. In S. Kunkel & J. Richards (Eds.), *United States Association for Small Business and Entrepreneurship—Sailing the Entrepreneurial Wave into the Twenty-first Century Proceedings,* pp. 519–534.

14. Granfield, M. (1993, June). Till debt do us part, How entrepreneurial couples—one of the fastest-growing small-business categories—keep their marriages and companies thriving. *Working Woman,* pp. 33–35; Bamford, J. (1995, May). The Working Woman fifty: America's top women business owners. *Working Woman,* pp. 37–45.

15. Marshack, K. (1998). *Entrepreneurial Couples: Making It Work at Work and at Home.* Palo Alto, CA: Davies-Black, 24. Specifically see: Knutson, D. (1994). Characteristics of business by gender [Online]. Available: http://www.census.gov/agfs/ gender/gend_res.htm [U.S. Census Bureau, Office of Statistics, revised April 24, 1997]. Foley, S., & Powell, G. N. (1997) have addressed important gaps that occur in business and marriage partner relationships as they impact the success of the business in a proposed model. Reconceptualizing work-family conflict for business/marriage partners: A theoretical model. *Journal of Small Business Management, 35*(4), 36–47.

16. Bamford, The Working Woman fifty; Chun, J. (1997, October). Entrepreneurial woman. *Entrepreneur,* p. 58.

17. Wiesendanger, B. (1999, May). Labors of love: 1999 Entrepreneurial Excellence Award Winners. *Working Woman,* pp. 46–47. There were 1,000 nominees for the seven awards.

18. F. N. Schwartz (1989). Management women and the new facts of life. *Harvard Business Review, 72*(1), 65–76. Cite from Brett, J. M. (1997). Family, sex, and career advancement. In S. Parasuraman, & J. H. Greenhaus (Eds.), *Integrating Work and Family: Challenges and Choices for a Changing World* (@ p. 149). Westport, CT: Greenwood Publishing.

19. Brush, C. (1992). Research on women business owners: Past trends, a new perspective and future directions. *Entrepreneurship Theory and Practice, 16*(4), 5–30.

20. See Moore & Buttner, *Women Entrepreneurs.* (See Corporate Climbers, pp. xiv, 3–4, 18, 52, 70–71).

21. Ragins, B. R., Townsend, B., & Mattis, M. (1998). Gender gap in the executive suite: CEOs and female executives report on breaking the glass ceiling. *Academy of Management Executive, 12*(1), 28–42.

22. Lancaster, H. (1996, August 13). Managing your career. *Wall Street Journal,* p. B1.

23. Touby, L. (1992, September). Starting a business on the side. *Working Woman,* pp. 44, 48, 103, citing Philip Holland, author of *How to Start a Business Without Quitting Your Job: The Moonlight Entrepreneur's Guide.*

24. For information on the interrelationship between organizational transitions and careers see Guest, D., Davey, K. M., & Prentice, G. (1996, February 22). Don't write off the traditional career. *People Management, 2*(4), 22–26.

25. Nicholson, N. (1996). Career systems in crisis: Change and opportunity in the information age. *Academy of Management Executive, 10*(4), 40–51.

26. For definition of broadbanding see Hequest, M. (1995, April). Flat and happy? *Training, 32*(4), 29–35. For additional information on broadbanding and career-banding see Tyler, K. (April, 1998). Compensation strategies can foster lateral moves and growing in place. *HRMagazine, 43*(5), 64–71.

27. Harvey, M., & Evans, R. (1995). Strategic windows in the entrepreneurial process. *Journal of Business Venturing, 10*(5), 331–347; Sullivan, The changing nature of careers.

28. Schneer, J. A., & Reitman, F. (1997). The interrupted managerial career path: A longitudinal study of MBAs. *Journal of Vocational Behavior, 51*, 411–434.

29. Lyness, K. S., & Thompson, D. E. (1997). Above the glass ceiling? A comparison of matched samples of female and male executives. *Journal of Applied Psychology, 82*(3), 359–375 (@ pp. 361, 367).

30. Brousseau, K. R., Driver, M. J., Eneroth, K., & Larsson, R. (1996). Career pandemonium: Realigning organizations and individuals. *Academy of Management Executive, 10*(4), 52–66.

31. Arthur, M. B., Hall, D. T., and Lawrence, B. S. (1989) Generating new directions in career theory: The case for a multi-disciplinary approach. In M. B. Arthur, D. T. Hall, & B. S. Lawrence, *Handbook of Career Theory* (p. 8). Cambridge, England: Cambridge University Press.

32. The term is from Cox & Jennings, The foundations of success.

33. Kanter, Careers and the wealth of nations.

34. Allred, B. B., Snow, C. C., & Miles, R. E. (1996). Characteristics of managerial careers in the twenty-first century. *Academy of Management Executive, 10*(4), 17–27.

35. Alfus, M. (2000). The Experiences and Lessons of a 20th Century Entrepreneur: How Relevant in the Next Millennium? United States Association of Small Business and Entrepreneurship/SBIDA-2000 Plenary Address, Feb. 18, 2000, San Antonio. http://www.USABE.ORG/CONFERENCES2000/PLENARY.HTM, p. 3.

36. Brush, C. G. (1992). Research on women business owners: Past trends, a new perspective, and future choices. *Entrepreneurship Theory and Practice, 16*, 5–30; Powell, G. N., & Mainiero, L. A. (1992). Cross currents in the river of time: Conceptualizing the complexities of women's careers. *Journal of Management, 18*, 215–237; Powell, G. N., and Mainiero, L. A. (1993). Getting ahead in career and life. In G. N. Powell (Ed.), *Women and Men in Management* (pp. 215–237). Thousand Oaks, CA: Sage.

Chapter 2

1. Moore, D. P., Buttner, E. H., & Rosen, B. (1992). Stepping off the corporate track: The entrepreneurial alternative. In U. Sekaran & F. Leong (Eds.), *Womenpower: Managing in Times of Demographic Turbulence* (pp. 85–110; @ p. 86). Thousand Oaks, CA: Sage.

2. Women's pay went from 64 percent of men's to over 80 percent, with young, childless professional workers of either sex working full-time often getting similar wages. Beck, B. (1998). Women and work: For better, for worse. *The Economist* (London), *348*(8077), 3–13 (@ p. 7).

3. Lyness, K. S., & Thompson, D. E. (1997). Above the glass ceiling? A comparison of matched samples of female and male executives. *Journal of Applied Psychology, 82*(3), 359–375. Catalyst. 1996. Census of women corporate officers and top earners. New York: Catalyst, as cited by B. R. Ragins, B. Townsend, & M. Mattis (1998) in Gender gap in the executive suite: CEOs and female executives report on breaking the glass ceiling. *Academy of Management Executive, 12*(1), 28–42 (@ p. 28).

4. Taylor, A., III. (1986, August 18). Why women managers are bailing out, *Fortune,* pp. 16-23. The term "glass ceiling" entered the lexicon with the publication of Morrison, A., White, R. P., & Van Velsor, E. (1988). *Breaking the Glass Ceiling: Can Women Reach the Top of America's Largest Corporations?* Reading, MA: Addison-Wesley; Lyness & Thompson. Above the glass ceiling?, p. 359.

5. Ragins, Townsend, & Mattis, Gender gap in the executive suite, p. 29. The authors cite the study of Korn/Ferry International. (1993). Decade of the executive woman. New York: [Author: Korn/Ferry International Federal Glass Ceiling Commission.] (1995). Good for business: Making full use of the nation's human capital. Washington, DC: U.S. Government Printing Office.

6. Kalleberg, A. L., Kooke, D., Marsden, P.V., & Spaeth, J. L. (1996). *Organizations in America: Analyzing Their Structures and Human Resource Practices.* Based on the National Organizations Study, Thousand Oaks, CA: Sage (pp. 276–300).

7. Kroeger, B. (1994, July). The road less rewarded, *Working Woman,* pp. 50–53, 82–83, citing Reaskin, B. and Roos, P. (1990). *Job Queues, Gender Queues.*

8. Kalleberg, Kooke, Marsden, & Spaeth, *Organizations in America,* pp. 276-300.

9. Helgesen, S. (1990). *The Female Advantage: Women's Ways of Leadership.* New York: Doubleday; Austin. (1992, March). When you're the new boss, *Working Woman,* p. 42.

10. Lindsay, C., & Pasquali, J. (1993). The wounded feminine: From organizational abuse to personal healing. *Business Horizons, 36*(2), 35–41; Gilson, E., & Kane, S. (1987). *Unnecessary Choices: The Hidden Life of the Executive Woman.* New York: Paragon House; Ely, R. (1995). The power in demography: Women's social construction of gender identity at work. *Academy of Management Journal, 38*(3), 589–634.

11. Ragins, Townsend, & Mattis, Gender gap in the executive suite; Safian, K., & Thomas, A. (1999, February 10). Climate for women in business relatively un-changed: Survey of top women in finance indicates mixed progress on key issues [Padilla Speer Beardsley Inc., New York Financial Women's Association, www.fwa.org.].

12. Jacobs, J.A. (1999). The sex segregation of occupations. In G. Powell (Ed.), *Handbook of Gender and Work* (pp. 125–144). Thousand Oaks, London, & New Delhi: Sage.

13. Carli. L. L., & Eagly, A. H. (1999). Gender effects on social influence and emergent leadership. In G. Powell (Ed.), *Handbook of Gender and Work* (pp. 203–222). Thousand Oaks, London, & New Delhi: Sage.

14. Ragins, Townsend, & Mattis, Gender gap in the executive suite.

15. Powell, G. N. (1999). Reflections on the glass ceiling: Recent trends and future prospects. In G. Powell (Ed.), *Handbook of Gender and Work* (pp. 325–345). Thousand Oaks, London, & New Delhi: Sage.

16. Maier, M. (1999). On the gendered substructure of organization: Dimensions and dilemmas of corporate masculinity. In G. Powell (Ed.), *Handbook of Gender and Work* (pp. 69–94). Thousand Oaks, London, & New Delhi: Sage.

17. Catalyst, the National Foundation for Women Business Owners (NFWBO), with support of the Committee 200 Foundation. (1998). *Women Entrepreneurs: Why Companies Lose Female Talent and What They Can Do About It.* New York: Catalyst, 43 pages. [References for leaving organization given on p. 13. In the private sector these are flexibility, 51%; glass ceiling, 29%; unhappy with work environment, 28%; unchallenged, 22%. See p. 22 for change in percentage of women starting businesses with an entrepreneurial idea: 20+ years = 51%; 10 to 19 years = 48%; and less than ten years = 35%.]

18. Moore, D. P., & Buttner, E. H. (1997). *Women Entrepreneurs: Moving Beyond the Glass Ceiling.* Thousand Oaks, CA: Sage.

19. Abelson, R. (1999, August 22). A push from the top shatters a glass ceiling. *New York Times,* pp. 1, 23.

20. Gatewood, E. J., Shaver, K. G., & Gartner, W. B. (1995). A longitudinal study of cognitive factors influencing start-up behaviors and success at venture creation. *Journal of Business Venturing, 10*(5), 371–391; Fagenson, E. (1993). Personal value systems of men and women entrepreneurs versus managers. *Journal of Business Venturing, 8*(5), 409–430. Brush, C. G., & Bird, B. J. (1996). Leadership vision of successful women entrepreneurs: Dimensions and characteristics. In W. D. Bygrave, B. J. Bird, S. Birley, N. C. Churchill, M. G. Hay, R. H. Kelley, & W. E. Wetzel, Jr. (Eds.), *Frontiers of Entrepreneurship Research* (Summary). Babson Park, MA: Center for Entrepreneurial Studies, Babson College; Srinivasan, R., Woo, C. Y., & Cooper, A. C. (1994). Performance determinants for male and female entrepreneurs. In W. D. Bygrave, S. Birley, N. C. Churchill, E. Gatewood, F. Hoy, R. Keeley, & W. E. Wetzel, Jr. (Eds.), *Frontiers of Entrepreneurship Research* (pp. 43–56). Babson Park, MA: Center for Entrepreneurial Studies, Babson College; National Foundation for Women Business Owners. (1994). *Styles of success.* Washington, DC.

21. Catalyst, National Foundation for Women Business Owners, with support of the Committee 200 Foundation (1998, February). *Paths to Entrepreneurship: New Directions for Women in Business.* New York: Catalyst [Sponsored by Salomon Smith Barney] (p. 3); Srinivasan, Woo, & Cooper, Performance determinants for male and female entrepreneurs.

22. Srinivasan, Woo, & Cooper. Performance determinants for male and female entrepreneurs; Gundry, L. K., Kowlake, C., & Robertson, B. L. (1992). Women-owned businesses in start-up and growth stages: A comparison of information needs and performance. In D. Naffziger & J. Hornsby (Eds.), *United States Association of Small Business & Entrepreneurship Proceedings: Emerging Entrepreneurial Strategies in the 1990s* (pp. 184–191). Chicago.

23. Drucker, P. F. (1999, March-April). Managing oneself. *Harvard Business Review,* pp. 65–72.

24. Brush, C. (1992). Research on women business owners: Past trends, a new perspective and future directions. *Entrepreneurship Theory and Practice, 16*(4), 5–30; Fischer, E. M., Reuber, A. R., & Dyke, L. S. (1993). A theoretical overview and extension of research on sex, gender, and entrepreneurship. *Journal of Business Venturing, 8*(2), 151–168; Cooper, A. C., Woo, C., & Dunkelberg, W. (1989). Entrepreneurship and the initial size of firms.

25. Moore & Buttner, *Women Entrepreneurs,* pp. 76–78.

26. Moore & Buttner, *Women Entrepreneurs,* pp. 29–30.

27. Sharp, C., & Sharp, D. (1999) argue this is the case. Cited in Sanders, D. (C.M.) (Ed.) (1999). Study shows women who are unhappy with corporate life plan to start own businesses. *Women in Management, 9*(2), 1–3. [Richard Ivey School of Business: The University of Western Ontario, London, Canada, N6A 3K7. Moore & Buttner, *Women Entrepreneurs,* disagree.]

28. For example: Atlas, J. (1999, July 19). Annals of education. The million-dollar diploma. The Harvard Business School struggles to remain worth it in the era of instant high-tech fortunes. *New Yorker,* pp. 42–51.

29. Fisher, A., & Moskowitz, M. (1998, January 12). The 100 best companies to work for in America. *Fortune, 137*(1) 69–74; Martinez, N. (1998). An inside look at making the grade. *HRMagazine, 43*(3), 61–67. [Moskowitz and Levering have been tracking the best places to work since 1981.]

30. Catalyst (1998). *Advancing Women in Business—The Catalyst Guide—Best Practices from the Corporate Leaders.* San Francisco: Jossey-Bass (@ pp. 66–67).

31. DiDio, L. (1998). Crashing the glass ceiling. *Computerworld, 32*(4), 72–75.

32. Brush & Hisrich, Strategic origins impact on growth; Cooper, Woo, & Dunkelberg, Entrepreneurship and the initial size of firms.

33. Moore & Buttner, *Women Entrepreneurs,* p. 54.

34. Ragins, B. R., & Sundstrom, E. (1989). Gender and power in organizations. *Psychological Bulletin,* pp. 105, 51-88; Moore & Buttner, *Women Entrepreneurs,* pp. 55–56.

35. Ragins, B. R. (1999). Gender and mentoring relationships: A review and research agenda for the next decade. In G. N. Powell (Ed.), *Handbook of Gender and Work* (pp. 347–370). Thousand Oaks, CA: Sage.

36. Catalyst, National Foundation for Women Business Owners, with support of the Committee 200 Foundation (1998, February). *Paths to Entrepreneurship: New Directions for Women in Business* [Sponsored by Salomon Smith Barney]. New York: Catalyst.

37. Moore & Buttner, *Women Entrepreneurs,* pp. 59–60.

38. Small Business Administration (1998, June 4). *Avon Survey Reveals Mentoring Matters.* New York: Online Women's Business Center [www.onlinewbc.org]. Over 2,000 men and women were surveyed.

39. Moore & Buttner, *Women Entrepreneurs,* p. 57.

40. Moore & Buttner, *Women Entrepreneurs,* p. 61.

41. Drucker, P. F. (1985). *Innovation and Entrepreneurship.* New York: Harper & Row; Hambrick, D. C., & Crozier, L. M. (1985). Stumblers and stars in the management of rapid growth. *Journal of Business Venturing, 1,* 31–45; Fagenson, Personal value systems of men and women entrepreneurs versus managers; Sharp, C., & Sharp, D. (see note 27 above), 1; Moore & Buttner, *Women Entrepreneurs,* p. 68; Duchesneau & Gartner, A profile of new venture success and failure in an emerging industry; Daily, C., & Dalton, D. Financial performance of founder-managed versus professionally managed small corporations. *Journal of Small Business Management, 30*(2), 25–34.

42. van Oldenborgh, M. (1992). Making it to the executive suite. *International Business, 5*(7), 54–60; Guy, M. E. (1994). Organizational architecture, gender and

women's careers. *Review of Public Personnel Administration, 14*(2), 77–90; Blum, T. C., Fields, D. L., & Goodman, J. S. (1994). Organization-level determinants of women in management. *Academy of Management Journal, 37*(2), 241–268; Hill, R. J. (1993). Women and work—Is the glass ceiling coming down? *Risk Management, 40*(7), 26–34; Moore & Buttner, *Women Entrepreneurs,* p. 60.

43. It is advisable to not only look at *Fortune's* list of 100 Best Companies to Work For in 1998, but to compare it with the most recent listings. The reports are usually issued around the first of the year. Fisher & Moskowitz, The 100 best companies to work for in America. Branch, S. (1999, January 11). The 100 best companies to work for in America. *Fortune, 139*(1) 118–144. For future reference you may also check www.fortune.com; Wilburn, D. A. (1998, October). 100 best companies for working mothers—Our thirteenth annual survey. *Working Mother,* pp. 14–96 (@ pp. 15, 17); Advancing Women (1998). 1998 Catalyst award winners—Proctor & Gamble and Sara Lee Corporation [http://www.advancingwomen.com/cataward.html], pp. 1-3; Wellington, S. W. (Foreword) (1998). *Advancing Women in Business—The Catalyst Guide, Best Practices from the Corporate Leaders.* San Francisco: Jossey-Bass; Cleaver, J. (1998). 25 top leading companies for women. *Working Woman, 23*(8), 50–64.

44. Wilburn, 100 best companies for working mothers, pp. 15, 17. See also references listed in above note.

45. Advancing Women, 1998 Catalyst award winners; *Advancing women in business—The Catalyst guide, best practices from the corporate leaders.*

46. Cleaver, 25 top leading companies for women.

47. For example, you can locate a host of online financial data finders [http://www.cob. ohio-state.edu/dept/fin/osudata.htm]. From this site you can click onto the Annual Report Gallery, a complete listing of annual reports published on the Internet with links to many company home pages, and also find DataMerge Financing Resources for Entrepreneurs, Dun & Bradstreet, and other worthwhile financial company data. The Career Development Center—Using Annual Reports to Research a Company [www.wpi.edu/Admin/Depts/CDC/Workshops/ann_rep.html] provides some excellent guidelines on how you can use annual reports to assess the present status of a career option or transition at a particular company. You can then go to the Online Women's Business Center, United States Small Business Administration, to identify links to Internet sites with the information you need, i.e., banking and finance, business magazines, business news, company research, women on the Internet, women's associations, and women's business [www.onlinewbc.org/ docs/links.html]. In each area you can click on the web site to get additional information. For example, finance: JP Morgan, www.jpmorgan.com, will take you immediately to the home page.

48. The Online Women's Business Center, the United States Small Business Administration, will assist in identifying a comprehensive list of links to Internet sites that includes all the major classifications of information you will need, i.e., banking and finance, business magazines, business news, company research, women on the Internet, women's associations, women's business [www.onlinewbc.org/docs/links.html] to use as resources in starting a business. Also visit each of the guidance pages provided by the center. In addition, you may return to earlier chapters of this book for specific information and resources.

Chapter 3

1. Gladwell, M. (1999, January 11). Six degrees of Lois Weisberg. *New Yorker*, pp. 52–62.

2. Moore, D. P., & Buttner, E. H. (1997), *Women Entrepreneurs: Moving Beyond the Glass Ceiling.* Thousand Oaks, CA: Sage, p. 126; Tjosvold, D., & Weicker, D. (1993). Cooperative and competitive networking by entrepreneurs: A critical incident study. *Journal of Small Business Management, 31*(1), 11–21.

3. Jacobs, M. A. (1997, March 4). "New girl" network is boon for women lawyers. *Wall Street Journal,* p. B1; Krackhardt, D., & Hanson, J. R. (1993, July-August). Informal networks: The company behind the chart. *Harvard Business Review,* pp. 104–111; Barbieri, S. M. (1993, August). How to win allies and influence snakes—Office politics in the nicer '90s. *Working Woman,* pp. 34–37.

4. Baker, T., Aldrich, H. E., & Liou, N. (1997). Invisible entrepreneurs: The neglect of women business owners by mass media and scholarly journals in the USA. *Entrepreneurship & Regional Development, 9,* 221–238 (@ p. 235); Cromie, S., & Birley, S. (1992). Networking by female business owners in Northern Ireland. *Journal of Business Venturing, 7*(3), 237–252, (@ p. 238); Moore, D. P. (1990). An examination of present research on the female entrepreneur: Suggested research strategies for the 1990s. *Journal of Business Ethics, 9*(4/5), 275–281 (@ p. 734).

5. Hays, C. L. (1997, November 14). Focus for MBAs turns to women: Harvard's case studies will include more female executives. *New York Times,* p. A14. See also Ruder, D. B. (1998, June 4). Kennedy school, business school develops women-related case studies. *Harvard University Gazette* website [http://www.news.harvard.edu/gazette]; Mallory, M. (1996, February 19). From the ground up—Women entrepreneurs build businesses and create jobs in a soft economy, U.S. News Online: Business, [www.usnews.com/usnews/issue/woman.htm], pp. 1–5 (@ p. 3).

6. Parker, S. G. (1998, September 15). Putting women front and center at Harvard Business School [http://ad.adsmart.net/accipiter/adclick.exe/SITE=Womenconnect/ AREA=Womenconnect.Business].

7. Moore & Buttner, *Women Entrepreneurs,* pp. 146–147.

8. Brass, D. J. (1985). Men's and women's networks: A study of interaction patterns and influence in an organization. *Academy of Management Journal, 28,* 518–539; Kanter, R. M. (1977). *Men and Women of the Corporation.* New York: Basic Books.

9. Barbieri, How to win allies and influence snakes, pp. 36–37.

10. Ibarra, H. (1993). Personal networks of women and minorities in management: A conceptual framework. *Academy of Management Review, 18*(1), 56–87; Ibarra, H. (1995). Race, opportunity, and diversity of social circles in managerial networks. *Academy of Management Journal, 38*(3), 673–703; Smeltzer and Fann (1989) (p. 25).

11. Washer, L. (1992, November). The best franchises for women: Fifteen companies that stand out for their integrity and support of women business owners. *Working Woman,* pp. 73–75, 97–101 (@ p. 74).

12. Cohen, C. E. (1994, May). Making the leap to entrepreneur. *Working Woman,* pp. 67–68.

13. Cohen, Making the leap to entrepreneur; Lancaster, H. (1996, October 1). Managing your career. *Wall Street Journal,* p. B1.

14. Moore & Buttner, *Women Entrepreneurs,* pp. 126–127.

15. Moore & Buttner, *Women Entrepreneurs,* p. 134.

16. Farnham, A. (1996, January 16). *Fortune,* p. 3.

17. Brown, C. M. (1995). A network of opportunities. *Black Enterprise, 25*(12), 40.

18. Moore & Buttner, *Women Entrepreneurs*, pp. 126–127.

19. Shulruff, L. (1992, December). Blood and money: The perils and payoffs that come with working in a family-owned business. *Working Woman,* pp. 49, 52.

20. Shellenbarger, S. (1996, May 29). Work and family: Five friends get the lift they need from a girl's night out. *Wall Street Journal,* p. B1.

21. Olm, K., Carsrud, A., & Alvey, L. (1988). The role of networks in new venture funding for the female entrepreneur: A continuing analysis. In B. Kirchhoff, W. Long, W. McMullen, K. Vesper, & W. Wetzel, Jr. (Eds.), *Frontiers of Entrepreneurship Research* (pp. 658–659). Wellesley, MA: Center for Entrepreneurial Studies, Babson College; Moore & Buttner, *Women Entrepreneurs,* pp. 118–120.

22. Moore & Buttner, *Women Entrepreneurs,* pp. 141–142.

23. Simurda, S. J. (1993, October). Five best business areas for women. *Working Woman,* pp. 30–38.

24. For networking tips see: Texas Center for Women's Business Enterprise, Austin, TX, Online Women's Business Center, (1997, June). Networking—the key to lifetime work, [www.onlinewbc.org/docs/manage/networking.html], pp. 1–3. Also see tips provided by the U.S. Small Business Administration, Office of Women's Business Ownership. (1998). *The Right Stuff: Evaluating Your Entrepreneurial Potential. Blueprint for Success: A Guide for Women Entrepreneurs* [Publication sponsored by Salomon Smith Barney], Ch. 1, p. 7 [online wbc.org/docs/whats_new/index.html].

25. Lerner, M., Brush, C., & Hisrich, R. (1997). Israeli women entrepreneurs: An examination of factors affecting performance. *Journal of Business Venturing, 12*(4), 315–339.

26. Applegate, J. (1994, February). Teaming up your business advisors. *Working Woman,* p. 55.

27. Moore & Buttner, *Women Entrepreneurs,* pp. 138–139.

28. National Foundation for Women Business Owners. (1994). New study quantifies thinking and management style differences between women and men business owners [http://www.NFWBO.org/rr003.htm] [press release, 1994, July 19]; Van Auken, H. E., Rittenburg, T. L., Doran, B. M., & Hsieh, S. F. (1994). An empirical analysis of advertising by women entrepreneurs. *Journal of Small Business Management, 32*(3), 11–28.

29. Andre, R. (1995). Diversity in executive networks: A national study of women's representation in private sector economic development. *Journal of Managerial Issues, 7*(3), 306–332.

30. Ibarra, H. (1993). Personal networks of women and minorities in management: A conceptual framework. *Academy of Management Review, 18*(1), 56–87.

31. Linn, S. (1990, July/August). Network news: Master the art of networking. *Entrepreneurial Woman,* pp. 90–93.

32. Moore & Buttner, *Women Entrepreneurs,* pp. 129–130.

33. Moore & Buttner, *Women Entrepreneurs,* p. 131.

34. Ericksen, G. K. (1997). Ernst & Young entrepreneur of the year success stories: How renowned entrepreneurs turned ideas into breakthrough success (Excerpted by Erickson from *What's Luck Got to Do With It? 12 Entrepreneurs Reveal the Secrets Behind Their Success.*) John Wiley & Sons [www.ey.com/industry/entrepreneur/eoy/magazine/success.asp], 8 pages, @ p.1.

35. Harding, F. (1996, May). How to build a network. *Journal of Accountacy,* pp. 79–82; Moore & Buttner, *Women Entrepreneurs,* p. 128.

36. Moore & Buttner, *Women Entrepreneurs,* p. 126.

37. Moore & Buttner, *Women Entrepreneurs,* pp. 134–135.

38. Cromie & Birley. (1992). Networking by female business owners in Northern Ireland. *Journal of Business Venturing,* 7(3), 237–252; National Foundation for Women Business Owners (1996, May 24). Women business owners: Leaders in volunteerism [http://www.NFWBO.org/ao19710.htm] [Press release].

39. Moore & Buttner, *Women Entrepreneurs,* pp. 144–145.

40. The countries are Argentina, Australia, Brazil, Canada, France, Germany, Greece, Hong Kong, India, Ireland, Italy, Japan, Malaysia, Norway, Philippines, Poland, Portugal, Scotland, Singapore, Sweden, South Africa, Taiwan, Thailand, United Kingdom, and United States.

41. U.S. Department of Commerce, (1996). SBA Office of Advocacy facts about small business—1996. [http://www.sba.gov/ADVO/stats/fact1.html], pp. 1–6.

42. Moore & Buttner, *Women Entrepreneurs,* p. 117.

Chapter 4

1. Hellriegel, D., Slocum, J. W., Jr., & Woodman, R. W. (1998). *Organizational Behavior* (8th ed.). Cincinnati, OH: South-Western College Publishing, pp. 299–359.

2. Yukl, G., & VanFleet, D. D. (1992). Theory and research on leadership in organizations. In M. D. Dunnette & L. M. Hough (Eds.), *Handbook of Industrial and Organizational Psychology* (Vol. 3) (pp. 147–198). Palo Alto, CA: Davies-Black.

3. Kouzes, J. M., & Posner, B. Z. (1995). *The Leadership Challenge.* San Francisco: Jossey-Bass; Spreitzer, G. M. (1996). Social structural characteristics of psychological empowerment. *Academy of Management Journal, 39,* 483–502; Hooijberg, R. A. (1996). A multidimensional approach toward leadership: An extension of the concept of behavioral complexity. *Human Relations, 49,* 917–946; Hellriegel, Slocum, & Woodman, *Organizational Behavior,* p. 301.

4. Council of Economic Advisors, 1998, Table B-40; Lynch, M., & Post, K. (1996). What glass ceiling? *The Public Interest, 124,* 27–37. [htt://web7.searchbank.com/infotra..., 6 pages, @ p. 5-6 on website.] Statistics also based on recent releases of information from the National Foundation for Women Business Owners, Catalyst, the U.S. Department of Labor, and the *Chronicle of Higher Education.*

5. Chronicle of Higher Education Almanac, 1999. Earned degrees conferred, 1994-1995. [http://www.chronicle.com/weekly/almanac/facts, p. 2.]

6. Mintzberg, H. (1974, September-October). The manager's job: Folklore and fact. *Harvard Business Review,* p. 91; Mintzberg, H. (1974, July–August). The manager's job: Folklore and fact. *Harvard Business Review,* pp. 49–61. See also Mintzberg, H. (1990, March-April). Retrospective commentary on "The Manager's Job: Folklore and Fact." *Harvard Business Review,* p. 170; Hart, S. L., & Quinn, R. E. (1993, May). Roles executives play: CEOs, behavioral complexity, and firm performance. *Human Relations,* pp. 328–342; Javidan, M., & Dastmalchian, A. (1993, September) Assessing senior executives: The impact of context on their roles. *Journal of Applied Behavioral Science,* pp. 328–342.

7. Moore, D. P., & Buttner, E. H. (1997). *Women Entrepreneurs: Moving Beyond the Glass Ceiling.* Thousand Oaks, CA: Sage (p. 183).

8. Lewis, et. al., *Management: Challenges in the Twenty-first Century,* pp. 26–28; Moore & Buttner, *Women Entrepreneurs,* p. 83.

9. Moore & Buttner, *Women Entrepreneurs,* pp. 91–92.

10. Lewis, et al., *Management: Challenges in the Twenty-first Century,* pp. 26–27.

11. Moore & Buttner, *Women Entrepreneurs,* p. 90.

12. Watson, C. (1994, April). Gender versus power as a predictor of negotiation behavior and outcomes. *Negotiation Journal,* pp. 117–127.

13. Nadler, D. A., & Tushman, M. L. (1997). *Competing by Design: The Power of Organizational Architecture,* New York: Oxford University Press (pp. 7–10).

14. Lewis, et. al., *Management: Challenges in the Twenty-first Century,* pp. 60–61; Smith, J. M. (1992, October). How I did it: Putting together a winning team. *Working Woman.* pp. 28–30.

15. Lewis, et. al., *Management, Challenges in the Twenty-first Century,* pp. 78–87.

16. Peters, T. J., & Waterman, R. H., Jr. (1982). *In Search of Excellence: Lessons from America's Best-Run Companies.* New York: Harper & Row.

17. Lewis, et al., *Management, Challenges in the Twenty-first Century,* p. 66.

18. Nadler & Tushman, *Competing by Design,* pp. 7–10; Moore & Buttner, *Women Entrepreneurs,* p. 106.

19. Austin, N. K. (1993, September). Reorganizing the organization chart. *Working Woman,* pp. 23–26, citing D. Quinn Mills, *Rebirth of the Corporation,* Michael Hammer and James Champy, *Reengineering the Corporation,* and James Belasco and Ralph Stayer, from whose *Flight of the Buffalo* the quotation is taken; Wheatley, M. J. (1994, October). Quantum management. *Working Woman,* p. 16; Holzman, D. (1993, August). When workers run the show. *Working Woman,* pp. 38–41, 72–73.

20. Isenhour, L. (1993, August). Managing in a disaster. *Working Woman,* 15–16; Vandermolen, M. (1992, November). How I did it: Shifting the corporate culture. *Working Woman,* 25.

21. Clift, E. (1992, September). The body politics. *Working Woman,* pp. 61–63, 98–99, 106; (1993, January). Clearing a new path to the top. *Working Woman,* p. 24; Lewis et al., *Management: Challenges in the Twenty-first Century,* p. 66; Sellers, P. (1997, September 8). Don't mess with Darla. *Fortune, 136*(5), 63–72. Invited to address the South Carolina General Assembly the next year after donating $20 million to the University of South Carolina School of Business (now named for her), she took the occasion to blast the legislators for the state's laggard support of public education.

22. Eagley, A., & Johnson, B. (1990). Gender and leadership style: A meta-analysis. *Psychological Bulletin, 108*(2), 233–256, Coppolina, Y., & Seath, C. B. (1987). Women managers: Fitting the moulding or moulding the fit. *Equal Opportunity International, 6*(3), 4–10; Korabik, K., (1982). Sex-role orientation and leadership style. *International Journal of Women's Studies, 5,* 328–336; Gilligan, C. (1982). *In a Different Voice.* Cambridge, MA: Harvard University Press; Desjardins, C. (1989, June). Gender issues in community college leadership. *American Association of Women in Community and Junior College Journal;* Fagenson, E. (1993). Personal value systems of men and women entrepreneurs versus managers. *Journal of Business*

Venturing, 8(5), 409–430; Fagenson, F. (1986). Women's work orientations: Something old something new. *Group and Organization Studies, 11,* 75–100.

23. Parker, S. G. (1998, September 15). Putting women front and center at Harvard Business School. [http://ad.adsmart.net/accipiter/adclick.exe/SITE=Womenconnect /AREA= Womenconnect.Business].

24. Moore & Buttner, *Women Entrepreneurs,* p. 109. Also see Koonce, R. (1997, September). Language, sex, and power: Women and men in the workplace. *Training & Development, 51*(9), 34–40. Author cites interviews with author Deborah Tannen, who says, " . . . women view conversation as a way to connect. . . [It] is about finding commonality and building networks of connection and intimacy."

25. Moore & Buttner, *Women Entrepreneurs,* p. 109.

26. Kaye, E. (1993, October). The face of power. *Working Woman,* pp. 50–53.

27. Gaines, L. (1994, November/December). When women managers talk and men don't listen. *Executive Female,* pp. 11-16.

28. Rosener, J. (1990, November-December). Ways women lead. *Harvard Business Review,* pp. 119–125.

29. Billard, M. (1992, March). Do women make better managers? *Working Woman,* pp. 68–71, 106–107; Austin, N. K. (1992, January). Leadership seminars: The good, the bad and the baloney. *Working Woman,* p. 22; Sellar, N. (1999). Financial Women's Association, 215 Park Avenue South, New York, NY 10003. See also New York Business Wire, Feb. 10, 1999, Climate for women in business relatively unchanged: Survey of top women in finance indicates mixed progress on key issues. AOLNews@aol.com.

30. Kelly, R. M. (1991). *The Gendered Economy: Work, Careers, and Success.* Thousand Oaks, CA: Sage (pp. 99–103); Watson, C. (1994, April). Gender versus power as a predictor of negotiation behavior and outcomes. *Negotiation Journal,* pp. 117–127.

31. Seyegorf, J. (1995, August). Confessions of a reengineered manager. *Working Woman,* p. 19.

32. Watson, Gender versus power as a predictor of negotiation behavior and outcomes.

33. Konek, C., & Kitch, S. (1994). *Women and Careers: Issues and Challenges.* Thousand Oaks, CA: Sage; Hardesty, S., & Jacobs, N. (1986). *Success and Betrayal: The Crisis of Women in Corporate America.* New York: Franklin Watts.

34. Helgesen, S. (1990). *The Female Advantage: Women's Ways of Leadership.* New York: Doubleday; Helgesen, S. (1995). *The Web of Inclusion.* New York: Currency Doubleday; Mintzberg, H. (1973). *The Nature of Managerial Work.* New York: Harper & Row; Yammarino, F. J., Dubinsky, A. J., Comer, L. B., & Jolson, M. A. (1997). Women and transformational and contingent reward leadership: A multiple-levels-of-analysis perspective. *Academy of Management Journal, 40*(1), 205–222; National Foundation for Women Business Owners. New study quantifies thinking and management style differences between women and men business owners. [http://www.NFWBO.org/rr003.htm] [NFWBO press release (1994, July 19), 2.]

35. Moore & Buttner, *Women Entrepreneurs,* pp. 106–107; Gilligan, *In a Different Voice.*

36. Sashkin, M., & Burke, W. (1990). Understanding and assessing leadership. In K. Clark & M. Clark (Eds.), *Measures of Leadership* (pp. 297-325). Greensboro, NC: Center for Creative Leadership; Kouzes, J. M., & Posner, B. Z. (1987). *The Leadership Challenge.* San Francisco: Jossey-Bass; Hellriegel, D., Slocum, J. W., Jr., & Woodman, R. W. (1998). *Organizational Behavior* (8th ed.). Cincinnati, OH: South-Western College Publishing (pp. 344–349); Bass, B. (1985). *Leadership and*

Performance Beyond Expectations. New York: Free Press; Bass, B. (1990). From transactional to transformational leadership: Learning to share the vision. *Organizational Dynamics, 18,* 19–31; Schein, E. H. (1983). The role of the founder in creating organizational culture. *Organizational Dynamics, 12*(1), 13–28; Parsons, T. (1960). *Structure and Process in Modern Societies.* New York: Free Press; Kelly, R. M. (1991). *The Gendered Economy;* Powell, G. (1993). Women and Men in Management (2nd ed.). Thousand Oaks, CA: Sage.

37. For a review of the literature see Moore & Buttner, pp. 99–101; Bycio, Hackett, & Allen, 1995; Brush, C. G., & Bird, B. J. (1996). Leadership vision of successful women entrepreneurs: Dimensions and characteristics. In W. D. Bygrave, B. J. Bird, S. Birley, N. C. Churchill, M. G. Hay, R. H. Keeley, & W. E. Wetzel, Jr. (Eds.), *Frontiers of Entrepreneurship Research* (Summary). Babson Park, MA: Center for Entrepreneurial Studies, Babson College.

38. Luthans, F., Envick, B. R., & Anderson, R.D. (1995). The need for achievement and organizational commitment of entrepreneurs: A gender comparison. In W. D. Bygrave, B. J. Bird, S. Birley, N. C. Churchill, M. G. Hay, R. H. Keeley, & W. E. Wetzel, Jr. (Eds.), *Frontiers of Entrepreneurship Research* (pp. 379–380). Babson Park, MA: Center for Entrepreneurial Studies, Babson College. According to Luthans, Envick, & Anderson, the need for achievement is significantly lower for women than for men, though their commitment to enterprise is similar. Parasuraman, S., Purohit, Y. S., & Godshalk, V. M. (1996). Work and family variables, entrepreneurial career success, and psychological well being. *Journal of Vocational Behavior, 48,* 275–300; Srinivasan, R., Woo, C. Y., Cooper, A.C. (1994). Performance determinants for male and female entrepreneurs. In W. D. Bygrave, S. Birley, N. C. Churchill, E. Gatewood, F. Hoy, R. Keeley, & W. E. Wetzel, Jr. (Eds.), *Frontiers of Entrepreneurship Research* (pp. 43–56). Babson Park, MA: Center for Entrepreneurial Studies, Babson College.

39. Podsakoff, P. M., MacKenzie, S. B., & Bommer, W. H. (1996). Transformational leader behaviors and substitutes for leadership as determinants of employee satisfaction, commitment, trust, and organizational citizenship behaviors. *Journal of Management, 22,* 259–299.

40. Moore & Buttner, *Women Entrepreneurs,* pp. 111, 105.

41. White, B., Cox, C., & Cooper, C. (1992). *Women's career development. A study of high flyers.* Cambridge, MA: Blackwell; Larwood, L., Falbe, C. M., Kriger, M. P., & Missing, P. (1995). Structure and meaning of organizational vision. *Academy of Management Journal, 38,* 740–769; National Foundation for Women Business Owners. (1998). NFWBO News, No. 1—Women business owners give priority to retirement plans [http://www.NFWBO.org/News9801.htm#980101] [Press release, 1998, March.]

42. National Foundation for Women Business Owners (1996). Women business owners: Leaders in volunteerism [http://www.NFWBO.org/ao19710.htm] [Press release: 1996, May 24]. National Foundation for Women Business Owners (1994). New study quantifies thinking and management style differences between women and men business owners. [http://www.NFWBO.org/rr003.htm] [NFWBO press release, 1994, July 19]; Higgins, C., & Duxbury, L. (1994). "Supportive" managers can change your life and the company's bottom line. *Western Business School's National Center for Management Research and Development's Women in Management Program Newsletter, 5*(1), 4; Goodwin, V., & Whittington, J. L. (1996, August). *A Field*

Study of a Cognitive Approach to Understanding Transformational and Transactional Leadership. Paper presented at the meeting of The Academy of Management, Cincinnati, OH; Korabik, K. (1990). Androgyny and leadership style. *Journal of Business Ethics, 9*(4), 28–290.

43. Moore & Buttner, *Women Entrepreneurs,* p. 111.

44. Billard, M. (1992, March). Do women make better managers? *Working Woman,* pp. 68–71, 106–107.

45. Moore & Buttner, *Women Entrepreneurs,* p. 110.

46. Moore & Buttner, *Women Entrepreneurs,* p. 108.

47. Helgesen, S. (1990). *The Female Advantage: Women's Ways of Leadership.* New York: Doubleday; Helgesen, S. (1995). *The Web of Inclusion.* New York: Currency Doubleday.

48. Burt, R. S. (1982). *Toward a structural theory of action.* New York: Academic Press. [Used here as cited in Ibarra, H., & Andrews, S. B. (1993). Power, social influence, and sense making: Effects of network centrality and proximity on employee perceptions. *Administrative Science Quarterly, 38,* 277–303 (@ p. 279)]; Brass, D. P. (1992). Power in organizations: A social network perspective. In G. Moore & J. Whitt (Eds.), *Research in Politics and Society* (pp. 295–323). Greenwich, CT; Ibarra, H. (1995). Race, opportunity, and diversity of social circles in managerial networks. *Academy of Management Journal, 38*(3), 673–703.

49. Moore & Buttner, *Women Entrepreneurs,* p. 106; You may wish to go to the Online Women's Business Center and assess your team-building approach on the four-item stem questionnaire to give you a sense of your style. For more accurate results you will wish to acquire an instrument with a Likert-type scale (5 to 7 points for rating) for a more accurate profile rating. See Developing your team building skills [www.onlinewbc.org/docs/manage/team.html].

50. Austin, N. K. (1994, September). What's missing from corporate cure-alls. *Working Woman,* pp. 16–19.

51. Grove, A. S. (1992, December) Manage Faster (and for Better Results). *Working Woman,* p. 24.

52. Scheele, A. (1993, January). Smarter decision making: The inability to make decisions is an automatic career killer, at any experience level. *Working Woman,* p. 22.

53. Popular publications are full of surveys offering ways to measure your leadership style. To be useful, a scale must be reliable and valid. Such scales are usually authored by professionals in the fields of business and psychology and are found only in the professional journals.

54. For an assessment of your leadership style I recommend Marshall Sashkin's validated *Leader Assessment Inventory* (1990), which permits you to measure your transactional or management style—transactional in terms of providing rewards in exchange for performance and transformational or visionary leadership. References: Sashkin, M. (1984). *The leader behavior questionnaire.* King of Prussia, PA: Organization Design and Development; Sashkin, M., & Burke, W. (1990). Understanding and assessing leadership. In K. Clark & M. Clark (Eds.), *Measures of Leadership* (pp. 297–325). Greensboro, NC: Center for Creative Leadership. Also see P. M. Poksakoff, S. B. MacKenzie, R. H. Moorman, & R. Fetter (1990), Transformational Leader Behaviors and Their Effects on Followers' Trust in Leader, Satisfaction, and Organizational Citizenship Behaviors, *Leadership Quarterly 1,* 2. 107–42.

Chapter 5

1. Most people are born with the ability to communicate in some fashion. In so doing, we are able to convey our needs and desires and assess those of other people. This is the essence of negotiation. Neale, M. A., & Bazerman, M. H. (1992). Negotiating rationally: The power and impact of the negotiator's frame. *Academy of Management Executive, 6*(3), 42–51.

2. Watson, C. (1994, April). Gender versus power as a predictor of negotiation behavior and outcomes, *Negotiation Journal*, pp. 117–127; Washer, L. (1995, March). Is bigger better? *Working Woman*, pp. 39–42, 90; Moore, D. P., & Buttner, E. H. (1997), *Women Entrepreneurs: Moving Beyond the Glass Ceiling.* Thousand Oaks, CA: Sage (p. 36).

3. Watson, Gender versus power as a predictor; For a full discussion of gender differences in the usage of power see Moore & Buttner, *Women Entrepreneurs,* pp. 106–114.

4. Lewicki, R. J. (1996). *Essentials of Negotiation.* Burr Ridge, IL: Irwin; Mintzbert, H., Dougherty, D., & Jorgensen, J. (1996, Summer). Some surprising things about collaboration: Knowing how people connect makes it work better. *Organizational Dynamics,* pp. 60–71.

5. Beck, C. E. (1999). *Managerial Communication—Bridging Theory and Practice.* Upper Saddle River, NJ: Prentice Hall (p. 283). Cited from Dangot-Simpkin, G. (1992, January). Eight attitudes to develop to hone your negotiating skills. *Supervisory Management, 37*(2), 10.

6. Pounds, M. H. (1997, August 29). Art of dealmaking demands open mind, creativity. *Sun-Sentinel,* Business Strategies, South Florida.

7. De Dreu, C. K. W., Giebels, E., & Van de Vliert, E. (1998). Social motives and trust in integrative negotiation: The disruptive effects of punitive capability. *Journal of Applied Psychology, 8*(3), 408–422; Beck, *Managerial Communication.* On page 283 Beck presents a model based on Levinger, G., & Rubin, J. Z. (1994). Bridges and barriers to a more general theory of conflict. *Negotiation Journal, 10*(3), 201–215; Perez-Greek, R. (1992, March-April). Resolving conflict. *Vibrant Life, 8,* 38–49.

8. Rubin, J. Z., Pruitt, D. G., & Kim, S. H. (1994). *Social Conflict* (2nd ed.). New York: McGraw-Hill. Cited from Brett, J. M., Shapiro, D. L., & Lytle, A. L. (1998). Breaking the bonds of reciprocity in negotiations. *Academy of Management Journal, 41*(4), 410–424 (@ p. 412).

9. Neale & Bazerman, Negotiating rationally; Lewicki, R. J., Litterer, J. A., Minton, J. W., & Saunders, D. M. (1994). *Negotiation* (2nd ed.). Boston: Irwin.

10. Adaptation by Beck, *Managerial Communication,* pp. 198–201, 294, from Dangot-Simpkin, G. (1992, January). Eight attitudes to develop to hone your negotiating skills. *Supervisory Management, 37*(2), 10. For communication elements see Gibb, J. R. (1964, September). Defensive communication. *Journal of Communication, 14*(3), 141–148, and Brett, J. M., Shapiro, D. L., & Lytle, A. L. (1998). Breaking the bonds of reciprocity in negotiations. *Academy of Management Journal, 41*(4), 410–425.

11. For a practitioner approach to negotiations see Adler, R., Rosen, B., & Silverstein, E. (1996). The art of tough negotiating: Thrust and parry. *Training & Development, 50*(3), 42–49.

12. Huber, V. L., Neale, M. A., & Northcraft, G. G. (1987). Decision bias and personnel selection strategies. *Organizational Behavior and Human Decision Processes, 40,*

136–147; Pinkley, R. L., & Northcraft, G. B. (1994). Conflict frames of reference: Implications for dispute processes and outcomes. *Academy of Management Journal, 37*(1), 193–205 (@ p. 194); Pinkley, R. (1990). Dimensions of conflict frame: Disputant interpretations of conflict. *Journal of Applied Psychology, 75,* 117–126.

13. For information on the two distinct perspectives of negotiation see Walton, R. S., & McKersie, R. B. (1965). *A Behavioral Theory of Labor Negotiations: An Analysis of a Social Interaction System.* New York: McGraw-Hill. For the integrative and distributive negotiation strategies see Tjosvold, D. (1991). *The Conflict-Positive Organization.* Reading, MA: Addison-Wesley. A more recent study of the role of cognitive ability and personality in negotiations is Barry, B., & Friedman, R. A. (1998). Bargainer characteristics in distributive and integrative negotiation, *Journal of Personality and Social Psychology, 74*(2), 345–359.

14. Pinkley & Northcraft, Conflict frames of reference, p. 201.

15. Thomas, K. W. (1992). Conflict and negotiation processes in organizations. In M. D. Dunnette & L. H. Hough, *Handbook of Industrial & Organizational Psychology* (2nd ed., Vol. 3, pp. 651–718). Palo Alto, CA: Davies-Black. Also see references to Thomas in Lewicki, R. J., Litterer, J. A., Minton, J. W., & Saunders, D. M. (1994). Negotiation (2nd ed.). Boston: Irwin (pp. 8, 330–332).

16. Thomas, K. W. (1977). Toward multidimensional values in teaching: The example of conflict behavior. *Academy of Management Review, 2,* 484–490; Thomas, K. W., & Kilmann, R. H. (1974). *Thomas-Kilmann Conflict Mode Instrument.* Palo Alto, CA: Consulting Psychologists Press. Thomas, K. W. (1976). Conflict and conflict management. In M. D. Dunnette (Ed.), *Handbook of Industrial & Organizational Psychology* (pp. 889–935). Chicago: Rand McNally; Thomas, K. W., Conflict and negotiation processes in organizations. The approaches to negotiation used by Thomas are related to the Myers-Briggs measure of personality styles and should be interpreted by understanding the importance of its validity and reliability.

17. Barry, B., & Friedman, R. A. (1998). Interpersonal relations and group processes: Bargainer characteristics in distributive and integrative negotiation. *Journal of Personality and Social Psychology, 74*(2), 345–359; For detailed coverage on distributive, integrative, and mixed bargaining processes see Lewicki, R., Minton, J. W., & Saunders, D. M. (1997). *Essentials of Negotiation.* New York: Irwin McGraw-Hill; Pinkley & Northcraft, Conflict frames of reference. Establishing trust is very important to receiving desired outcomes in the integrative bargaining process as noted in the research of De Dreu, Giebels, & Van de Vliert. Social motives and trust in integrative negotiation. See reference above to Thomas, 1992, as reported in Lewicki, et. al, *Negotiation* (2nd ed.), pp. 8, 331–332; Byrnes, J. F. (1987). Negotiating: Master the ethics. *Personnel Journal, 66*(6), 97–102.

18. Regarding the time dimension in negotiations, remember to consider "past decisions, precedents, arbitration decisions, or other objectively fair outcomes and processes that can be used as benchmarks for legitimizing the fairness of the current settlement." Cited from Lewicki, R., Minton, J. W., & Saunders, D. M. (1997). *Essentials of Negotiation.* New York: Irwin McGraw-Hill (p. 80); Mannix, E. A., Tinsley, C. H., & Bazerman, M. (1995). Negotiating over time: Impediments to integrative solutions. *Organizational Behavior and Human Decision Processes, 62*(3), 241–251. Mannix, Tinsley, & Bazerman found three steps to reaching integrative agreements across time: "Discovering that such an agreement is possible, wanting it enough to wait for it, and trusting that the short-term

sacrifice will be reciprocated by one's negotiation opponent." What appears to be important here is the level of mobility in reaching the optimal agreement.

19. Thompson, L. (1998). *The Mind and Heart of the Negotiator.* Upper Saddle River, NJ: Prentice Hall. Adapted from French & Raven (1959). The bases of social power. In D. Cartwright (Ed.), *Studies in Social Power.* Ann Arbor: University of Michigan Press.

20. Brett, Shapiro, & Lytle, Breaking the bonds of reciprocity in negotiations.

21. Brett, Shapiro, & Lytle. Breaking the bonds of reciprocity in negotiations.

22. Byrnes, J. F. (1987). Negotiating: Master the ethics. *Personnel Journal, 66*(6), 97–102.

23. Steward, J. K. (1999, August) The '99 salary survey. *Working Woman,* pp. 46–50.

24. Major, B., & Konar, E. (1984). An investigation of sex differences in pay expectations and their possible causes. *Academy of Management Journal, 17*(4), 782; Wendleton, K. (1992). *Through the Brick Wall: How to Job-Hunt in a Tight Market.* New York: Villard Books. (p. 244). Cited from Locker, K.O. (1999). *Business and Administrative Communication* (4th ed.). New York: Irwin McGraw-Hill. (p. 569).

25. Locker, K. O. (1996, July 26-27), as based on Jan Harding, *Closing the Circle: Collaboration with Recent Graduates.* Mini-Conference on Accounting and Business Communication (p. 569). Columbus, OH.

26. Pollan, S., & Levine, M. (1996, February). Asking for a lateral move. *Working Woman,* p. 57.

27. In addition to examining the text above for references to each of these negotiation styles also see Whetten, D. A., & Cameron, K. S. (1998). *Developing Management Skills.* New York: Addison-Wesley Longman (pp. 319-320, 562); Fritz, S., Brown, F. W., Lunde, J. P., & Banset, E. A. (1999). *Interpersonal Skills for Leadership.* Upper Saddle River, NJ: Prentice-Hall (pp. 208-221); Johnson, D. W., & Johnson, F. P. (1994). *Joining Together Group Theory and Group Skills.* Boston: Allyn & Bacon.

Chapter 6

1. Flamholtz, E. G. (1990). *Growing Pains—How to Make the Transition from an Entrepreneurship to a Professionally Managed Firm.* San Francisco: Jossey-Bass (p. 35); Kansas, D. (1993, October 15). Small business warm-ups: Don't believe it, "I can do it on a shoestring"—and other myths about starting a business. *Wall Street Journal,* p. R8; Carter, N. M., Williams, M., & Reynolds, P. D. (1997). Discontinuance among new firms in retail: The influence of initial resources, strategy, and gender. *Journal of Business Venturing, 12,* 126–145. The Online Women's Business Center (1999) has four web pages that help identify entrepreneurial passages: Introduction to Charted Courses [www.onlinewbc.org/docs/chart_courses/index.html]; What Stage Is My Business In? Characteristics of Developing Businesses [www.onlinewbc.org/docs/chart_courses/char.html]; Common Roadblocks for Developing Businesses [www.online wbc.org/docs/chart_courses/blocks.html]; Entrepreneurial Passages: Making the Growth Transition [www.onlinewbc.org/docs/growing/growstage.html]

2. Catalyst, National Foundation for Women Business Owners, with support of the Committee 200 Foundation (1998, February). *Paths to Entrepreneurship: New Directions for Women in Business.* New York: Catalyst [Sponsored by Salomon Smith Barney].

3. While this listing is from Kansas, Small business warm-ups, similar cautions have been posted by many in the entrepreneurship field. See American Women's

Economic Development Corporation (1997, April), Stamford, CT. Ten myths about starting a business [www.onlinewbc.org/docs/starting/myths.html], pp. 1-3, and U.S. Small Business Administration, Office of Women's Business Ownership (1998, June). *Blueprint for Success: A Guide for Women Entrepreneurs,* sponsored by Salomon Smith Barney [www.onlinewbc.org/docs/whats_new/index.html], Ch.1, 1–4.

4. Abedon, E. (1998, April 19). Ooooh, scary! Entrepreneur's idea becomes monster hit. *Charleston Post and Courier,* pp. F1, F10.

5. The Hammer Award recognizes new standards of excellence achieved by teams helping to reinvent government. About 600 Hammer Awards have been presented to teams composed of federal employees, state and local employees, and private citizens.

6. Willard, G. E., Krueger, D. A., & Feeser, H. R. (1992). In order to grow, must the founder go: A comparison of performance between founder and non-founder-managed high-growth manufacturing firms. *Journal of Business Venturing, 16,* 181–194; Hanks, S. H., Watson, C. J., Jansen, E., & Chandler, G. N. (1994). Tightening the life-cycle construct: A taxonomic study of growth stage configurations in high-technology organizations. *Entrepreneurship Theory and Practice, 19*(2), 5–30; Whisler, T. L. (1988). The role of the board in the threshold firm. *Family Business Review, 1,* 309–321; Daily, C., & Dalton, D. (1992). Financial performance of founder-managed versus professionally managed small corporations. *Journal of Small Business Management, 30*(2), 25–34; Busenitz, L. W., & Barney, J. B. (1997). Differences between entrepreneurs and managers in large organizations: Biases and heuristics in strategic decision making. *Journal of Business Venturing, 12*(1), 9–30.

7. Lorrain, J., & Dussault, L. (1987). Management behaviors and types of entrepreneurs: The case of manufacturing businesses in the survival and establishment stage. In M. Wyckham, & Bushe (Eds.), *The Spirit of Entrepreneurship* (pp. 77–94). Burnaby, BC: Simon Fraser University; Flamholtz, *Growing Pains.*

8. Begley, M. (1995). Using founder status, age of firm, and company growth rate as the basis for distinguishing entrepreneurs from managers of smaller businesses. *Journal of Business Venturing, 10*(3), 249–264; Willard, Krueger, & Feeser, In order to Grow, Must the Founder Go; Daily, & Dalton, Financial performance of founder-managed versus professionally managed small corporations, pp. 30-31.

9. Flamholtz, *Growing Pains;* Dodge, H. R., & Robbins, J. E. (1992). An empirical investigation of the organizational life cycle model for small business development and survival. *Journal of Small Business Management, 30*(1), 27–37; Buchele, R. B. (1967). *Business Policy in Growing Firms.* San Francisco: Chandler.

10. Begley, T. M. (1995). Using founder status, age of firm, and company growth rate as the basis for distinguishing entrepreneurs from managers of smaller businesses, p. 249; Miller, L. E., & Simmons, K. A. (1992). Differences in management practices of founding and nonfounding chief executives of human service organizations. *Entrepreneurship Theory and Practice, 16*(4), 31–39; Ginn, C. W., & Sexton, D. L. (1990). A comparison of the personality type dimensions of the 1987 Inc. 500 Company Founders/CEOs with those of slower-growth firms. *Journal of Business Venturing, 5*(5), 313–327; Daily & Dalton, Financial performance of founder-managed versus professionally managed small corporations; Schein, E. H. (1983, Summer). The role of the founder in creating organizational culture. *Organizational Dynamics,* pp. 13–28; Schein, E. H. (1985). *Organizational Culture and Leadership.* San Francisco: Jossey-Bass; Miner, J. B. (1990). Entrepreneurs, high-growth entrepreneurs, and managers: Contrasting

and overlapping motivational patterns. *Journal of Business Venturing, 5*(4), 221–235; Dyer, W. G. (1986). *Cultural Change in Family Firms.* San Francisco: Jossey-Bass; Busenitz & Barney, Differences between entrepreneurs and managers in large organizations.

11. NFWBO Recent Facts '99. Fact of the Week, (February 8, 1999). The National Foundation for Women Business Owners [http://www.nfwbo.org/publications.html]. Fact of the Week, (January 25, 1999). The National Foundation for Women Business Owners [http://www.nfwbo.org/publications.html].

12. Scollard, J. R. (1989). *Risk To Win—A Woman's Guide to Success.* New York: Macmillan.

13. Farren, C. E. (1999). *Planning and Managing Interior Projects.* (2nd ed.) Kingston, MA: R.S. Means.

14. Moore, D. P., & Buttner, E. H. (1997). *Women Entrepreneurs—Moving Beyond the Glass Ceiling.* Thousand Oaks, CA: Sage, ch. 7; Scollard, Risk To Win; Hisrich, R. D., & Brush, C. G. (1984). The woman entrepreneur: Management skills and business problems. *Journal of Small Business Management, 22*(1), 30–37; Chaganti, R. (1986, October). Management in women-owned enterprises. *Journal of Small Business Management, 24,* 18–29.

15. Gatewood, E. J., Shaver, K. G., & Gartner, W. B. (1995). A longitudinal study of cognitive factors influencing start-up behaviors and success at venture creation. *Journal of Business Venturing, 10*(5), 371–391; Srinvasan, R., Woo, C. Y., & Cooper, A. C. (1994). Performance determinants for male and female entrepreneurs. In W. D. Bygrave, S. Birley, N. C. Churchill, E. Gatewood, F. Hoy, R. Keeley, & W. E. Wetzel, Jr. (Eds.), *Frontiers of Entrepreneurship Research* (p. 43–56). Babson Park, MA: Center for Entrepreneurial Studies, Babson College; National Foundation for Women Business Owners. (1994, September 30). Credibility and independence: Women business owners voice greatest challenges and biggest rewards of entrepreneurship [http://www.NFWBO.org/rm012htm] [Press release]; National Foundation for Women Business Owners, Women business owners' economic impact reaffirmed; Moore & Buttner, *Women Entrepreneurs,* chap. 7.

Chapter 7

1. Alfus, M. (2000). The Experiences and Lessons of a 20th Century Entrepreneur: How Relevant in the Next Millennium? United States Association of Small Business and Entrepreneurship/SBIDA-2000 Plenary Address, Feb. 18, 2000, San Antonio. See website: http://www.USABE.ORG/CONFERENCES2000/PLENARY.HTM, pp. 1–2.

2. Alfus, M. The Experiences and Lessons of a 20th Century Entrepreneur, pp. 5–6.

3. Ortega, B. (1998). *In Sam We Trust—The Untold Story of Sam Walton and How Wal-Mart Is Devouring America.* New York: Times Books, Random House (pp. 157 and 278).

4. American Women's Economic Development Corporation, Stamford, CT, and Women in New Development, Bemidji, MN, 1/97 (http://www.onlinew-bc.org/docs/starting/test.html).

5. Tannenbaum, J. A. (1999, June 24). Business Bulletin, A special background report on trends in industry and finance: New entrepreneurs appear vital to healthy economic growth. *Wall Street Journal,* p. A5, 1.

6. Dolinsky, A. L., Caputo, R. K., Pasumarty, K., & Quazi, H. (1993). The effects of education on business ownership: A longitudinal study of women. *Entrepreneurship Theory*

and Practice, 18(1), 43–54; Dolinsky, A. L., Caputo, R. K., & Pasumarty, K. (1994). Long-term entrepreneurship patterns: A national study of black and white female entry and stayer status differences. *Journal of Small Business Management, 32*(1), 18–27.

7. Stevenson, H. H., Grousbeck, H. I., Roberts, M. J., and Bhide, A. (1999). *New Business Ventures and the Entrepreneurs* (5th ed.). Boston: Irwin McGraw-Hill (pp. 21–22).

8. The Chronicle of Higher Education Almanac (1998–1999). Earned degrees conferred, 1994–1995. [http://www.chronicle.com/weekly/almanac/1998/facts/9stu.html] @ 2 of 9. Women earn 68.7% of the associate degrees, 47.9% of the bachelor's degrees, 36.9% of the master's degrees, and 27.26% of the doctorates. For information on AACSB—The International Association for Management Education—see updated information [http://www.aacsb.edu/aboutus.html]. As of April 2000, of the 392 accredited programs, "382 are in North America, four in Europe, three in Asia, one in Central America, and two in South America."

9. Stroh, L. K., & Reilly, A. H. (1999). Gender and careers: Present experiences and emerging trends. In G. Powell (Ed.), *Handbook of Gender and Work*. Thousand Oaks, CA: Sage.

10. Catalyst, National Foundation for Women Business Owners, with support of the Committee 200 Foundation (1998, February). *Paths to Entrepreneurship: New Directions for Women in Business*. New York: Catalyst [Sponsored by Salomon Smith Barney].

11. Catalyst, National Foundation for Women Business Owners, with support of the Committee 200 Foundation, *Paths to Entrepreneurship*.

12. Gallucci, J. (1999, July 11). When casual becomes crass. *New York Times*, pp. BU, 9.

13. Scollard, J. R. (1989). *Risk To Win—A Woman's Guide to Success*. New York: Macmillan (pp. 94–95).

14. Scollard, *Risk to Win*, pp. 95–96.

15. Calvey, M. (1997) Shock treatment: Waving good-bye to corporate America for your own venture? Be prepared for culture shock. *Special Report: Fast Track Quarterly. San Francisco Business Times, 11*(36) 2A(2). [web4.searchbank.com/infotrac/session/699/ 547/1263618w5/93!xrn_19].

16. Mincer, J. American women leave frustrating corporate jobs to seek better lifestyles. *Knight-Ridder/Tribune Business News* [http://web2.infotrac-custom.com/in...618/6449745w5/20!xrn_20_0_A53166658], four pages, p. 2.

17. Cohen, C. E. (1994, May). Making the leap to entrepreneur. *Working Woman, 19*(5), 67–69. [http://web3.searchbank.com/infotrac/session/196/200/1287620w5/27!xrn_22], p. 1 of 3.

18. Moore, D. P., & Buttner, E. H. (1997). *Women Entrepreneurs: Moving Beyond the Glass Ceiling*. Thousand Oaks, CA: Sage (p. 181).

19. Online Women's Business Center, SBA, Office of Women's Business Ownership, (1998, Dec. 5). SBAExpress Provides Easy Access to Revolving Credit. http://www.onlinewbc.creditaccess.sba.html.

20. The National Foundation for Women Business Owners (1998, June 29). Fact of the Week [www.nfwbo.org/factndx.html], p. 8 of 18. Cite comes from: *Women Business Owners of Color: Challenges and Accomplishments*, NFWBO, 1998.

21. Dyer, W. G., Jr. (1992). *The Entrepreneurial Experience: Confronting Career Dilemmas of the Start-Up Executive*. San Francisco: Jossey-Bass (pp. 40–41).

22. The Online Women's Business Center home page is http://www.onlinewbc.org.

23 SBA, The Office of Women's Business Ownership (1999). Changing the face of America's economy. [www.sba.gov/womeninbusiness/] last modified 5/26/99 (p. 1 of 3). Also see U.S. Small Business Administration, Office of Communications and Public Liaison News Release (1999, June 18). SBA Administrator announces the addition of 25 new sites to the Women's Business Center Network, Release #99-60 [www.sba.gov/news/], p. 1 of 4.

24. Online Women's Business Center (1999). About WBENC . . . [www.onlinew-bc.org/docs/whats_new/WBENC.htm], two pages.

25. Online Women's Business Center (1999). Forms of business ownership. [Forms of ownership.sba.htm], seven pages. (From Small Business success sessions, a workshop series sponsored by NationsBank and Ohio Women's Business Resource Network.)

26. NFWBO (1997, December 29). Fact of the Week [www.nfwbo.org/ factndx.htm], Retirement Plan Trends in the Small Business Market: A Survey of Women- and Men-Owned Firms, p. 12 of 18. See a series of financial decisions that women make that are distinctly different from those made by men. Also see NFWBO (1998, Jan. 12). For factors influencing purchasing decisions, see *Embracing the Information Age: A Comparison of Women and Men Business Owners,* NFWBO (1997). For differences in profit sharing with employees, see From Retirement Plan Trends, NFWBO (1998, January 26).

27. Online Women's Business Center (1997, May). Insurance—Do I need it? What kind? How much? [types of insurance.sba.htm], three pages. (Entrepreneur's Network for Women, Watertown, SD and Online Women's Business Center).

28. NFWBO (1999, March 22). Fact of the Week [www.nfwbo.org/facts 1999.html], p. 2 of 5. "Women business owners continue to have less bank credit than their male counterparts. Forty-six percent of women business owners with bank credit, compared to 34% of men business owners with bank credit have less than $50,000 available for use in their business. Thirty-four percent of women with bank credit have $50,000 or more available to them for use in their business, compared to nearly six in ten (58%) men business owners." From Capital, Credit and Financing: An Update Comparing Women and Men Business Owners' Sources and Uses of Capital, NFWBO 1998 [http://www.nfwbo.org/publications.html].

29. Advancing Women, 1998 [sysop@advancingwomen.com, p. 1]. For a summary report contact the North Carolina Institute of Minority Economic Development, Inc., at 919-831-2467 or ncimed@interpath.com.

30. The Community Affairs Office (CAO) of the Federal Reserve Bank of Richmond (1998).

31. NFWBO and Dun & Bradstreet (1998); Kallenberg, A. L., & Leicht, K. T. (1991). Gender and organizational performance: Determinants of small business survival and success. *Academy of Management Journal, 34*(1), 131–161.

32. Aida Alvarez, administrator, U.S. Small Business Administration, Office of Women's Business Ownership, Office of Advocacy. (1999, July). New Sources of Private Equity Capital for Women Entrepreneurs—A Case Study: The Women's Growth Capital Fund [http://www.onlinewbc.org/docs/Venture Capital/VCR1.html], p. 1 of 18.

33. Source: Above text and Semas, J. Harkham. (1996, Sept. 2). Women entrepreneurs still find it difficult to get capital. *The Business Journal Serving Greater Sacramento, 13*(24),

[http://web2.infotrac-custom.com/infotrac_...on/895/529/6514487w5/ 22! xrn_8_0_A18740450], p. 4 of 7.

34. Fay, M., & Williams, L. (1993). Gender bias and the availability of business loans. *Journal of Business Venturing, 8*(4), 363–377.

35. NFWBO (1998). Women of all races share entrepreneurial spirit—women of color start businesses in record numbers. NFWBO News, 1998, No. 3 [http://www.nfwbo.org], p. 2 of 4. See also: Fact of the Week, April 19, 1999. "Women business owners of color continue to be less likely than their counterparts to have bank credit. Less than one in three (29%) women business owners of color surveyed currently have bank credit, compared to 53% of Caucasian women business owners surveyed." From "Capital, Credit and Financing: An Update Comparing Women and Men Business Owners' Sources and Uses of Capital."

36. NFWBO (1998, Sept. 28). Fact of the Week, [www.nfwbo.org/factndx.htm] p. 5 of 18. "Women Business Owners of Color: Challenges and Accomplishments."

37. NFWBO (1996). Women business owners make progress in access to capital: Still lag men-owned businesses in credit levels. [http://www.NFWBO.org/rr010.htm] [Press release, 1996, Oct.] @ p. 1; The same pattern continues in 1999. NFWBO (1999, Mar. 22 Fact of the Week). See reference by NFWBO to: *From Capital, Credit and Financing: An Update Comparing Women and Men Business Owners' Sources and Uses of Capital, NFWBO 1998.* [http://www.nfwbo.org/facts1999.html] @ p. 2 of 5.

38. Allen, K. R., & Carter, N. M. (1996). Women entrepreneurs: Profile differences across high and low performing adolescent firms. In W. D. Bygrave, B. J. Bird, S. Birley, N. C. Churchill, M. G. Hay, R. H. Kelley, W. E. Wetzel, Jr. (Eds.), *Frontiers of Entrepreneurship Research* (Summary). Babson Park, MA: Center for Entrepreneurial Studies, Babson College. (See allen.html at www.babson.edu, 1996) @ p. 2 of abstract.

39. Dedyna, K. (1999, Jan. 4). Woman entrepreneurs "willing to work for less," Monday Business, *The Gazette* (Montreal), p. F2; http://web.lexis-nexis.com/universe/docum @ p. 1.

40. AVON-Women—Women on the Move (1999). Women of Enterprise: Meet the 1998 Women of Enterprise Awards Honorees. [http://www.avon.com/about/women/move/enterprise/biosfull98.html] 1-6.

41. Kallenberg, & Leicht, Gender and organizational performance; Chaganti, R., & Parasuraman, S. (1996). A study of the impacts of gender on business performance and management patterns in small business. *Entrepreneurship Theory and Practice, 21*(2), 73–75.

42. Semas, J. H. (1996, Sept. 2). Women entrepreneurs still find it difficult to get capital. *The Business Journal Serving Greater Sacramento, 13*(24), [http://web2.infotrac-custom.com/infotrac_...on/895/529/6514487w5/22!!xrn_8_0_A18740450] @ p. 4 of 7.

43. U.S. Small Business Administration Office of Advocacy Report (1995). The third millennium: Small business and entrepreneurship in the Twenty-first century. Washington, DC: U.S. Government Printing Office. See also more recent statistics: Office of Advocacy (1998, Oct.). Women in business. [http://www.sba.gov/ADVO/stats/wib.pdf].

44. Stanley, F. D. (1998, Sept. 15). *Accessing Capital: Start to Finish—Community Development Marketwise Reports,* Community Affairs Office of The Federal Reserve Bank of Richmond, 10.

45. Ratner, Hedy, & Carol Dougal, codirectors; Linda Darragh, project director, Women's Business Development Center (WBDC), Extension 22, 8 South Michigan Avenue, Suite 400, Chicago, IL 60603 [email: wbdc@aol.com].

46. Stahura, B. (1997, Jan. 11). Microloans offer more than just money; microenterprise development organizations; includes list of resources. *Executive Female, 20*(1) [http://web.lexis-nexis.com/universe/docum...5a3&_md5=ecb-dbbfbf82a13d4fcd988ab1f7b59b], p. 2.

47. Aida Alvarez, administrator, U.S. Small Business Administration, Office of Women's Business Ownership, Office of Advocacy. (1998, Sept. 18). SBA News Release, 1-2. Also see SBA 1999 News Press Office releases. What's New? and Other News? [www.sba.gov/news/indexwhatsnew.html] for information on new or updated forms, e.g., SBA Form 4—Application for Business Loan, SBA Form 4_SHT—Application for Small Business Loan (short form for $50,000 and under) released on June 24, 1999, and for notification that 12 more SBA forms are fillable on line (1999, May 20).

48. Online Women's Business Center. (date not given). Existing Business Quiz—Can I Qualify for a Business Loan? [http://www.onlinewbc.org/docs/whats-new/quiz1.html]. Start-Up Business Quiz—Can I Qualify for a Start-Up Business Loan? [http://www.onlinewbc.org/docs/whats-new/quiz2.html]; Borrowing and Lending—The Five "C's" of Credit. Women's Economic Self-Sufficiency Team, Alburquerque, NM; (1997, April). Borrowing and Lending—How Do I Qualify for a Loan? (Key points to consider; questions your banker will ask; commercial loan evaluation factors; self-assessment checklist). Women's Business Development Corporation, Chicago. [http://www.onlinewbc.org/docs/finance/loanqual.html]. U.S. Small Business Administration Office of Communications and Public Liaison Press Office Contact: Patricia L. Young. (1999, June 18). Presently there are over 80 women's business centers in 47 states, District of Columbia, Puerto Rico and the Virgin Island. For a complete updated list see: SBA, The Office of Women's Business Ownership, April 27, 2000 [http://www.onlinewbnc.org/docs/wbcs/index.html or call 202-205-6673 or SBA at 1-800-8-ASK-SBA].

49. California, Florida, Georgia, Kansas, Kentucky, Maryland, Massachusetts, Michigan, Mississippi, Missouri, New Jersey, New York, North Dakota, Oklahoma, Pennsylvania, Texas, and Washington (http://www.sba.gov/onestop/facts.html) and [http://www.sba.gov/gopher/Local-Information/Business-Information-Centers/Onestop/, 4/28/99].

50. Contacts include Capital Across America (615-254-1515) and Women's Growth Capital Fund of Washington, DC [http://www.womensgrowthcapital.com or call 202-342-1431].

51. Online Women's Business Center. See note 47 [http://www.onlinewbc.org].

52. Drury, T. (1999, January 11). WNY women's directory opens more doors to capital. *Business First of Buffalo, 15* [http://web2.infotrac-custom.com/in.../618/6449745w5/5!xrn_1_0_A53747122], p. 5.

53. Dutton, G. (1998). Wanted: A practical visionary. *Management Review, 87*(3), 33–37. [web3.searchbank.com/infotrac/session/196/200/1287620w5/68!xrn_85].

54. High, K. (1999, February 17). Briefs—Money is out there, go get it. *Fortune,* [http//cgi.pathfinder.com/yourco/briefs/0,2246,157,00html], pp. 1–2.

55. Thomas, P. (1999, February 24). When mars decides to invest in venus's promising start-up. *The Wall Street Journal Interactive Ed.,* p. 1 of 4. Regarding factoring see p. 2.

56. Online Women's Business Center. (1997). Capital Alternatives—What Type of Capital Does Your Business Need? Women's Business Development Center, Chicago (1997, April). [http://www.onlinewbc.org/docs/finance/captoo.html], p. 1–2 of 6. See also Online Women's Business Center (1997, June). The role of factoring as a source of funding. [www.onlinewbc.org/docs/finance/factor.html]. (Jeanne Manley, CFS, in connection with Women's Business Development Center, Chicago, IL).

57. Mallory, M. (1999, February 5). From the ground up—Women entrepreneurs build businesses and create jobs in a soft economy. *U.S. News Online: Business* (http://www.usnews.com/usnews/issue/woman.htm).

58. Online Women's Business Center (1999, April 30). SBA-Backed Venture Capital Companies Owned by Women, [www.onlinewbc.org/docs/whats_new/nr0430.html], pp. 1–2. Also see Capital Across America (1999). About Capital Across America Home Page [www.capitalacrossamerica.org/aboutus.htm],; Growth Capital from Capital Across America, A Small Business Investment Company [www.capitalacrossamerica.org], p. 1 of 2.

59. Online Women's Business Center (1999, April 30). SBA-Backed Venture Capital Companies owned by women, [www.onlinewbc.org/docs/whats_new/nr0430.html], 1-2.

60. Women's Business Development Center, 1997, p. 2 .

61. Web sources include the National Venture Capital Association (nvca.org), the Mid-Atlantic Venture Funds (mavf.com), Venture Capital Online (vcapital.com), and the Women's Growth Capital Fund (womensgrowthcapital.com).

62. U.S. Small Business Administration. (1998, June 29). SBA Web site offers new comprehensive guide for business resources and information (News Release No. 98-55, Press Office). [Resource Directory, www.sba.gov/news].

63. Online Women's Business Center (1997, May). Capital alternatives—Understanding money sources. [http://www.onlinewbc.org/docs/finance/capital.html], 14 pages. Adapted from Financial Management for Small Business, University of Wisconsin Small Business Development Center by Charlotte Taylor, Venture Concepts, in association with New Jersey Association of Women Business Owners, Inc.

64. Online Women's Business Center, Ohio Women's Business Resource Network, Columbus, OH (1997, August). When do you need to contact a professional? [www.onlinewbc.org/docs/finance/pro_help.html]. Also see Assessing of a Financial Specialist by Jade Knapp, CPA, MBA (2000). Identification of financial service comparison. An unpublished MBA manuscript, The Citadel, Charleston, SC. You may also wish to consult your local chapter of SCORE for advice.

65. Mallory, From the ground up, p. 4.

INDEX